Pickups

Windings and Magnets...and the Guitar Became Electric **by Mario Milan**

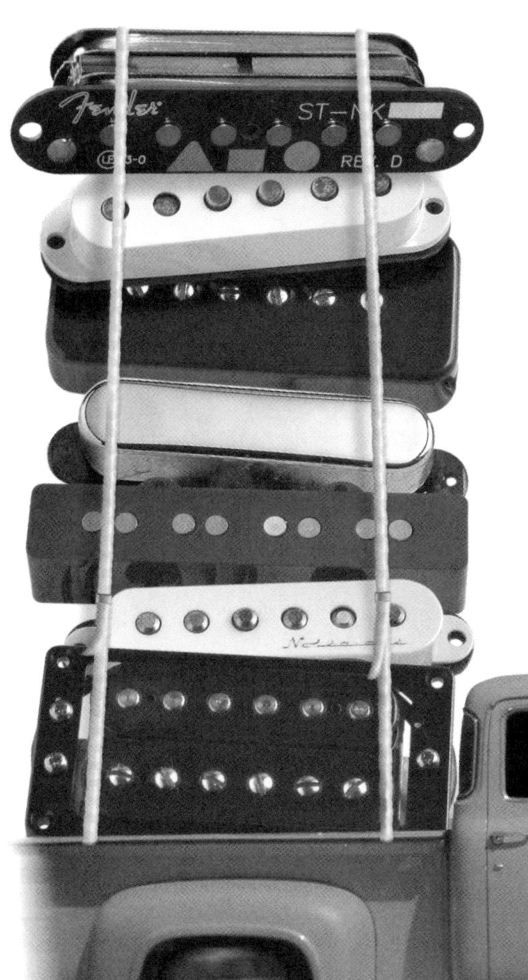

Page layout by Mario Milan and Claudio Prosperini

Photographs by Claudio Prosperini and Claudio Caldana

Drawings by Mario Milan

English translation revised by Valerie Nurse and Susan Law

Cover photo by Ron Middlebrook

Cover pickups courtesy of Fender Guitar Co.

Cover design by Design Associates

ISBN-13: 978-1-57424-209-6
ISBN-10: 1-57424-209-1
SAN 683-8022

P.O. Box 17878 – Anaheim Hills, CA 92817

TABLE OF CONTENTS

Mario Milan was born in Mestre, near Venice, Italy, on October 11, 1949.
He started playing guitar in the sixties and in the early seventies worked for a while as a composer for RCA in Rome. The restrictions of commercial music didn't suit him well and he left to play in underground bands.
At the same time his main interest became the blues and he specialized in slide playing having Earl Hooker, Mick Taylor and Duane Allman as style models. Since the eighties he writes articles for the Italian guitar magazine "AXE", contributing with instruments and record reviews, vintage instruments' history and answering to "impossible questions" from the readers.

Claudio Prosperini, was born in Roma on October 24, 1951. He started playing in the sixties and in 1974 founded the rock band "Strada Aperta".
They recorded a couple of records on their own and backed the Italian singer Antonello Venditti on most of his albums.
Even after the band's dissolution, in 1985, Prosperini continued to pursue his interest in vintage instruments collecting and playing as well as photography.
Since then he's also busy running his own recording studio "Zoo Symphony", having as customers many Italian top players.

Able to make a clean guitar sing, he's very fond on tasteful use of effects and his collection of vintage pedals is impressive. Whatever he does, creativity is always the main issue.

Acknowledgments

This work should be thought of as a collective effort to which several friends contributed greatly. Thanks go to Claudio Prosperini, who shot most of the pictures and has been very helpful in finding information and items concerning the European models. Claudio Caldana supplied articles and other documents. Alex Angelucci kindly provided several pickups and shared a lot of information about vintage instruments (he was also the pickup's driver!). Some pickups have been supplied by the luthiers Paolo Benedettini, Franco Cavolata and Franco Di Filippo, other units have been supplied by Franco Bandiera's musical instruments shop (thank you, Carlo), players' player Nicola Distaso, Mauro Parretti, Gerardo Bellanti and Angelo Flamini. We are extremely grateful to all the photographers, credited under each picture. Giovanni Gaglio, maker of the Red Push pickups, contributed with lots of information on old and new models, given with his usual generosity, an article and some hard to find items. A special mention is due to Mr John Hall (Rickenbacker), for his kindness and the permission to use freely images from original catalogues, and to Mr Roger Ball (Gibson) for allowing us to use Gibson material. Mr Leo Valdes kindly let us use the Charlie Christian's pictures, showed on his beautiful web site "Solo Flight", http://home.elp.rr.com/valdes/, dedicated to the famous musician. We would also like to say thank you to Mr Peter Liebert for his permission to use the pictures from his web site www.nipperhead.com, dedicated to old phonographs and other Edison related stuff. Amps and electronics' specialist Vincenzo Tabacco patiently answered many technical questions. He also designed the first Broadcaster's circuit for this project from a Leo Fender's drawing and shot some of the pictures. Riccardo Milan has been very helpful with his computer advice, making it possible to enrich several chapters with the drawings and illustrations. We would like to give thanks to all the friends and family members who sustained us with love: Franco and Enrica Bandiera, confident in this project since the beginning and whose help has been invaluable, Rong Li and her family, for their love and fantastic food, "Mama" Elena, for excellent coffee and infinite patience, "Zia" Pia, who carefully read the manuscript hunting for mistakes. Gianfranco Molle supplied friendship and computer servicing. A very special thank you is deserved to Fabrizio Dadò, director of "AXE" magazine, in suggesting the writing of this book, encouraging its realization and supplying many original catalogues.

Mario Milan

The Authors and all the people involved in this project are very grateful to the readers who will have the patience to follow us in this journey through the world of the magnetic pickups for guitar. We hope to have been able to make it informing as well as entertaining.

It was hard work, but we also had lots of fun, so we wish some of that fun would reach you, the reader, as well as our enthusiasm for good instruments from any era.

For all the opinions expressed, the author takes full responsibility, as they are based on personal experience and taste and are meant in no way to be definitive or detrimental to any eventual different point of view.

Actually every time we come across a new instrument, or an old one which is new to us, we have to change a bit, exposed as we are to a never ending learning process. What doesn't change, over time, is our love for tones and our appetite for new sounds or for rediscovering old sounds.

Some makers work to reproduce as faithfully as possible tones from the past, others try to bring new recipes for the musician looking for unexplored sounds, this gives to the present guitar player an unprecedented variety of choices.

Our aim was to help the player to know more about the humble but essential component making an electric guitar what it is and to pay homage to the designers who worked on its development, people like George Beauchamp, Walter Fuller, Leo Fender, Seth Lover, Bill Lawrence, Larry DiMarzio, Seymour Duncan and the many craftsmen producing countless pickups every day.

To them all, as players, we must be, and we are indeed, extremely grateful.

Mario Milan

Introduction (Guitar players, wake up!)

On December 1st 1939, Charlie Christian wrote an article to incite other guitar players to adopt the electric guitar, urging them to wake up, and, with the amplified instrument, be finally heard.

Charlie Christian with a Gibson ES 250

According to this musician, one of the credited founders of bebop and a pioneer of the electric guitar, thanks to amplification, new soloing spaces are open to the guitar player. These were usually relegated to simple rhythm roles, often barely perceivable in the orchestras of the time.

With the amplified guitar a revolution is finally possible! Now the rhythm parts will be audible and the compulsory lines and solos can have the same effectiveness of those played by the brass players and it will be possible to explore more complex harmonic textures without fear of them being obscured by the volume of the piano.

A forecast surely confirmed by facts, considering that since then the electric guitar has gone a long way, indeed!

Born as a novelty many used to laugh at, the electric guitar has conquered jazz, propelled rock 'n roll, brought new energy to the blues and has become the motive power for hard rock, star of fusion's virtuosity and main component of the eclectic modern rock.

Charlie Christian used a Gibson ES 150, the first electric guitar to be produced in series, which was mainly a classic Archtop made “special” by the pickup destined to become famous with the nickname of "Charlie Christian" model.

Charlie Christian with a Gibson ES 150

Charlie Christian was born in Bonham, Texas, on July 29, 1916. Later the whole family moved to Oklahoma City. In this town Charlie attended school and played baseball. At that time he was also playing bass in a school band. During the '930s Charlie earned a good reputation as a guitar player. John Hammond, the man who discovered Billie Holiday and, later, Bob Dylan and Stevie Ray Vaughan, in 1939 went to Oklahoma City to listen to Charlie's playing. Hammond was informed about this new musician by a well known jazz guitar player: Mary Lou Williams. Impressed by his fully developed style, Hammond invited Christian to Los Angeles to introduce him to Benny Goodman. At first Goodman didn't seem to be impressed by the young guitar player, but after a version of "Rose Room" in which Christian played several solos extending the tune's length to more than 47 minutes, any doubts disappeared. With Charlie in the band, the radio broadcasts and the recordings of Benny Goodman, made a nationwide audience finally aware of the style of a new musician and the voice of a new instrument: the electric guitar (the Gibson ES 150, soon followed by the fancier ES 250).

The connection of Charlie Christian with the pickup, as the namesake so created seems to remark, goes beyond the simple case of an extraordinary musician who conceived the language for the electric guitar. Christian was a man who saw into the future, understood the potential of new technology and actively worked in a unique way to make it known and successful.

Of course Hendrix, Clapton, Van Halen and many others certainly promoted the use of new instruments and opened new technical and expressive ways to use them, but never with this distinctive trait of novelty or such personal commitment.

Since then many pickup models have followed the "Charlie Christian Model" and have become collector's items and part of the myth: the Rickenbacker Horseshoe - the real number one, then the Gibson P 90, the "Patent Applied For", the Minihumbucking, the Fender models for the Telecaster and the Stratocaster, the DeArmond, the Gretsch Filter 'Tron, the humble but clever Danelectro.

Right now the world is teeming with models from DiMarzio (responsible for a second revolution), Seymour Duncan, Lindy Fralin and Rio Grande. Fender and Gibson are trying to recapture the qualities of a wonderful past with reissue models while introducing new designs.

In Italy new makers such as Red Push are showing up, with new ingredients for tone enthusiasts.

At first, the main reason for the development of this component was to give a stronger voice to the old six strings, but then things evolved in two different directions.

One route was to obtain simple amplification of the acoustic instrument, while preserving as much as possible its natural timbre.
The other route was the development of a new class of instruments in which electrification represented the main source of sound, up to the point where some models lost the traditional acoustic soundbox in favour of a solid body.
At this point the acoustic amplified guitar and the specialized electric instrument underwent different evolution paths, with distinctive characteristics and playing techniques.

Charlie playing a Vega guitar through a Vega amplifier.

The different systems of amplification for acoustic or classical guitars (the modern circuits and improved piezo pickups, plus mixed systems of pickup and microphone), were aimed at reproducing the natural voice of the instrument by modifying it as little as possible. The ideal system of acoustic amplification would be one whose presence is not even perceptible.

The electric guitar pickup, on the contrary, was designed to add character to the final sound, by contributing to the colour of the instrument's voice.
In the beginning this was due to technological limitations, but then players accepted the new voice.

With the amplified guitar, the player has no fear of being obscured by the volume of other instruments...

A smiling Charlie with his Gibson ES 250

All the Charlie Christian pictures are courtesy of Leo Valdes from his web site “Solo Flight”.

The charm of this small but however important component, is determined by its contribution to the personality of the guitar, with both it's qualities and it's defects: this charm we plan to honour by exploring it in detail in all its evolution.

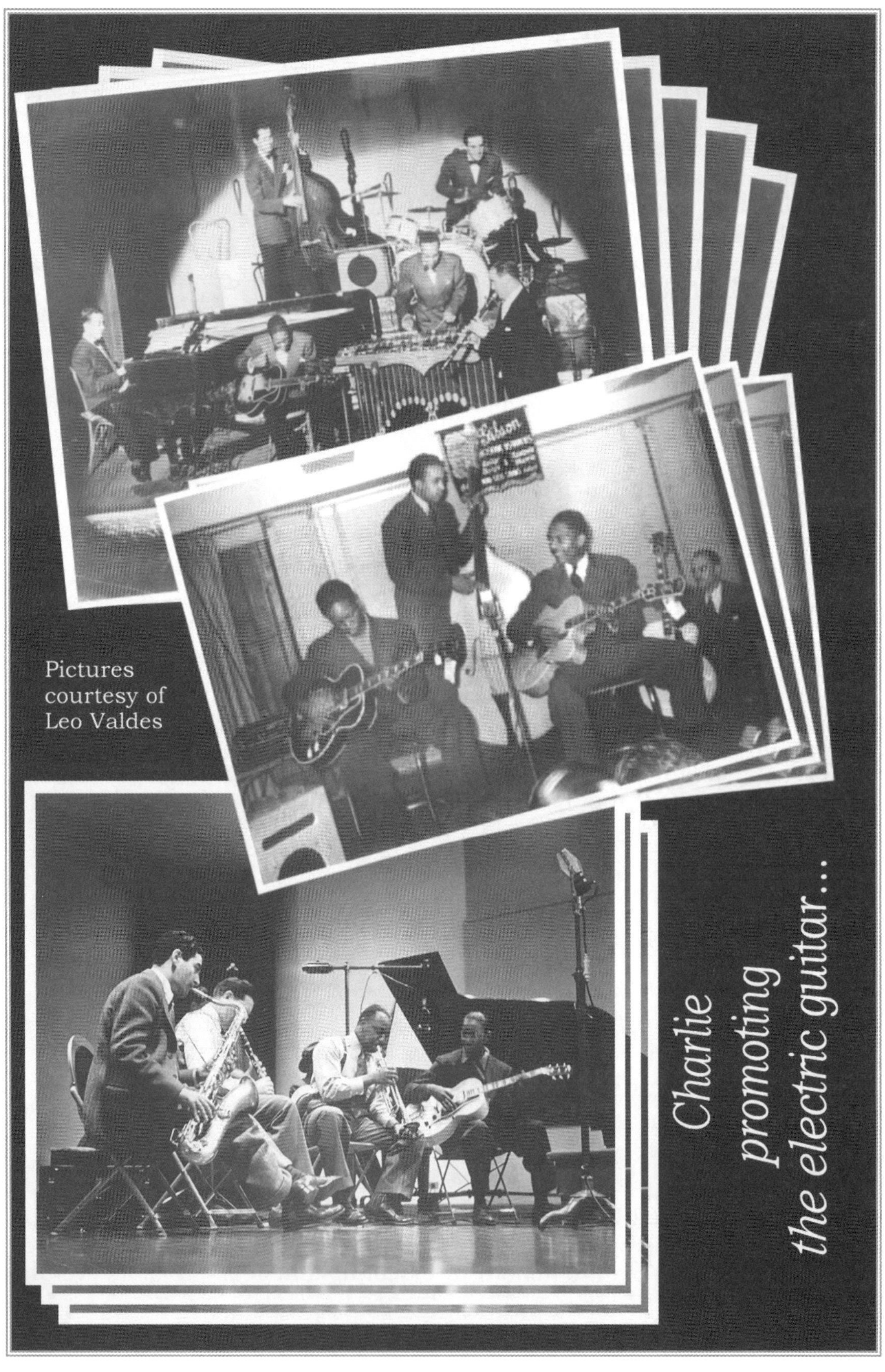

Pictures courtesy of Leo Valdes

Charlie promoting the electric guitar...

Prologue: searching for a louder voice

The problem of relatively feeble voice on string instruments is an old one. While the sound of many lute types made during the centuries all over the world, from Africa to Europe, and from China to Japan presented a variety of timbre, they never obtained a volume capable of competing with percussion and wind instruments.

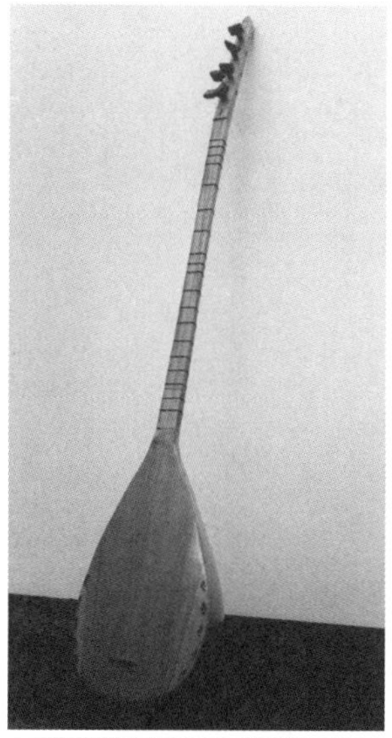

Oud, bouzouki, vihuela, pi'pa, biwa, sitar, shamisen, are only a few of the many components of the great family of string instruments developed around the World...

An infinite research brought to life an unbelievable number of stringed instruments, but it was only during the nineteenth century that a guitar was designed loud enough to fill a concert hall.

In Spain, around the middle of the century, the luthier Antonio De Torres made a six string instrument, which had the same dimensions and shape we know today (the six string guitar was becoming popular in Europe, but in Spain the five course version still predominated). The result was a guitar which, thanks to additional technological details, (such as the fan patterned bracing of the soundboard), was relatively strong but light weight. It had good resonant properties and was louder than any stringed instrument of the time. The length of the fingerboard scale was standardized at cm. 65, creating the basis of modern classic guitars which today are made, with minor variations, as those designed by De Torres (*).

Lute type instruments (Claudio Prosperini)

In the meantime, across the ocean, the best known guitar maker was Christian Frederick Martin, an immigrant from Markneukirchen, near Dresda, Saxony. Martin founded his company in 1833 in New York and moved to Cherry Hill, not far from Nazareth, Pennsylvania. In 1839, his guitars started to become less influenced by Stauffer, a Viennese luthier who had a distinctive headstock with tuners on a line, a solution which today reminds us of Fender. Gradually Martin developed his original design and the Stauffer style headstock disappeared from his instruments. By the turn of the century the factory, now under the management of his son Christian Frederick Jr, had already gained a good reputation due to the high quality of its products, which offered several improvements, such as the X bracing, a method already known in Europe and perfected by Martin making it a distinctive American achievement.

Flamenco guitar, Vicente Arias, Madrid, 1910 (C. P.)

Gibson harp-guitar, about 1919 (Alex Angelucci).

The instruments offered had a simple yet elegant shape and a good tone balance, from the humble 018, introduced in 1854, to the top of the line 00045, added in 1904.
These represented for many a state of the art in American guitars and had an undeniable influence on contemporary makers who promptly imitated them.

As good as they were, Martin guitars could not compete in volume, with the best classical models and the bulky Style O made by Orville Gibson, which had more possibilities due to it's larger body and use of steel strings.

The use of metallic strings, which Martin adopted only in 1927, was typical of some European instruments such as mandolins and the "chitarra battente", a seventeenth century Italian guitar.

Musician Orville H. Gibson, was born in Chateaugay in 1856. He moved to Kalamazoo in 1881, worked as a clerk in a shoe shop until he had the possibility, in 1896, to open a luthier's shop.

He made mandolins, guitars, lutes and other stringed instruments combining characteristics of guitar and harp.

The uncommon attention to aesthetics and the fancy inlay work gave his products a look which recalled Renaissance instruments, although the use of carved solid wood for the soundboard, sides and back, as used in violin making, was really innovative applied to guitars and mandolins.
The sound top, as on violins, was arched rather than flat. Another original feature of Orville's guitars was that they were unusually big for the time. His Grand Concert Model measured a width of 16" against the 15" of the Martin 00028.

In 1902 five Kalamazoo investors decided to fund the production of instruments based on the innovative ideas of Orville Gibson and founded the Gibson Mandolin & Guitar Manufacturing Company Limited. These new Gibson-made instruments were different in more than a few details from those originally made

by Orville. They were louder, better sounding and cheaper to make (Orville's use of only carved solid wood, good for small instruments such as the violin, applied to guitars rendered a costly and limited production with dubious results).
The basic ideas of the original luthier were respected and the models produced now (Style L, L-1, L-3, Style 0, 0-2, 0-3) have their place in history. A disinhibited and effective style of advertising was also adopted from Orville. Bold to say the least, it offered catalogues giving 41 reasons for choosing a Gibson instrument, the only way to ensure the most powerful sound. Competitors lacked potential simply because they hadn't followed the same rules.

Literature of the time went as far as to say that whoever tried to denigrate these innovations, was really only attacking the ghost of their own imagination and finally proclaimed that mandolins and Gibson guitars were the only instruments of their kind made in a professional manner, for professionals. This was later summed up by the classical motto: "Only a Gibson is good enough" which they have recently readopted.

A late twenties' Gibson L3 (Alex Angelucci).

Thanks to it's good reputation, Martin received orders for Hawaiian guitars, ukuleles and some mandolins from different manufacturers, most important of whom was distributor and editor Oliver Ditson.
The manager of Ditson's New York branch, Harry. L. Hunt designed a guitar especially for him which was bigger than Martin's triple O series and had a less curvaceous shape.
Martin made the guitar as a special limited production for Ditson, in three sizes: Standard, Concert and Extra Large.

The Extra Large guitar evolved into a new model which became the folk guitar "par excellence": the Dreadnought.

Introduced in 1931, in two versions, D1 and D2, they then became the present classic models D18 (1932) and D28 (1935). Top of the Dreadnought line was the D 45, at first available on special order only, then added to the line in 1938 until 1942. The model was reintroduced in 1968.

A seventies' Martin D 45 (Renato Bartolini)

Although these instruments were louder than previous designs, the increment was barely significant.

A six string banjo. The instruments of the banjo family were the loudest available before amplification, the most popular is still the five string version. (C. Prosperini).

Another advance in volume arrived in 1919, when a famous musician of the time, Lloyd Alayre Loar, was employed by Gibson to take charge of quality control, product development, customer service, design of strings, bridges and other accessories, plus other jobs in advertising, teaching and music publishing. The line designed under his direction, Style 5, with the mandolin F-5, the H-5 mandola, the K-5 mandocello, the TB-5 banjo and the L-5 guitar, gave evidence of his professionalism and are still today regarded as the best quality of Gibson's production of all times.

The innovative features of these instruments are the "F" holes, the raised finger rest, designed and patented by George D. Laurian in 1917, the adjustable truss-rod to counter-act the strings' tension on the neck, invented by Gibson artisan Ted McHugh (the patent was applied for in 1921 and granted in 1923), the fingerboard extended on the body, though suspended to allow the arched soundboard to be free to vibrate, and the parallel bracing.

The L-5 guitar is capable of a sound level higher than other contemporary models, almost halfway between those and the banjo, with a brighter tone and better projection.

These qualities make the L-5 a favourite of the professionals and became a classic in the hands of jazz player Eddie Lang (who had already used the excellent but not so loud L-4) and country artist Maybelle Carter substituted her L-1 with this model.

The combination of arched top and F holes proved efficient to the point that Gibson, whose most impressive model was the Super 400, was soon imitated and similar models were made, during the '30s, by brands such as Epiphone, D'Angelico, Stromberg and, although briefly, by Martin.

By the turn of the century, Hawaiian music was increasingly popular and the technique used to play this style prompted more research.

The Hawaiian guitar is played holding the instrument flat on the thighs, with the soundboard towards the top and sliding a metallic bar on the strings, kept high on the firngerboard.

This technique causes the sound to go upward, reaching the listener indirectly, thus the need for more volume.

Chris Knutsen, a Norwegian immigrant, took into consideration the characteristics of many hand made Hawaiian musical instruments made after 1909.

Knutsen started to make instruments reflecting his research and the result was a deeper guitar with a longer body, and a hollow square neck, which had more internal volume. The wood mostly used was Koa, similar to mahogany and indigenous of Hawaii.

Knutsen produced under the Kona brand, other makes of similar instruments were the well respected Weissenborn and Hilo.

Though interesting for their tonal quality and original structure, Hawaiian guitars were destined to be clouded by the success of a Czech immigrant's invention.

In 1927 John Dopyera patented a really unusual guitar, completely metallic, neck included, with the bridge suspended on three aluminium cones facing the base. The cones were meant to amplify the sound and the base to reflect it toward the holes on the upper part of the soundboard. The neck had a square section because the instrument was aimed at the Hawaiian musician.

The instrument, strange as it looked, worked well and, according to contemporary advertising, was seven times louder than a normal acoustic guitar: the Resophonic guitar was born.

At first only Hawaiian style instruments were produced, but soon other versions were added with conventional guitar necks and the success of the National Tricone became popular in all musical styles and appeared in orchestras as well as in jazz combos or in the arms of blues players. It was favoured by Hawaiian wizard Sol Hoopii and jazz virtuoso Carlos Alomar (**).

A 1929 National Tricone
(Claudio Prosperini)

In Europe the research didn't end with De Torres, in 1932, indeed, the French Selmer introduced a new guitar designed by the Italian Mario Maccaferri and made with extreme attention to details in a climate controlled environment.

The instrument had laminated rosewood sides and back, solid spruce top, sealed lubricated tuning machines, similar to modern Schaller or Grover, and a large "D" shaped sound hole.

Under the sound hole a curved panel reflected the sound of an internal sound-box, which had really thin sides so as to vibrate as a diaphragm, improving clarity and sound projection with a more balanced emission of all frequencies.

Other innovations were the cutaway (a first for a mass produced instrument), a fingerboard extending over the sound hole on the treble side for a range of 24 frets on the first string, helicoidal bridge for a more exact intonation, tailpiece made to accept loop or ball-end strings.

Good, sweet tone and a powerful, long sustaining voice, permitted the Maccaferri guitar to compete favourably with the American archtop models, though not with the cutting Nationals. However contractual disagreements between the designer and Selmer stopped production at only 300 instruments (***).

In the meantime Rickenbacker introduced the first Hawaiian electric guitar (1931), then Gibson produced the ES 150, an archtop with a magnetic pickup (1936) and a new era began, the era of the electric guitar player.

Even Django Reinhardt, the gipsy jazz wonder, usually a Maccaferri user, in his last performances and recordings chose the amplified guitar (L-5).

The invention of the magnetic pickup around the 1930's, caused a general decrease in interest in experiments aimed at obtaining more volume from pure acoustic instruments and the standard remained the Dreadnought, the only exception being the big and much imitated Gibson J 200.

The new star, offering previously unavailable possibilities to the guitar player and favouring the birth of new musical styles, was this simple but fascinating item known as the magnetic pickup...

The Gibson Super 400, held by Arnold Covay, was the Queen of the acoustic guitars, but the bar pickup gave to the smaller ES 150, in the arms of a smiling Charlie Christian, a much stronger voice. Witness: Benny Goodman.
(picture courtesy of Leo Valdes).

Notes

(*) The most important development concerning the classical guitar, which did not arrive until the first half of the twentieth century, was not related to structural elements, but to the strings. Andres Segovia's concerts in the United States, proved to American people how efficient the bracing conceived by De Torres was, in small sized instruments, and how only the big archtop and the dreadnought with steel strings can rival the Spanish guitar for volume.

The great player's much sought after solution to the weak point was in the kind of strings used. The gut strings deteriorate easily and are unpredictable in consistency and difficult to keep in tune. Segovia tried to involve all the string makers he could find and finally met Albert Augustine, from New York, who accepted the challenge.

Finally in 1947, Augustine found the solution in a new material; nylon, invented by Wallace Carothers in 1935. The resulting nylon strings were long lasting, had a balanced tone and were easy to tune; at last the classical guitar was complete.

(**) After just about one year, John Dopyera, owing to arguments with his partners, quitted National and founded a new company which made similar instruments, the difference being a wooden body and a cone of different design, under the Dobro brand.

(***) Maccaferri guitars are famous because of their connection with Django Reinhardt who, judging from the pictures of the time, used both the original model and the version produced by Selmer after Maccaferri left. These later models had an oval sound hole and lacked the internal soundbox.

The guitar shown could be a Fabbricatore from Napoli, Italy, 1791, but is more likely a 1820's copy made by Franciolini, a well known maker of fakes from the same town (C. P.).

Now, let's follow the "pickup" for a journey through history ...

PART 1 – A BIT OF HISTORY

Adolph Rickenbacker and the Lap Steel's prototype, handmade by Harry Watson from a single piece of maple, fitted with the pickup designed by George Beauchamp.

Courtesy of Rickenbacker

1) The pioneers

The connection between string instruments and electricity had been explored since the end of the nineteenth century, but very little is known about those first experiments. In 1919 the power of a new technology to amplify sounds was proved by the radio sets and, a few years later, by the introduction of cone speakers and the tube amplifier.
During the 1920s, though solutions specifically studied for guitar's amplification had been tried, none of them proved to be commercially suitable.

A Victor ad for the successful Victrola, a record player introduced in 1906 (Peter Liebert)

Lester Polfuss, later known as les Paul, often claimed to have been the first person to amplify a guitar using a phonograph cartridge. Eddie Durham was credited as the first guitar player to record, using an amplified guitar, though it could have possibly been a resophonic guitar. George Barnes first documented the use of an amplified guitar, which had a pickup and amplifier built by his brother, and later recorded blues sessions in Chicago, often with the nickname of "Hot Box" Johnson. Anyway it's clear that after the 1920s many individual and independent experiments were carried out, although rarely with convincing results.

Lloyd A. Loar, with the help of Lewis Williams, general manager at Gibson and a pioneer in the field of sound reproduction and loudspeaker design, carried out a systematic laboratory research into a product to launch on the professional market. Loar, well known as the designer of the F series, including the outstanding L-5 and the equally appreciated mandolin F-5, was a firm believer in the possibility and necessity to produce electrical instruments and worked with a commitment to the project.

Unfortunately at that time it seemed there was no market for such instruments, so Gibson decided to stop the experiments. Consequently Williams in 1923 and Loar in 1924, resigned from Gibson and together they founded the Vivitone Company in 1933, producing mainly electrical instruments, including a solid body prototype and an electric piano based on principles used at the time and again many years later, to design the Wurlitzer and the Fender Rhodes. The amplifier accompanying the piano was not less innovative, with an impressive power of 33 Watts when the usual power, at that time, was about 3 Watts. These instruments, however, were considered too bizarre by contemporary players, and Vivitone had to face a bad commercial failure.

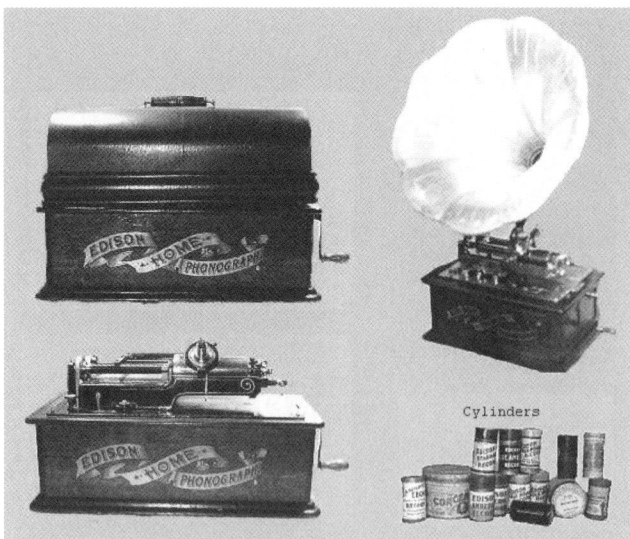

Edison's phonograph (courtesy of Peter Liebert).

In order to understand the difficulty in proposing electrical instruments in the 1930s, we must remember that the simple idea that a sonic event could be preserved was a recent achievement and sound diffusion was still in its infancy. It was 1887 when Edison announced the realization of a machine from which a sound could be recorded on a support, and reproduced: the phonograph. The first version worked with recorded cylinders of two or three minutes capacity, but there were no sound diffusion systems and it was only possible to listen through a horn reproducer.
Proper amplification of a signal became available only by the end of the 1920s*.

The connection between electricity and musical instruments was still, from any point of view, pure science-fiction.

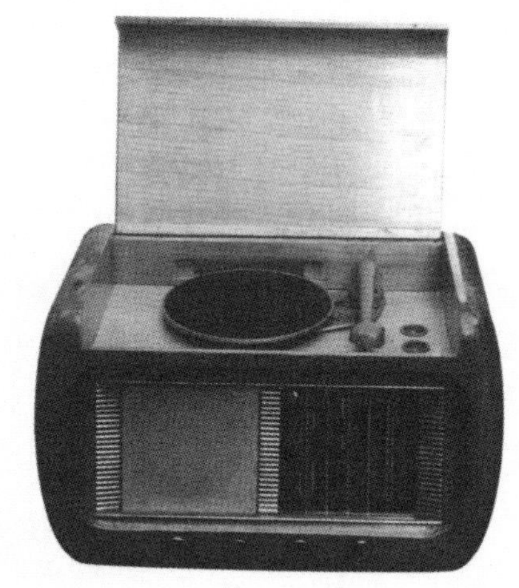
Radio sets and phonographs, in the same box in this forties' Dynacord offering, were the inspiration for guitar's amplification (courtesy of Giovanni Gaglio).

The Loar-Williams system consisted, as can be deducted from a Gibson prototype, in a condenser model with copper plates of coin dimensions and protected in a bakelite container, looking very similar to recent contact mikes such as those made by Barcus-Berry, DiMarzio and others. Both on the Gibson prototype and today's contact mikes, the pickup is applied to the soundboard, but instead of being on the external surface, as on the modern contact mikes, it was glued internally, with the output on the back of the instrument through a jack and strap-holder combination. The pickup, however, was excessively sensitive to humidity and its very high impedance, necessitated the use of short cables in order to avoid signal degeneration. This seems to explain, at least partially, Loar's failure; the vision was right, but the technology still too raw.

George Beauchamp (pronounced Beecham) was a fine guitar player, especially in the Hawaiian style, and a first rate contributor to the development of the National. His main interest was to carry out experiments on electric amplification of the guitar, but it was not shared by the Dopyera brothers and in 1930 he was out of the company.

Adolph Rickenbacher, who in 1925 founded the Rickenbacker Manufacturing Company and changed the spelling of his name to Rickenbacker, built the metal bodies of the National guitars in 1927 and became a good friend of George. In 1931 he allowed Beauchamp to carry out experiments, with Paul Barth, to develop a pickup suitable for guitar amplification in his laboratory.

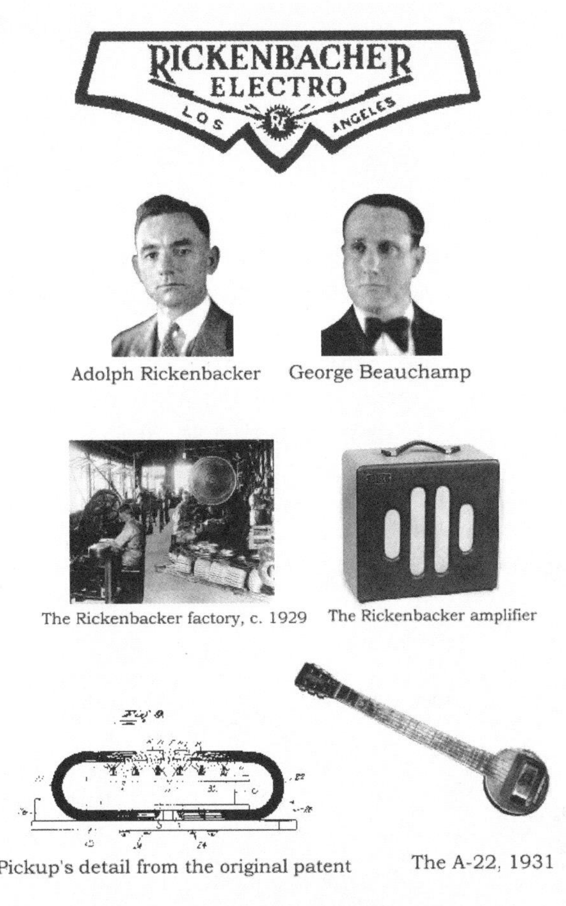

Adolph Rickenbacker George Beauchamp

The Rickenbacker factory, c. 1929 The Rickenbacker amplifier

Pickup's detail from the original patent The A-22, 1931

Pictures courtesy of Rickenbacker

Together they founded the Ro-Pat-In Corporation (later renamed Rickenbacker Electro, with the old "Rickenbacher" spelling on some early labels) and after a long research a completely new pickup was produced.

In Loar's condenser type, two thin plates facing each other, vibrated, thus reducing and increasing the distance between them which induced a variation in their capacity.

This process caused an alternating tension, the modulation of which was related to the sound waves soliciting the system, sending them to an amplifier, thereby increasing its level. Electrodes controlled the current produced, so it was necessary for the plates to be electrically charged inducing a permanently retained tension. In a magnetic pickup a magnet extends a magnetic field under the strings.

When this field is disturbed by the vibration of the strings, which are made from magnetic materials such as nickel, the resulting variations are converted by a coil surrounding the magnet into a weak electrical signal which is sent to an amplifier to boost the level.

On Rickenbacker's version the coil is under the strings, while two massive magnets, with a moderate attractive force, extend over them in a configuration shaped like a horse-shoe (from here the nickname given to this unit). Six cylindrical polepieces inside the coil direct the magnetic flux towards the strings. George Beauchamp, actually, tried different solutions before finding the final one; some drawings show pickups with the magnets parallel to the strings and two coils, one on top, one under the strings.

Some prototypes have the same structure as the horseshoe but with a blade polepiece.

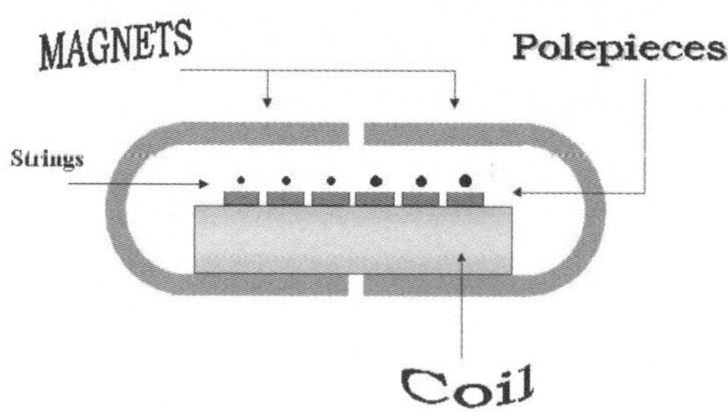

The production model has magnets which are 1.5" wide and a winding of more than 5000 turns of AWG 38 wire around six cylindrical ferrous polepieces.

Less delicate than condenser models, the magnetic pickup puts Rickenbacker on the right path.

The principle behind this pickup is the same as the one on which magnetic pickups are still based, making the Rickenbacker the first modern pickup.

The prototype guitar was made from wood, but the production models were completely made from aluminium and had a hollow neck, later filled with newspapers to improve the sound. Aluminium proved too sensitive to changes in temperature and so was substituted by bakelite, others were once again made from wood.

The complete six String Hawaiian Guitar Outfit consists of instrument, speaker, unit and necessary cords and plugs. Complete with three ply Veneer shell Keratol covered case. $140.00

The complete seven String Hawaiian Guitar Outfit consists of instrument, speaker, unit and necessary cords and plugs. Complete with three ply Veneer shell Keratol covered case. $150.00

The "MIDGETS" of the Tonal World Attain to GIANTS Stature!

A MIRACLE has come to pass in the realm of beautiful tone. The soft, fairy-voiced Hawaiian guitar, the tinkling mandolin, the ethereal Spanish guitar—all have been liberated, dignified, and given their rightful place among orchestral instruments.

HOW?

Touched with the magic wand of electrical genius the quality they lacked has been conferred upon them—

VOLUME!

CONTROLLED VOLUME—more than sufficient for the largest orchestra.

As much or as little as you want. You can start the tone softly and build up a tremendous crescendo, or execute a musicianly swell, without stroking the strings again. You can follow every dynamic effect of wind or percussion with no trouble at all. Marvelous, isn't it? Hardly believable till you hear it.

In addition to the added volume, the tonal qualities of each instrument have been vastly improved. The building of the instruments and the adjustment of the sound magnifying device have all been pointed to that end. There are no dissonances, or *noises* picked up to mar pure tone or damp vibration.

What would you say of a Hawaiian guitar you could hear a quarter of a mile on a clear day, or a Spanish Guitar louder than any piano? That's what we have in the new

RICKENBACKER ELECTRO INSTRUMENTS

The 1931's catalogue (courtesy of Rickenbacker).

Introduced in 1931, the A-22, nicknamed, as the prototype, "Frying Pan", for it's shape, was not an immediate success, but after two years sales increased and lawyers were forced to protect the product from imitations. Even Sol Hoopii, a National endorser, left his Tricone in its case and recorded with an electric Rickenbacker lap steel (on some very early instruments, curiously, the name is spelled the old way: Rickenbacher).

1931's Rickenbacker catalogue (courtesy of Rickenbacker).

Rickenbacker also built the amplifiers, which were very similar in design to radio sets of the time. He was also influenced by the developments in sound equipment used in the new industry of motion pictures, which was rapidly evolving in neighbouring Hollywood. It's not surprising that the most important lap steel players were professionals working on exotic movie soundtracks.

In catalogues from that era the price stated for the lap-steel included the loudspeaker, which meant the amplifier. An industry around this element had still not developed and all makers produced instruments with amplifiers which were made exclusively (Epiphone, for instance, had them built by Nat Daniel, who later became famous with his own brand: Danelectro).

During the 1930s a new shape, similar to that of a normal guitar but smaller, substituted the round shape of the first lap steels. A model named simply "Spanish Guitar" was added to the line and to many, it's the first solid body ever produced. The instrument had a bakelite body as aluminium had now been completely abandoned. It was a little larger than a lap steel, partially hollow for weight reduction (as some modern solid body models), had a horseshoe pickup and a regular round neck.

In an attempt to maintain a reasonable weight, as the same material used for bowling balls was used, the body was very small and consequently musicians didn't take the guitar seriously because it looked like a toy, unsuitable for a professional player.

Notwithstanding these characteristics, most players still found the new Rickenbacker too heavy.

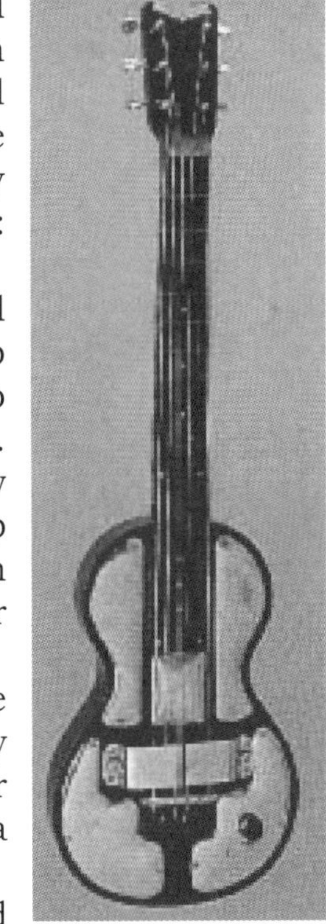

1935's Spanish Guitar (courtesy of Rickenbacker).

The pickup was also sold in different versions as an after market item.

Bakelite steel with matching amplifier, 1941 (courtesy of Rickenbacker).

A thinner model was designed for the amplification of the acoustic archtop, which was removable if so desired. Success led to imitation and the Rickenbacker pickup was soon copied by other makers. It would seem that only Epiphone paid a royalty to produce a similar unit, before designing his own model in 1937. Even after the golden days of the lap steel, the Horseshoe was used on guitars and basses. In fact it continued to be used right up until the sixties, when the price for tungsten, the material used for the magnets, became too high to competitively produce the pickup. The magnets had a relatively weak magnetic field surrounding the strings with a wider magnetic window than most single coil pickups, this produced a clear but full sound even in the usual position which was close to the bridge. This is the main reason why it's still held in high esteem by many players.

After World War Two, narrower magnets were used and the specifications of the pickup were changed to obtain a brighter tone, although most players preferred previous versions.

Sol Hoopii was the main promoter of the use of the resophonic guitar and later adopted the electric lap steel.

Beauchamp was not the only one, nor the first, to try a magnetic pickup, in 1929 Stromberg-Voisinet offered amplifiers and several instruments amplified by a pickup directly capturing the top's vibrations. Loar, with Vivitone, seems to have tried a magnetic pickup inserted inside the body of the instrument.
Those systems were less efficient than Rickenbacker's model which was certainly less acoustic sounding, but louder and more effective.

Beauchamp applied for a patent in 1932, but it was granted only in 1937, a situation which favoured the proliferation of copies.

Sometimes the results were unusual, as with a Slingerland model on which, instead of simple polepieces as on the Rickenbacker had real magnets in the coil and the magnetic interference between those and the big horseshoe magnets gave a sort of "vibrato" sound. In 1939 Vega produced a version with two out of phase coils, creating the first humbucking, though with a different structure than that used by Gibson in 1957.
The lap steel was fashionable and sales of Rickenbacker, National, Supro and Epiphone instruments overshadowed those of the resophonic guitars, making it impossible, for Gibson, to ignore the electrical instrument (in 1932 even Dobro introduced an amplified guitar).

Gibson relied on the amplification experience of a Chicago company, Lyon & Healy, by giving their engineer John Kutalek the job to design a pickup with the help of Alvino Rey, a popular lap steel player.

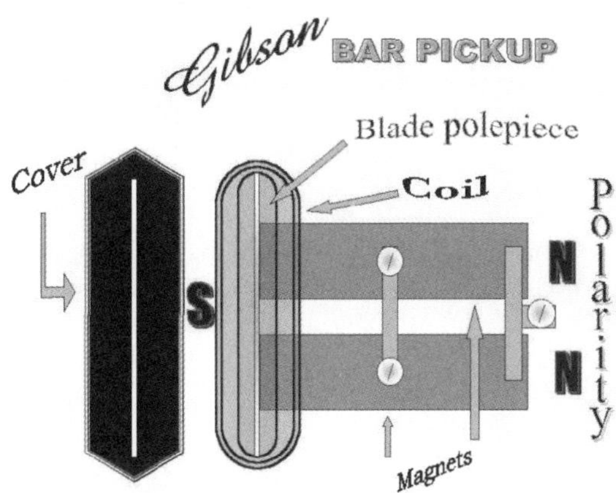

After several months of research a marketable design was still unavailable and Gibson decided to find a solution on it's own. Their employee Walter Fuller, expert in electronics, was asked to solve the problem.

The result was a magnetic pickup structured very differently from the Beauchamp designed unit and complying with Gibson's desire to avoid infringing the Rickenbacker patent. The magnetic field for the pickup was created by two bar magnets, made from an alloy containing 36% cobalt and steel, with the opposing poles on the shortest sides, the south ones touching a blade polepiece, around which the coil is wound, therefore transferring the magnetic field toward the strings. Nickel & steel magnets were also used until 1937.

These long magnets extended under the soundboard, parallel to the strings. The polepiece was notched under the three top strings giving the impression of separate smaller blades, probably to balance the sound by reducing the magnetic field under the thinner strings, which were naturally more sensitive.

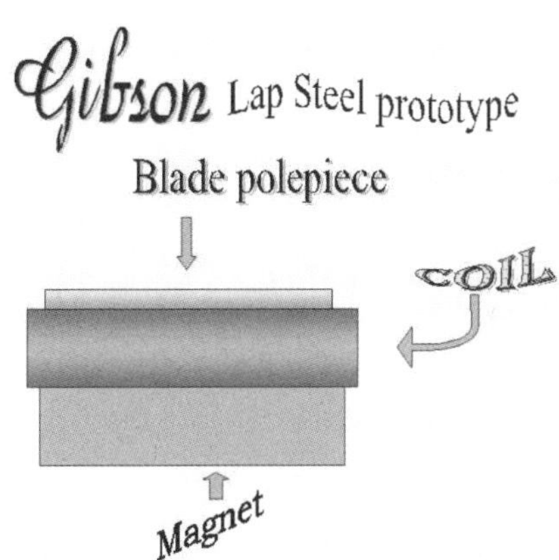

Some very early prototype lap steels probably had a pickup with a single magnet under the coil.

Completed in 1935, the pickup was used at first on a Gibson aluminium body lap steel and only in 1936 was it used on an archtop guitar. The guitar version was slightly different, with a blade polepiece without notches and had three spring-loaded screws to adjust the pickup's height and tilt the magnets under the soundboard for minor tone changes. The magnets were slightly smaller than those used on the lap steels.

Some variants of this pickup have been made, the first with a big coil of the relatively thick AWG 38 wire, with a low resistance, using, on the first few samples, two different kinds of magnets. These differed in the formula of cobalt percentage; respectively 17% and 36%, the second one then became the standard.

In 1938 the coil was changed to 10000 turns of AWG 42 wire for a resistance of about 8 kOhms, with a 20% tolerance, setting the standard, regarding coil

1938's Gibson ES 150 and 1939's ES 100 (Claudio Caldana).

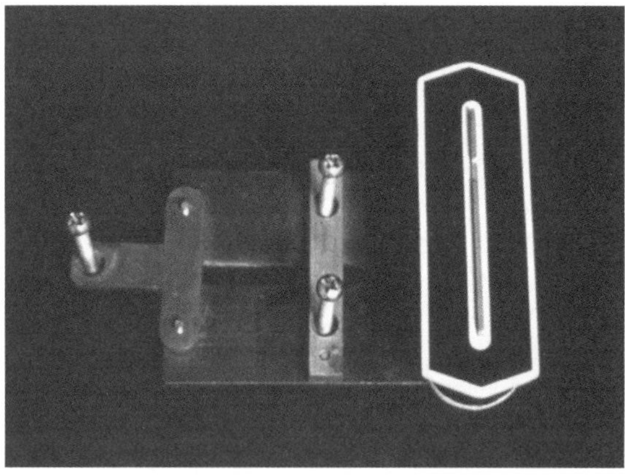

The late seventies' Gibson reissue bar pickup used on the ES 175 CC Limited Edition (Claudio Auriemma).

specifications, for later models up to the sixties.
In 1940, the ES 250 was introduced, as the top of the line. This new version had six individual small blades as polepiece, replacing the long one.

The guitar player Charlie Christian had a very important role and actively contributed to the popularity of the new instrument and his use of the ES 150 and ES 250 connected his name so powerfully to these pickups that they are still known as "Charlie Christian" models. The clean and clear timbre of these pickups was so popular, especially by jazz players, that Gibson in the sixties still offered, on special order, a version of the basic model and in 1977 a reissue was fitted to the limited edition ES 175 CC. A cheaper version of the pickup, composed of 17% Cobalt magnets, was used for the ES 100, a guitar intended to be an economical version of the ES 150.

Although undoubtedly, the bar pickup was designed by Walter Fuller, the patent was signed by Guy Hart. Hart, who was the general manager of the company at that time, established Gibson as the sole owner of the project, as was common practice in those years. This was very important in a competitive market.

The secrecy regarding technical details reached a point in which some makers, but not Gibson, used to soak the coil in wax or dark lacquer, not done, at that time, in order to prevent feedback. This was barely a problem with low wattage amplifiers. This technique was used, instead, to obscure information from competitors as to which kind of wire and how many turns were used.

Notes

(*) In 1887 Edison introduced a revolutionary change in the life of North Americans, by improving the telegraph, and bringing electric light into their homes. This also included the application of new energy to rail transport, and rendered the cylinder phonograph more reliable. In 1890 he advanced further by creating the basics for another item which was fundamental for the diffusion of popular music: the jukebox.

In 1988 Emile Berliner introduced the 7" flat record, which had a two minute capacity, and could be mass-produced from a zinc master.

In 1998, in Denmark, Valdemar Poulsen patented the first wire recorder, called Telegraphone.

In South America, in 1902 Ademor Petit patented a double face 10" record with a ten minute capacity.

The German company Odeon took care of sales while the American company Victor imported recordings of Enrico Caruso and classical repertoires with great success, despite the necessity to split the recording into several records to obtain a full symphony.

In 1906 the American Graphophone Company, acted on Marconi's suggestion and produced Velvet-tone records, which were made from shellac and had a paper core, with reduced background noise. That same year Victor introduced the Victrola, the first phonograph with the loudspeakers in the same box.

The radio was beginning to become well known and finally reached it's peak of popularity in 1912, when an assistant of Marconi, from New York, announced the Titanic disaster. This first broadcasted news was limited in most cases to listening through earphones.

AT&T developed a public amplification system which was devised only to amplify the speakers voice during conferences but not music. It involved horn loudspeakers which were very efficient, but still had a limited range.

In 1925 cone speakers were available and real amplification, involving the output signal being louder than the input, appeared only in 1929. Technology continued to evolve and in 1935 AEG, in Germany, made the first recordings on a magnetic tape. Meanwhile, cinema in the United States, realising the importance of novelty in sound, carried out thorough research in amplification. Only after World War Two, the United States and the United Kingdom discovered the invention of the magnetic tape, used by Germans to record allied radio communications.
Then in 1946 Ampex, in the USA, produced tape recorders for broadcasting. In the meantime NTC became the first TV network and television substituted radio as the most important showcase for musicians. Colour TV was finally available in 1954.

(**) AWG stands for American Wire Gauge and is relative to the diameter of the wire in respect to the thickness; e.g.: an AWG 43 (mm. 0,056) is thinner than AWG 42 (mm. 0,063) and so on.

CHARLIE CHRISTIAN
LIVE SESSIONS AT MINTON'S PLAYHOUSE
NEW-YORK • MAY 1941
JAZZ ANTHOLOGY
DIGITALLY REMASTERED DIRECTLY FROM THE ORIGINAL ANALOG TAPES
CHRISTIAN
CBS JAZZ MASTERPIECES
Charlie Christian
The Genius of the Electric Guitar
Gibson
G 30779
S O L O F L I G H T · THE GENIUS OF CHARLIE CHRISTIAN
John Hammond Collection

2) A fast evolution

During the first half of the century, the industrial progress was advancing rapidly and constantly making new materials. In 1939 G. B. Jonas invented a new kind of magnet, made from an alloy of aluminium, nickel, cobalt and other elements in varying percentages, plus steel or iron.

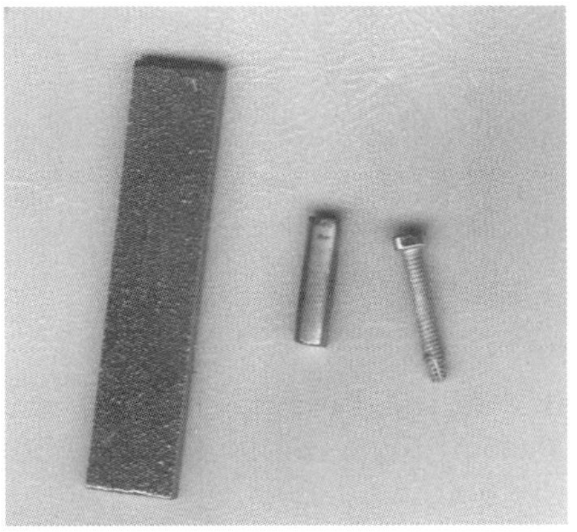

Alnico magnets and screw-type polepieces. Available in different shapes and dimensions, the magnets usually used for pickup making are bar or cylinders.

The new magnet, called "AlNiCo" derived from the initials of its' main components, had a stronger magnetic flux than the previous cobalt and steel type, and was available in a variety of dimensions. It soon became the standard in speaker and pickup making.
Another great innovation was the screw type adjustable polepiece.

Epiphone was the first manufacturer to use adjustable polepieces, issuing a model designed by Herb Sunshine, which was rather crude looking. It was made in variations up to 1951, when a new model, with smaller polepieces, placed on the side of the coil instead of inside, was introduced.

Jensen speaker with Alnico 5 magnet (Claudio Prosperini).

In October 1940 Walter Fuller, at Gibson, placed two Alnico magnets under the coil, through which, six adjustable polepieces transferred the magnetic flux towards the strings, thus designing a less bulky model which was more efficient than previous units, and was completed by a metallic cover.
The coil was the same as that of the latest "Charlie Christian" pickups, although the new magnets produced more output, enhanced middle frequencies and gave fuller basses, while its position close to the bridge emphasized clarity.

Gibson had experimented on the adjustable polepieces before the introduction of this model as there is evidence of the existence of an ES 150 model equipped with two "Charlie Christian" pickups with screw poles.

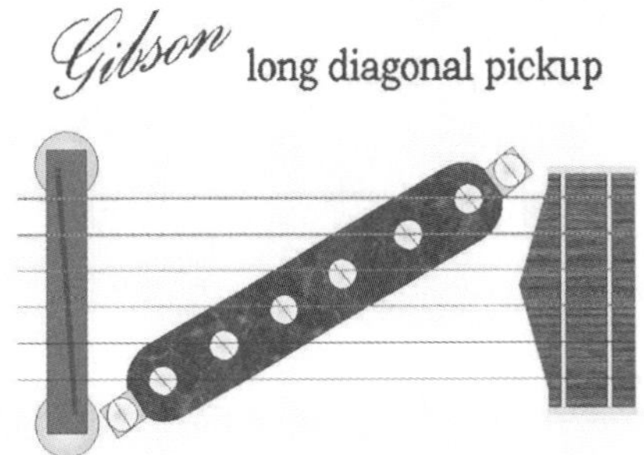

In an attempt to acquire a more "acoustic" sound, a new model was realized around the end of 1940. This pickup had a tortoise-like plastic

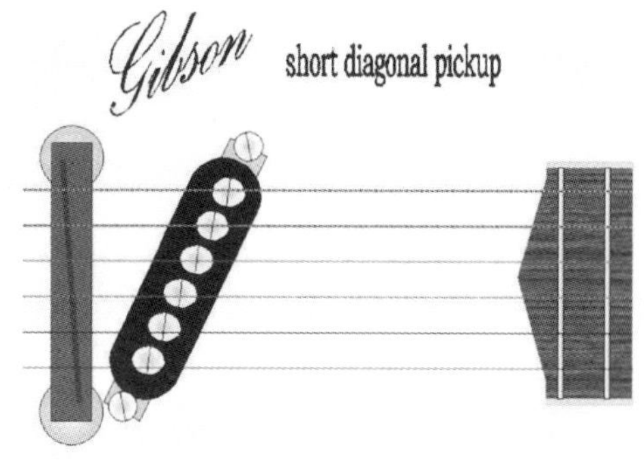

cover, was mounted diagonally and extended from the fingerboard (bass side) to the bridge (treble side), with two pairs of magnets under the long coil.

The long diagonal pickup was not successful and was replaced by a new model, similar to the 1939 version, with two magnets only. This was mounted close to the bridge and slightly slanted (thereby preceding the Telecaster).

It was used on the ES 300 and some L-5 and Super 400 models. Introduced in 1941 this model had the 10.000 turn winding but only two Alnico magnets under the coil.

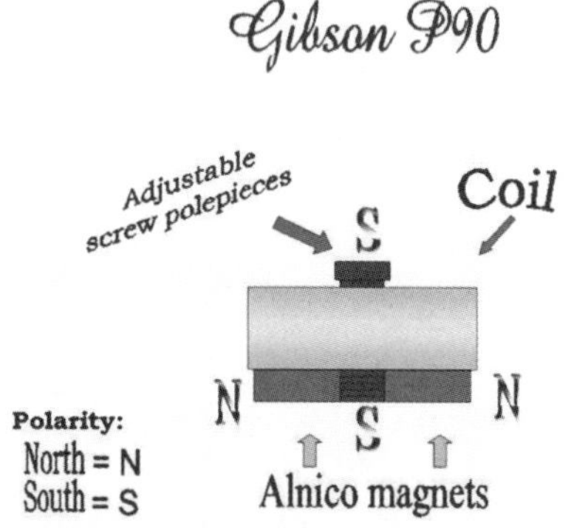

When World War Two broke out, production became limited due to the fact that most of the employees were occupied with military duties.
At the Gibson factory, for instance, only ten per cent of its workers continued to manufacture instruments while the rest was busy making radar assemblies and other war-related items.
Because of metal restrictions almost all production of electrical instruments and amplifiers had to be suspended and even acoustic guitars were often made without truss-rods (a few electric guitars, however, were made).

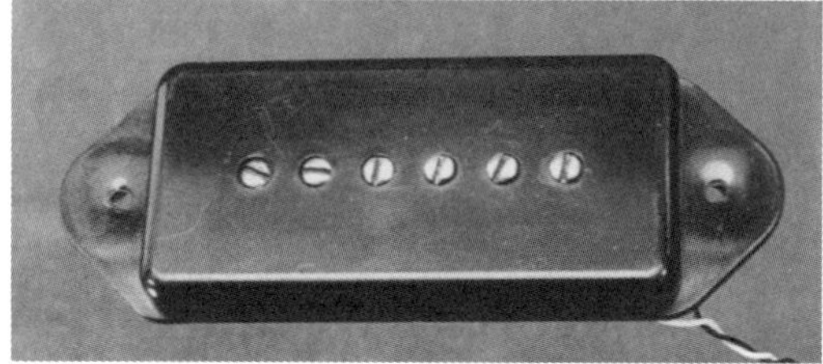

Gibson P 90 with "dog ear" cover (Claudio Prosperini).

When the war ended, production was resumed. A wave of optimism and enthusiasm brought unprecedented energy to the industry and new models were issued.

P 90s on a Gibson ES-5 (C. Caldana).

The Gibson pickup received a new black plastic cover, with distinctive "ears" at both ends, through which two screws secured it to the body of the guitar (the cover is nicknamed "dog ear"). In 1946, the new pickup, factory coded as PU-90, was introduced. It had the same technical specifications of the short diagonal model, identical to those of the metallic covered one, but it was mounted near the fingerboard for warmer sounds. The design of this model had two Alnico magnets and a coil winding of 10000 turns of AWG 42 Plain Enamel wire, but due to continuing lack of materials some earlier samples, were made with only one magnet and no adjustable polepieces.

Early fifties ES 5 with '61 Fender Twin Amp. Introduced in 1949 as the top of the line of the electric models, the ES 5 has three P 90s, volume control for each and master volume (C. Caldana).

This Gibson model, commercially known as the P 90, had an output level higher than any pickup of the time and a sound which was well balanced between warmth and aggressiveness. Due to these qualities the P 90 remained popular and Gibson offered several reissues. This model had also been copied by other manufacturers, as many players favoured it over the humbucker, although hum, from the powerful pickup, became a problem in certain circumstances.

Fuller, not a man to rest on his laurels, designed a simplified and cheaper version for the ES 125, made with six non adjustable cylindrical Alnico magnets directly in the coil, which was the same as on the P 90. The sound of this version was brighter and had a more immediate attack and for that reason some musicians preferred the ES 125 over other models (during the fifties the ES 125 was also fitted with P 90 pickups).

After 1946 the range of Gibson amplified guitars was broadened and two pickup models were offered. Top of the line was the ES-5 introduced in 1949, with three pickups, volume control for each, and master volume.

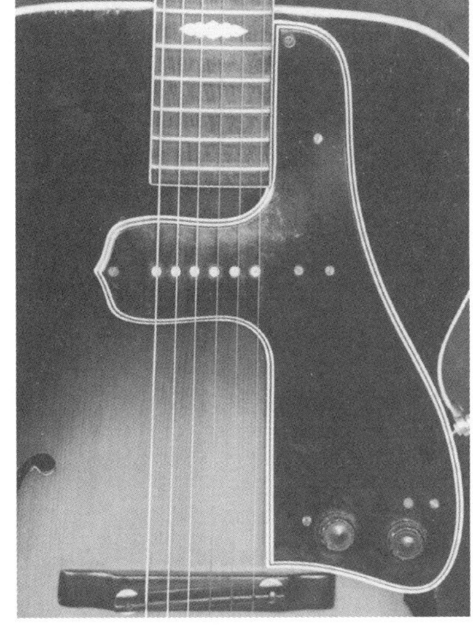
McCarty unit on an early 1930s L-7 (Claudio Caldana).

A new item, that same year was credited to Ted McCarty, a pickguard for acoustic archtops which were fitted with one or two pickups and controls for volume and tone. They also had small sized potentiometers because of the reduction of space. The pickups were flat, with a wide coil of reduced height, made with 25% less turns than on a regular P 90, with six cylindrical Alnico magnets inserted through the coil.

Compared to a P 90 the new McCarty pickups were brighter and had a more pronounced attack, but nonetheless had that unmistakable Gibson voice. It was therefore now available to owners of acoustic archtops, offering a more practical and elegant solutions than previous attempts.

At the same time, in California, Leo Fender was getting ready to enter the competition with a guitar which would force all instrument makers to think better of their ideas on the design of electric guitars.

Fender and Kaufman had produced electric lap steel guitars in the forties, with pickups partially inspired by the Rickenbacker model (Kauffman and Beauchamp had been friends since the 1930s), with some differences: instead of two tungsten horseshoe magnets, two Alnico bar magnets on the top and bottom of a coil, perpendicular to the top of the guitar, (as if it were lying on it's side), with the strings passing through.

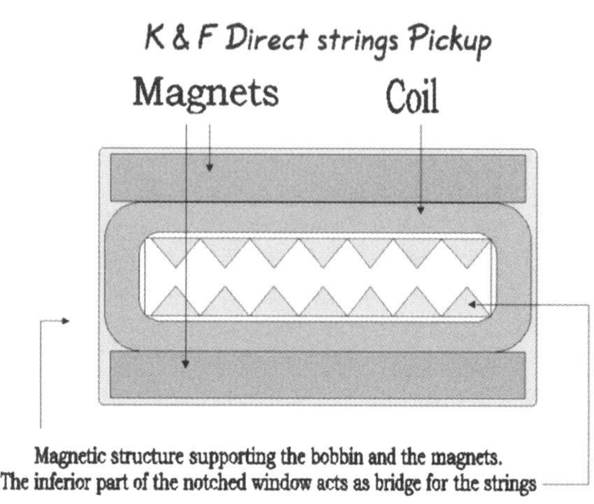

The idea came from a phonograph cartridge, on which the needle was inside a small coil. The entire pickup was held together by a metallic structure with a notched front window. The lower side acted as a bridge for the strings.
Even after the introduction of the pickups still universally connected to the Fender name, many are still fond of this unit for its broad range of sounds. (Fender applied for a patent, calling the model "Direct Strings Pickup", granted some years later).

Fender lap steels, 1949, produced when the F & K Company was already over (C. Caldana).

The electric guitar, to most, was simply an acoustic guitar fitted with pickups for electric amplification, but Fender's idea was different, conceiving the instrument more as a lap steel designed to be played like a regular guitar.

The body lacked a real soundbox and was made from solid wood. The signal was provided mainly from the vibrating strings and the pickup.

The idea was not really new; as Lloyd Loar at Vivitone had experimented with a solid body and in 1942 O. W. Appleton, in Arizona, built a prototype with a body strikingly similar in shape to that of Gibson's still to come Les Paul (it seems that Appleton tried, without luck, to interest Gibson in his invention).

In 1947 Paul Bigsby made some solid body guitars with a headstock similar to the one later designed for the Stratocaster, with six on line tuners. The pickups made by Bigsby were similar to the Gibson P 90, but with the two Alnico magnets vertically put to the sides of the coil, and with a ferrous sheet on the base which transferred the magnetic flux to the bar polepiece inside the winding (some units had screw-type polepieces). The polarity was north toward the strings.

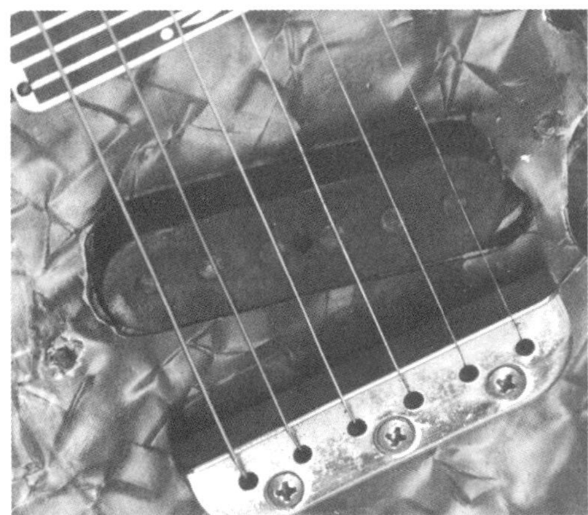
Fender lap steel pickup, 1949 (C. C.).

But Fender, at that time, was still working on his lap steels, for which a new pickup was being designed. Simple, relatively cheap to produce, and possibly, looking less bulky than the Direct Strings and Rickenbacker models.

By the end of the forties Alnico magnets were available in a variety of formats and Leo, after many experiments carried out with magnets of different shapes and dimensions, found a solution which remained as the basis of almost all the models he later designed. This had six cylindrical magnets around which the wire is wound directly (actually the magnets were soaked in lacquer to separate them from the winding).

Fender Broadcaster (1950) and Deluxe amp (1955) (C. Caldana).

The bridge unit for the guitar had a structure very similar to the lap steel's pickup and had the following specifications: AWG 43 wire for the coil (about 10000 turns) with a resistance close to 10 kOhms and six Alnico magnets. The top and the bottom plates, which kept the magnets and the coil together, were made of black vulcanized fibre.

Under the bottom of the unit there was a tin sheet, not used on the lap steel version, which had been copper plated since 1951, for shielding and grounding. This also intensified the magnetic field, improving sensitivity to high frequencies. The pickup was mounted on a slant, with the bass side farther from the bridge, to give more body at the bottom end. In the early fifties Fender changed the winding with a slightly bigger wire gauge, AWG 42, and about 9000 turns in the coil,

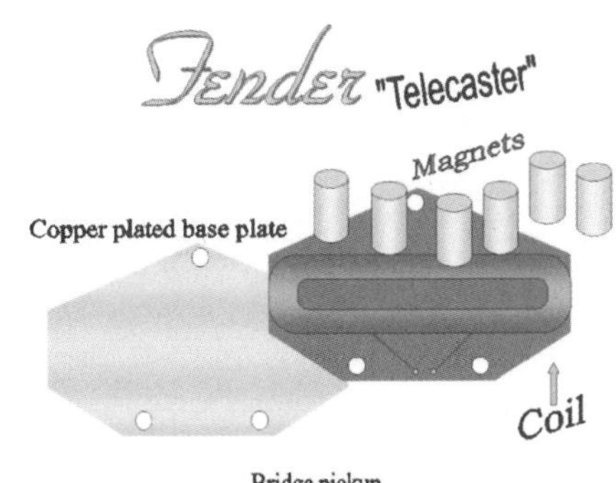

Fender Telecaster, 1967 (C. Caldana).

for a resistance ranging from 7 to 7,8 kOhms, creating a brighter sound. In the neck position a different model was used, with a smaller coil, made from the same AWG 43 wire used for the first version of the bridge model, but with fewer turns and a resistance of about 8 kOhms; a nickel cover protected the unit. The sound achieved with this model was soft and warm, and was aimed at jazz players.

With this arrangement Fender succeeded in his project thus producing a guitar with the clear and full sound of a lap steel.

This was particularly true of the first version of the bridge model, and versatile enough to be used for any kind of music, from country to jazz. In those years the big novelty was television and the most visible guitars were the big blonde finished archtops, contrasting against the black suits of professional musicians. Leo builds the regular production guitars from ash with a blonde finish (Fender made the very first experimental guitar with a white finish and the first one introduced was made from black finished pine wood).

P 90 with cream "soap bar" cover on a Gibson Les Paul (Claudio Prosperini).

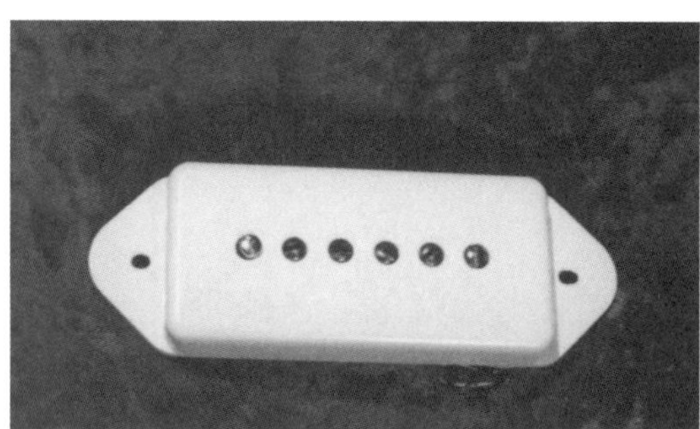

Gibson P 90 with cream "dog ear" cover, used on the ES 295, similar to the ES 175 but with a gold finish and trapeze bridge-tailpiece (C. Prosperini).

The first production model was a one pickup instrument called Esquire, then the two pickup model called Broadcaster was introduced and later renamed Telecaster (*).

Following the success of the Telecaster, Gibson was convinced that the solid body guitar could no longer be ignored, and introduced the Les Paul in 1952.

It had a structure which required specific tools which were unavailable to the average maker. The new guitar was built from solid seasoned mahogany and a carved maple top, with aesthetic and functional details rooted in the rich lutherie tradition.
Gibson was justifiably proud of this model and claimed to produce the "brand of the professionals".

Electrically, however, there were no changes, as the control layout was the same as on most archtop models.

The only difference was in the P 90's covers, which were rectangular, had round edges without "ears", and were cream coloured instead of black. The P 90s with this kind of cover were known as "Soap Bars", to distinguish them from the "Dog Ears" (most "dog ear" covers were black, except for the ones used on the ES295, introduced in 1952, which were cream coloured, while some "soap bar" covers, such as those on the Les Paul Special, were black).

In 1954 an acoustic jumbo, the J 160, was built with a P 90 mounted to the base of the fingerboard. The guitar received good exposure in the hands of the Beatles.

In the early sixties the P 90s used on Gibson and Epiphone guitars received a "dog ear" nickel cover.

Black "soapbar" P 90 on a 1953 Utratone lap steel (Claudio Prosperini).

In 1954 Leo Fender announced a new guitar, the Stratocaster, with several novelties, such as a bridge/vibrato system, which would become an industry standard, a more comfortably shaped body and three pickups.

Advertising claimed this feature as a "first" from Fender, but actually the first model with three pickups was the Gibson ES-5. Fender could properly claim to have built the first "solid body" guitar so equipped, which was to many the best one (an opinion still shared today by lots of players).

This time the units were identical for any position, and had a structure similar to the Telecaster models, with an AWG 42 gauge wire for the coil, having a 6 kOhms resistance, six cylindrical magnets, no metallic bottom plate and a white cover.

The first covers had rounder edges and were shinier, but after a few months a less shiny material was used, and by the end of 1955 Fender switched to a more durable injection moulded nylon-based plastic.

The control layout consisted of a master volume, tone controls for the neck and middle pickups. The bridge unit lacked a tone control for maximum clarity.

The pickups, the three position switch for single pickup selection and the potentiometers were all mounted on a large pickguard and the magnets were staggered, at different heights to compensate for the varied output of the strings, and were calibrated for the gauge in use.
For some reason Fender did not think it convenient to use adjustable poles.

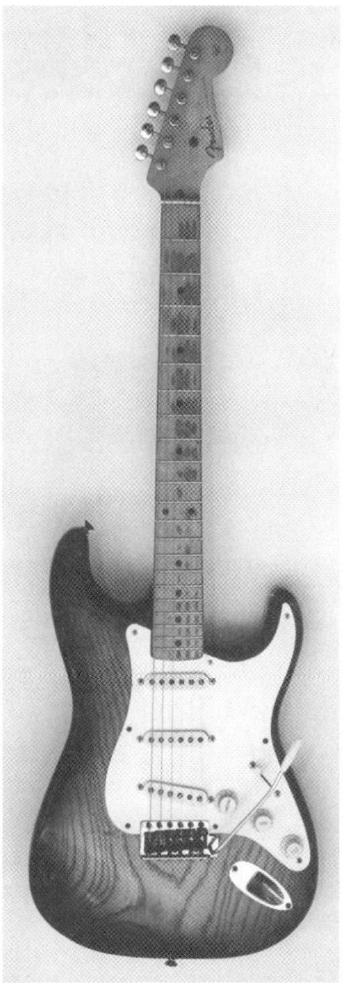

1955 Fender Stratocaster (Claudio Caldana)

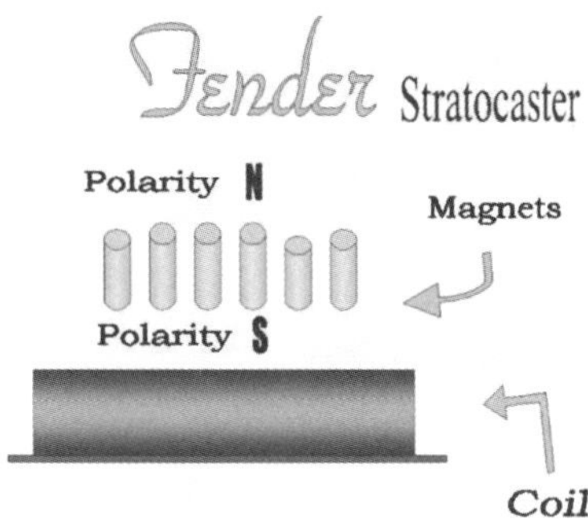

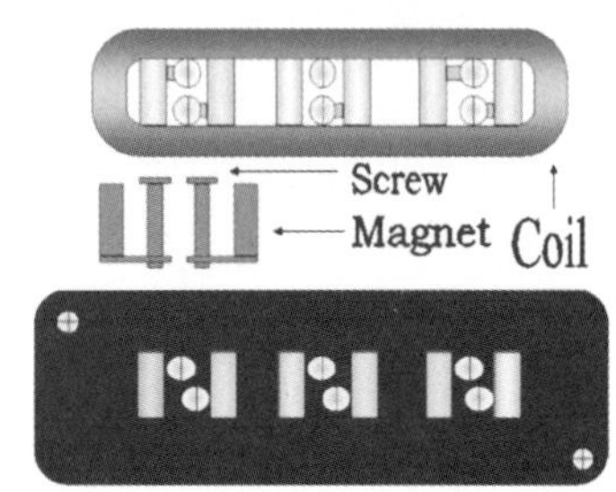

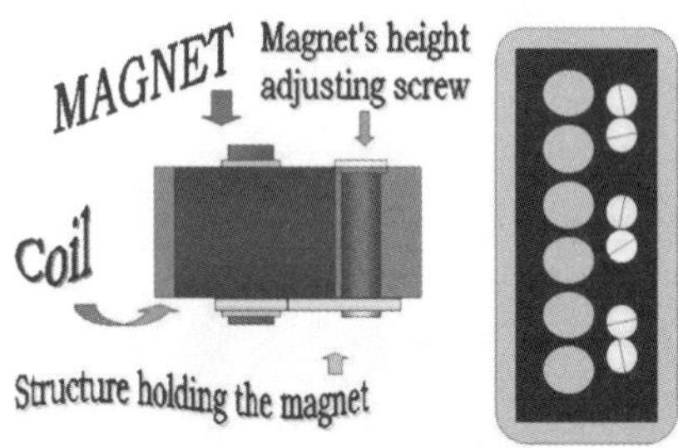

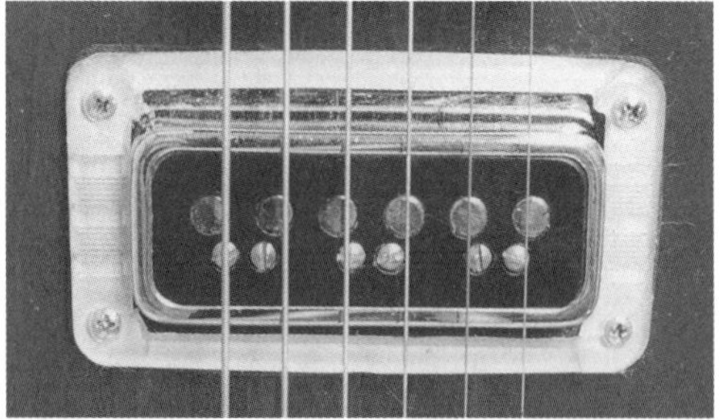
DeArmond pickup (Dynasonic) with black top, as used on Gretsch guitars (Claudio Caldana).

With an ever expanding range of guitars, Gibson felt it was time to introduce a new pickup model.

In 1952 Ted McCarty gave the job to Seth Lover, who had just left the Navy. In 1953 the Lover designed pickup was completed. It had the same coil as the P 90, but had six square Alnico 5 magnets directly in the wiring. The whole unit was height adjustable, as was each single magnet.

The use of magnets in the coil might have appeared to be a Fender influence, but Gibson was in fact competing with DeArmond (after all Gibson used direct magnets before Fender).

While Rickenbacker, Gibson and Fender made their own pickups, other guitar builders, such as Gretsch, Harmony and Kay, rely on units produced by specialized makers, the most popular being DeArmond after the 30's. Lots of guitars had been amplified with a Rowe-DeArmond RHC-B, a model for acoustic guitar electrification which had six Alnico magnets and a resistance of about 9 kOhms. These were appreciated more for sturdiness and dependability than sound quality.

In 1950 DeArmond produced an electric model with a screw parallel to each of the six Alnico magnets in order to adjust their height, a feature which made it the most advanced unit of the time.

A coil with about 9000 turns of AWG 44 wire, for a resistance of 12 kOhms, gave it plenty of power and the timbre was clear but sweet. It had qualities such as a good attack on the low strings, which is why this model is still loved unconditionally by many players.
Called Model 200, the pickup became standard equipment on guitars made by Gretsch, which in his brochures renamed it Fidelatone and later Dynasonic.

Later the pickup was also used on Guild guitars, and although otherwise identical, had a white top instead of a black one. This provoked resentment on the part of Gretsch who considered this model a Gretsch exclusive.

Considering the DeArmond's success, Gibson decided to fight back by introducing a more refined model of the P90 which was capable of giving an extra finesse, to the higher range guitars such as the L5 and the super 400, thereby differentiating them from the more economic models.

Alnico pickups on a Gibson Byrdland (Claudio Caldana).

The "Alnico" pickup, as was known, had a sound similar to the P 90, but was a bit louder and brighter. The new model was also chosen for a new kind of guitar, the thin hollow body, designed for Billy Byrd and Hank Garland, hence the name Byrdland. The prototype was still equipped with a "Charlie Christian" bar pickup near the fingerboard and a P 90 close to the bridge.

A less expensive version of the instrument, the ES 350, received two regular P 90s.
In 1955 the new Les Paul Custom was equipped with an "Alnico" model in the neck position and a regular P 90, with a "soap bar" style cover, at the bridge.

The "Alnico" pick up exceeds Gibson's expectations, but its inventor Seth Lover checks its flight toward success by producing an even better model: the humbucking pickup.

Notes

(*) The name given to the first solid body by Fender was Esquire, introduced in the spring of 1950, which at first only had the bridge pickup. After a few months, a two pickups version was added. In the following autumn the model was renamed Broadcaster and the name Esquire was kept for the single pickup version. In 1951, in order to avoid problems with Gretsch, who had produced a drum set called Broadkaster, Leo Fender changes the name of the guitar to Telecaster, inspired by the growing popularity of the television. The idea for the name seems to belong to Don Randall, then responsible for distribution. During the transition from Broadcaster to Telecaster, between April and August 1951, the instruments carried the old labels simply with the word "Broadcaster" cut off. These guitars were therefore nicknamed "Nocaster".

Alnico pickup on a Les Paul Custom

(**) After the split with Doc Kauffman, Leo Fender continued to produce lap steels that had a pickup similar to the one later used on Esquire, Broadcaster and Telecaster guitars, but its base was square instead of pentagonal and was missing the base metallic plate. As for the guitar models, the specifications were elusive and on original samples resistance values were measured ranging from as low as 6 kOhms to as high as 9 kOhms.

FENDER
FENDER

3) War to hum

As the power of the amplifiers increased, musicians had to face another problem with their pickups: excessive sensitivity to external interference sources, such as stage lights and transformers, produced "hum". The average power, for amplifiers in the forties, was 20 / 30 watts, although in the early fifties 40 watts was not uncommon and in 1952 Fender introduced the Twin Amp, which would evolve, in the late '50s, in an 80 watt monster.

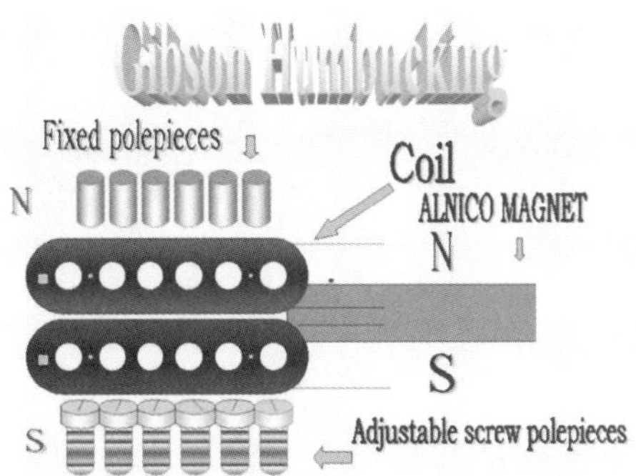

Aware of the problem, Gibson committed Seth E. Lover to find a solution to the excessive sensitivity, and in 1955 Lover designed a pickup, which was immediately patented, and thanks to design research carried out to reduce hum on amplifiers, greatly improved.

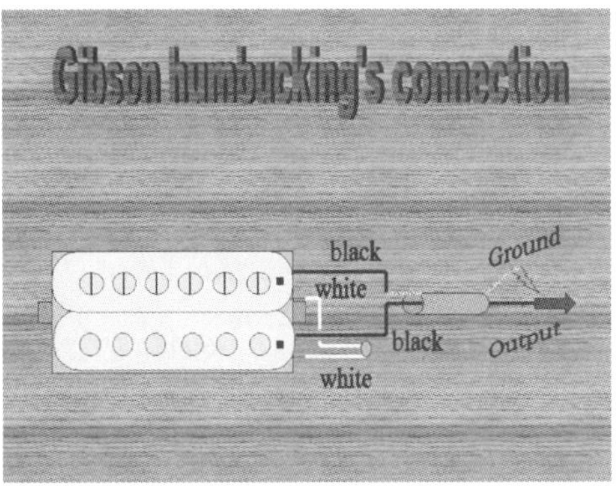

Two bobbins were connected in series out of phase, with a M55 magnet at the bottom, and the opposite magnetic fields transferred to six polepieces in each coil. This way the sound crossing the windings became out of phase and therefore cancelled. The signal picked up by the poles however was in phase and thus not affected.

The new model, codified as PU 490, was named "humbucking". The wire used was the same as that used on the P 90 (10000 turns of AWG 42 plain enamel), but split in the two bobbins (5000 turns in each) with a resistance of 8 kOhms (+/- 20%).

The pickup was not used immediately, perhaps because they had to wait for the patent to be granted, but in 1957 Gretsch applied for a patent on his own humbucking model.

Gretsch's model, Filter'Tron, was designed by Ray Butts, had a clear sound and earned Chet Atkins' approval.

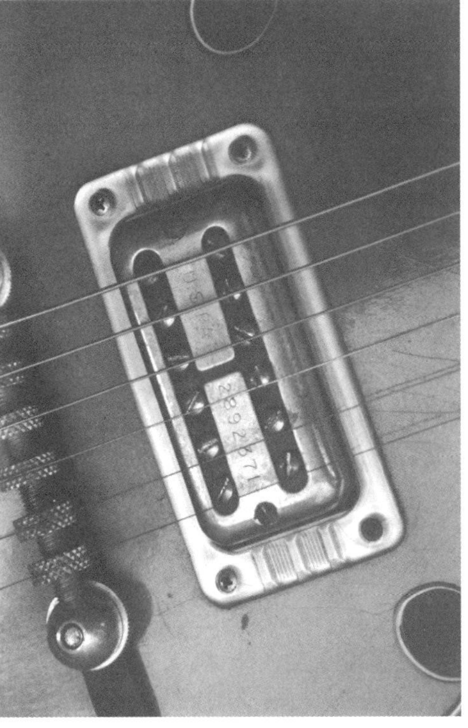

Gretsch Filter'Tron (Claudio Caldana).

Chet Atkins, who at the time was a Gretsch consultant, was not fond of the DeArmond pickups used on this brand of guitar and was enthusiastic about Butts' model.

1959's Gibson Les Paul with humbucking pickups (A. A.)

As early as 1954 another maker, Rickenbacker, had introduced the Combo-800, a guitar with a horseshoe pickup (two coils; one emphasizing trebles, the other bass frequencies). When both coils were selected you had "humbucking", but in 1957, strangely enough, instead of capitalizing on that novelty, the layout was changed in favour of a conventional single coil horseshoe.

All this prompted Gibson to hurry, in order to keep competitors behind, so the new model had to be put on the market without waiting for the patent.

The first instruments to receive the new unit were pedal steels, such as the Console Grand and the Electraharp, but later it substituted for the "Alnico Model" on top of the line guitars, while the P 90 remained standard equipment on cheaper models.

To protect his invention, Gibson put a label, with the words "Patent Applied For", on the base of each unit.

Gibson "Patent Applied For" pickups on a 1961's ES 335 TD. While on other instruments the humbucking pickup substituted for previous models, the ES 335, since it's introduction in 1958, had it from the start (C. Prosperini).

This method was also adopted by Gretsch, who engraved the words on the pickup cover, between the two rows of polepieces.

The Filter'Tron was structurally similar to Lover's model, but had a lower D. C. Resistance, (max 4 kOhms), due to fewer turns of a slightly thicker wire, a slightly bigger magnet and adjustable polepieces on each bobbin.

The very early units had no engraving and in the early sixties a patent number substituted the "Patent Applied For". Even though the two models were issued at almost the same time, there was no doubt that Seth Lover's design came first. Gibson had never experienced success such as that of the humbucker since the "Charlie Christian" model invention.

McCarty also gave his attention to the lower end of the market, and in 1959 a new solid body was introduced, the Melody Maker.

Similar to a Les Paul, the new model had a thinner body and a new pickup.

The unit, already in use on some lap steel guitars, had a coil with 15% less turns than a P 90 and a bar magnet M 56, slightly smaller than the M 55 used on P 90 and humbucking models.

Pickup and controls were on a large pickguard and later a two pickup version was added.

The Melody Maker pickup was also mounted on the ES 120 T, introduced in 1962. The bobbin used on the earlier units was made from grey fibre, replaced during the sixties by a thinner one made from nylon. The fifties ended with Gibson as the undisputed leader in the field of the electric guitar, leaving a step behind competitors like Rickenbacker, Gretsch and Guild.
Only in the field of the acoustic guitar does Martin still prevail.

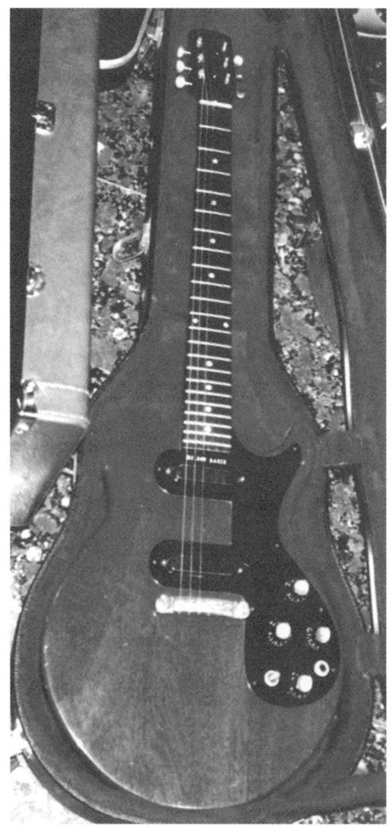

1960's Melody Maker
(Alex Angelucci)

In the fifties the new big event was the stereophonic sound and guitar makers started to offer stereo circuits on some models.

The first to put such a circuit on the market was Gretsch, with the Project-O-Sonic, consisting in two specially wound Filter'Tron pickups, with polepieces for only the three bass strings on the unit near the fingerboard and the three high strings on the bridge unit. The signal of the two pickups was sent to different channels. Later the layout was changed to two full pickups with coils split in half to give more possibilities of selection.
The system was introduced in 1959 on the White Falcon, then also used on the Country Club after 1960.

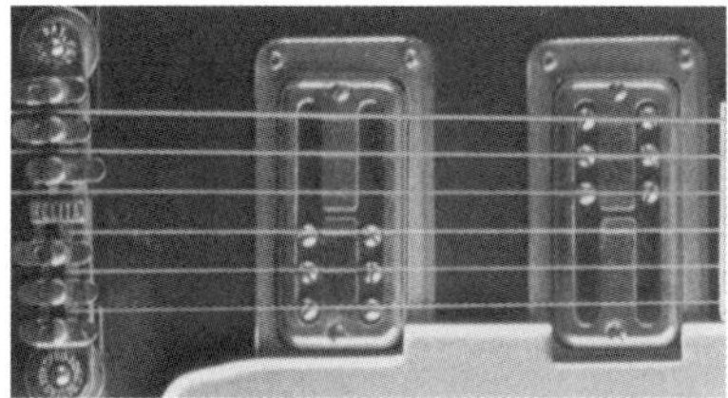

Gretsch Stereo Filter'Trons

In the meantime the range of models offered was growing and Gretsch added the Hi-Lo'Tron (1961), a single coil with a lower output than the Filter'Tron, and the Super'Tron (1964), a humbucker with blade polepieces for a brighter and louder sound.
Another addition, always in 1964, from the same maker, was the Super'Tron 2, with large solid polepieces for a smoother sound.

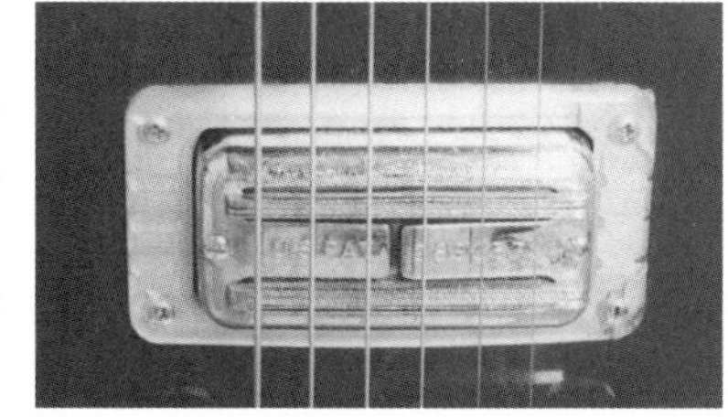

Gretsch Super'Tron (C. C.)

In 1959 Gibson introduced his stereo system, coupled with a new control, the Varitone, on the ES 345 TD. After a while ES 355 was also on offer in stereo version such as the ES 355 TD-SV.

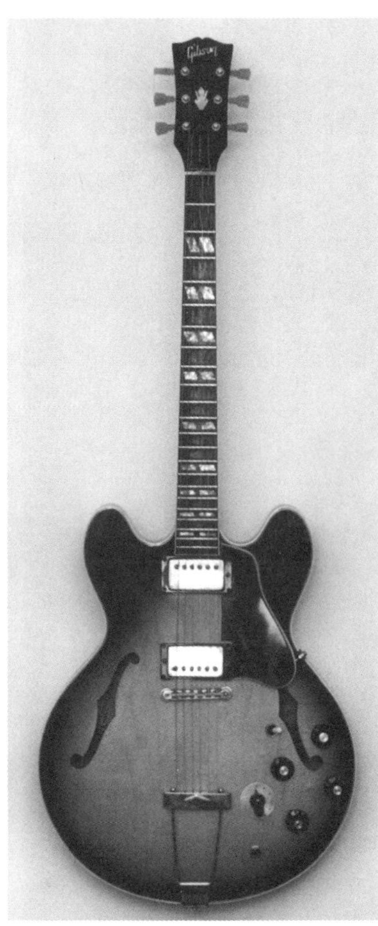

1967's Gibson ES 345 TD-SV
(Claudio Caldana)

The circuit was available for any other model on special order for $50 extra. As a matter of fact it had been seen on some L-5 CES, Byrdland, ES 335 TD, Super 400 CES and Les Paul Custom.

The circuit consisted of a filter which sent the signal from each pickup through a selectable series of capacitors and resistances of different values for a gradual reduction of the middle frequencies, a sort of passive equalizer, creating a total of 18 sounds. A stereo output with the use of a special cord sent each pickup signal to a different amplifier channel or to separate amps.

The Varitone was also available in a mono version, for $25.

Rickenbacker offered high end models with a stereo system called Rick-O-Sound, which is simply a separate output for each pickup.

Requiring the use of two amplifiers and special cords, the stereo systems had never been popular and most players actually used those high end guitars as normal mono instruments.
Some musicians had the guitars rewired for mono operation and even the Varitone disconnected.

All three systems, however, were cleverly designed and offered great versatility and unusual effects to the adventurous player, especially in the studio.

While some guitar makers still relied on specialized pickup makers, such as DeArmond, others made their own units inspired by the most famous ones, as some National models, which looked similar to Gibson humbuckings, but only had one coil under the cover.

In the fifties the electric guitar was not only the instrument of blues and jazz professionals, but also of young rock 'n roll rebels.

Most young players, however, could not afford to buy a Gretsch, a Gibson or a Fender; Harmony and Kay were cheaper, but they looked too traditional.

Nat Daniel, found the right solution: instruments made with cheap materials (masonite) but functional, attractively priced and available in a range of colours in order to compete with Fender's custom colour and the fancier Gretsch models.

The pickups were not less original, made by winding a coil directly around a bar Alnico magnet, with electric tape holding the whole in a cigar shape and then inserted into a lipstick tube which had holes for the output cables.

The D. C. Resistance of the Danelectro pickup varied between 3,7k and 4,7 k with a very bright tone, but still with some warmth. The use of 100k potentiometers rounded out the highs thus avoiding a shrill sound. Another original feature, on guitars with two pickups, was that they were connected in series, instead of being parallel as on most guitars, which produced a distinctively fuller sound when both units were selected.

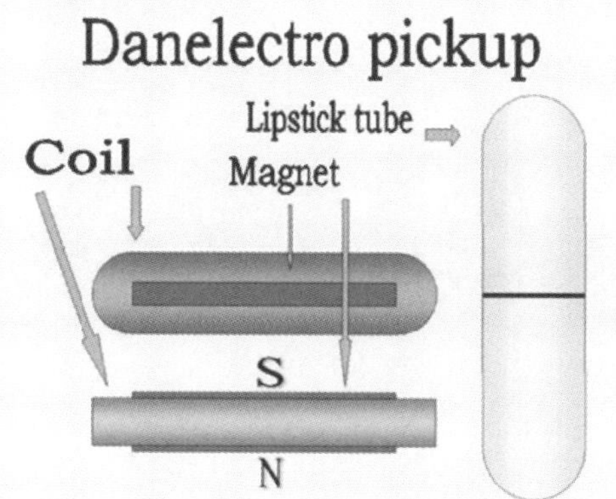

Not only was it used on Danelectro guitars, but also on the models Daniel produced for Sears, (a mail order distributor), under the brand name Silvertone. The pickup was versatile and had it's own personality, a quality which made it a favourite with blues musicians (very good for slide).

Many rock stars such as Dickey Betts, Jimmy Page, Warren Haynes and others, have occasionally used a Danelectro or a Silvertone. In the USA there were very few musicians who didn't start their career by learning the basics on a Danelectro or Silvertone. This continued at least until the invasion of cheap instruments from the Orient during the sixties.

Sears-Silvertone 1448, about 1963, made by Danelectro (C. C.).

Fender too, in the late fifties, introduced new guitar models, naturally fitted with new pickup designs. In 1956 the Duosonic, a low end model, arrived with two pickups similar to the Stratocaster's unit, but with level rod magnets and a plastic cover without the top holes, which rendered the poles invisible.

In 1958 the top of the line was the Jazzmaster, a guitar meant to be the Fender of the jazz player, with pickups looking similar to a P 90, but built with direct rod magnets. The accompanying circuit differed from Fender's usual simplicity, with separate tone controls for rhythm and lead playing.

Jazzmaster (C. C.) and Jaguar (C. P.)

The guitar failed to conquer the jazz musician's heart, but had a moderate success with the surf players.

Next, in 1962, comes the Jaguar, a 24 3/4" scale model with a new unit similar to

Epiphone's "New York" single coil pickup, introduced in 1951 (C. P.).

the one for the Stratocaster, but with a notched metallic ring around the coil reinforcing the magnetic field for better highs.

In 1957 Gibson acquired for a bargain price of $200,000, Epiphone, his long time competitor and maker of fine archtop guitars.

At first the stock parts which were still available were used on the new brand models, but then Gibson decided to update the specifications on the whole line. The P 90 gradually substituted the relatively low output Epiphone single coil pickup on low end models, while Seth Lover was asked to design a new unit based on his successful humbucking for the high end guitars. It is possible that in order to distinguish the instruments made for Epiphone from those distributed under the name of Gibson, the new pickup was smaller in size than the normal humbucker, with slightly less turns in the coils and smaller adjustable headless screw polepieces. A single bar polepiece was used for the other bobbin. It seemed that Epiphone now part of the family, would also be able to have a humbucking model, although only a real Gibson could have the full sized one.

Epiphone Casino, one of the models introduced by the new owners, similar to the Gibson ES 330, and fitted with P 90 pickups (Claudio Prosperini).

Known as the mini-humbucking, the new model had a lower output, compared to that of the Gibson, but was brighter, recalling, at least partially, the tone of earlier Epiphone models. As on the Gibson humbucking, the Epiphone's earlier units had the "Patent Applied For" label on the base.

Epiphone Mini-humbucking pickup, designed by Seth Lover (C. Prosperini).

In 1963 Gibson produced the Firebird series, a line of guitars aimed at fighting Fender's competition, in as far as image and sound were concerned.

These guitars were advertised as offering deep basses and cutting highs, with good sustain. The timbre of these fine instruments was due to the neck-through-body design, but well complemented by the clear sound of the new pickups, based on the minihumbucking model. The coils were identical to those of the Epiphone unit, but without adjustable polepieces. Two slightly smaller bar Alnico magnets were inserted directly into the bobbins, for increased attack and brilliance. With their distinctive look, bright but elegant sound, original pickups and several custom finishes on offer, the Firebird line represented the last of the great designs from the McCarty era.

Gibson Firebird V, 1963 (C. Caldana).

Other variants of the minihumbucking were: one designed for the "Johnny Smith" archtop electric and one similar to the Epiphone unit, but with offset poles. The last one was sold to other companies such as Harmony, who used it on some Silvertone models they were making at that time.

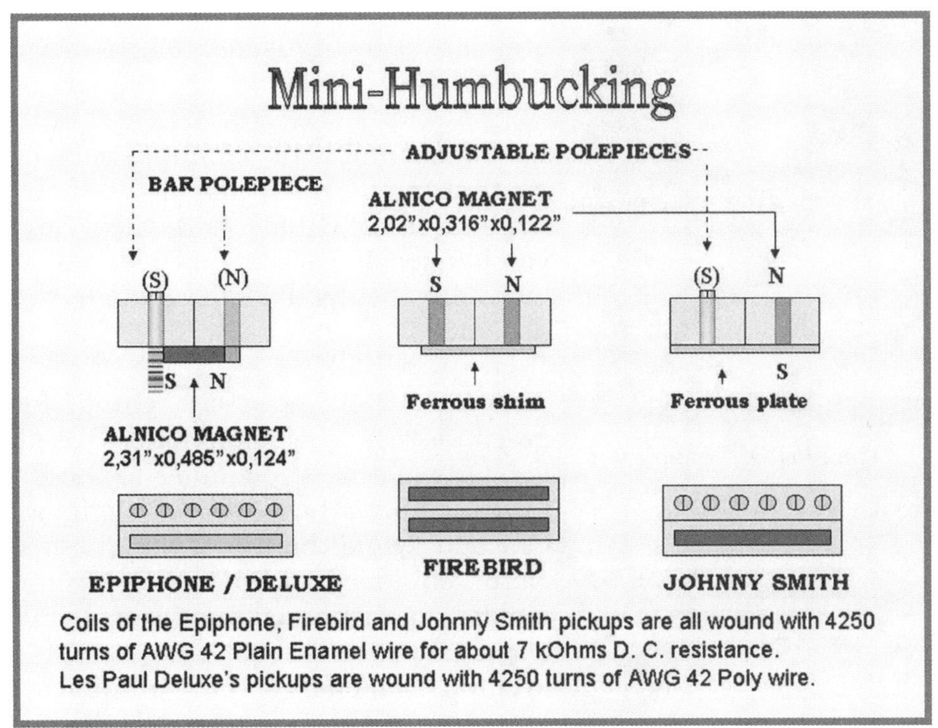

While widening the range of his electric guitar pickups, Gibson also carried out research in the field of acoustic guitar amplification, trying to preserve the natural sound of the instrument. In May 1960 Chauncey Richard Evans, an engineer from Salt Lake City, applied for a patent on a piezoelectric system, installed on the bridge, for classical guitar amplification.

A piezoelectric transducer consists of a crystal which converts the mechanical vibrations into voltage, a phenomenon known since it was discovered by Pierre and Paul Jacques Curie in 1880. It was used in microphone and phonograph cartridge making, but Evans was the first to apply it to acoustic guitar amplification. The system was made up of six transducers on the bridge, each notched to act as a saddle for the string, so as to pick up the whole vibration. The reduced weight, of only grams 1,5, reduced the sensitivity to undesired noise, reproducing the pure sound of the strings.

Gibson needed a chief engineer for a new electronics division and Evans was hired and in late 1960 the system was applied to a classical guitar, the CE-1, for which an amplifier was especially designed, the GA 100.

Charlie Byrd, a famous bossa nova and jazz player, in 1962, recorded the long playing "Jazz Samba" with Stan Getz using the CE-1 and in 1963 was voted best guitar player of the year in Down Beat. Notwithstanding all this plus an enthusiastic advertising campaign, the guitar was not a success and Gibson ceased production in 1968. Ironically that same year Ovation entered the market with a guitar using a similar system.

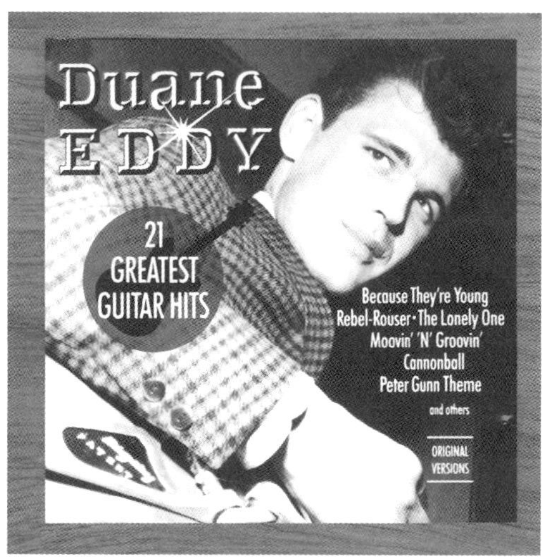

Duane Eddy, "The King Of Twang", used a Guild DE 500 with DeArmond pickups.

Had research been continued Gibson, could probably have remained at the top in that field as well, as the system was valid and was still the base of all piezoelectric systems still in use.

As far as magnetic pickups were concerned, at that point most major brands, such as Gretsch and Guild, had their humbucking version, each with its own sound character, although they could not compete with Gibson design.

Between 1952 and 1959, Guild, founded by ex-employees of Epiphone, used several versions of a pickup similar to the P 90, but of lower quality. These were made by a factory in Chicago, while the top of the line instruments were equipped with a DeArmond model similar to that used by Gretsch but without adjustable magnets. On most acoustic archtops models the amplification was provided by the DeArmond M-1000, a pickup suspended at the fingerboard end.

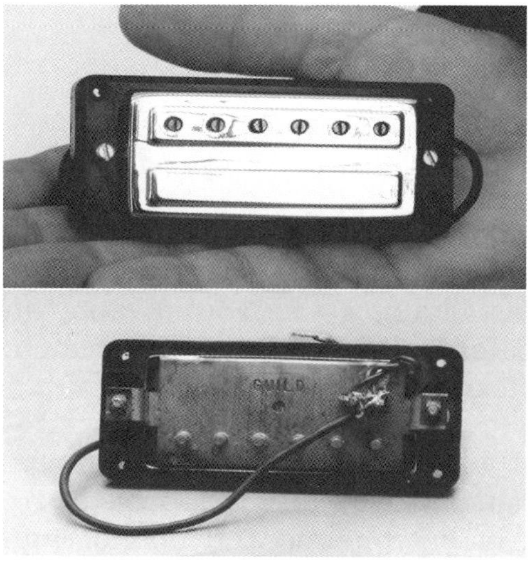

Early Guild humbucker (F. Dadò).

In 1959 Guild guitars were equipped with the same DeArmond Model 200 used by Gretsch (Dynasonic), but with a white top instead of black. Then in 1963 the factory produced its own models, a single coil similar to the DeArmond units used previously and a humbucking similar to Gibson's model, but slightly narrower and with a clearer sound.
The pickup cover had a distinctive relief over the two polepiece rows.

In late 1970 a new humbucking, HB-1, substituted the old one. It was slightly larger but similar in style, with three screws in the mounting ring allowing height adjustment and inclination of the guitar top.

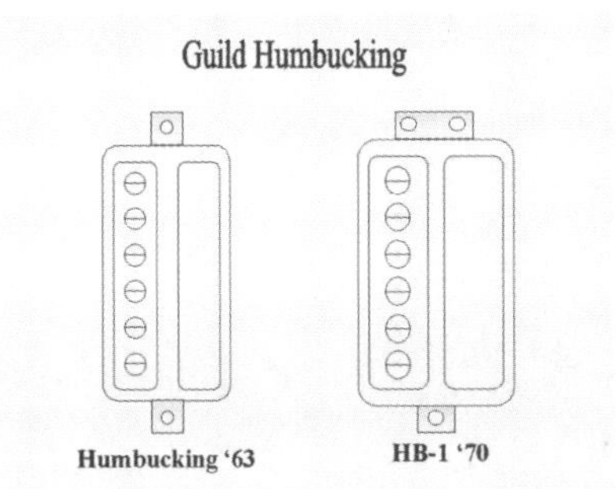

In the late sixties the magnets used on Gibson pickups were probably full power Alnico 5, which gave a brighter sound.
At the same time the Les Paul range, discontinued in 1960, was reintroduced, with the Standard model.

It was a gold top with two P 90 (1968), replaced by the Deluxe (1969), equipped with two mini-humbucking pickups similar to those previously used on some Epiphone guitars, then followed by the Custom, with a black finish, gold hardware and two new humbuckers.

In 1970 Seth Lover, who had left Gibson in 1967 having received a better offer from Fender, was asked to design a humbucking pickup for the now CBS owned brand.

Gibson Les Paul Standard, 1968 (Claudio Prosperini)

The new unit was for a new thin line Telecaster planned to compete with the successful ES 335 Gibson.

Lover, instead of trying to emulate the warm sound of Gibson pickups, decided to design a model with the brilliant tone associated to the Fender name, but hum-free.

The solution was a pickup made with twelve Cunife magnets machined as screws, directly inserted into the nylon bobbins.
Three of these protruded from the cover, under the E, A and D strings in the bobbin closest to the fingerboard, while the magnets referring to G, B and high E strings protruded from the other bobbin.
The remaining magnets were upside down, hidden under the cover. In this way the six protruding poles were adjustable and offset under the strings, creating a magnetic field similar to that of a slanted Stratocaster pickup, the others acted as fixed poles.

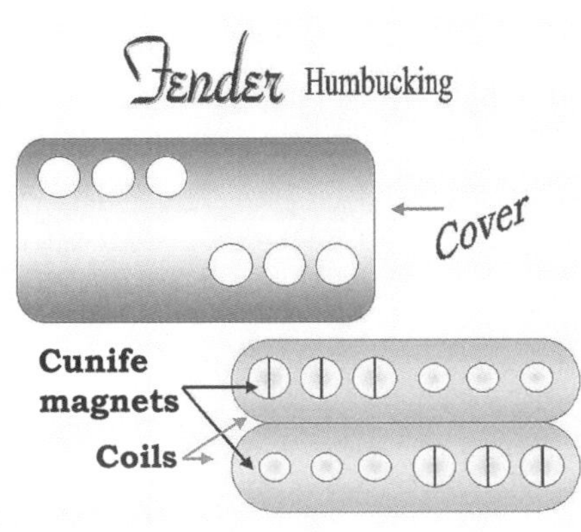

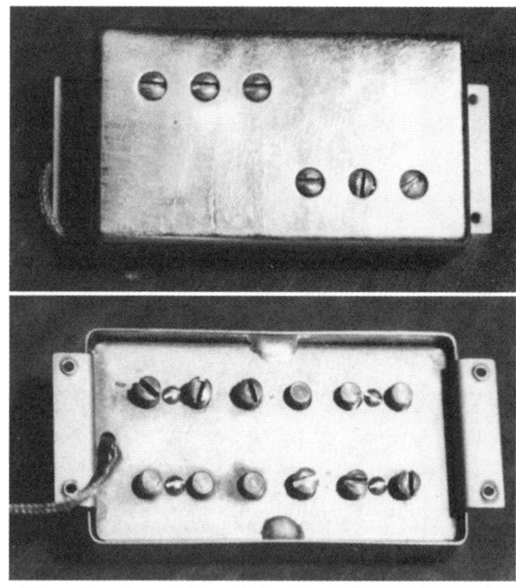

Fender humbucking pickup (C. P.).

Cunife is an alloy made from copper, nickel and steel and was the only material which could be machined at that time, allowing, used as adjustable polepieces, to obtain a more concentrated magnetic field than that of regular Alnico magnets under the coils, giving a clear sound, while a D.C. resistance of 10 kOhms made for a strong output. The wire was AWG 42 Poly and four mounting strings permitted full adjustment of the pickup.

The new model became standard equipment on three Telecaster guitars: the Thinline, the Custom and the Deluxe.
In 1976 Fender introduced the Starcaster, a semi solid guitar in the ES 335 style, with two of the Lover designed humbucking pickups.

Some players used to replace the neck pickup on the Telecaster with a Gibson humbucker (C. Caldana).

Although Keith Richards of the Rolling Stones gave great exposure to a Custom Telecaster, the Fender humbucking and the Telecasters on which it's used had a relatively limited success, while the Starcaster was a total flop.

After CBS acquired the brand, production methods were changed and the choice of the materials being used was not always wise, including the wire for pickup's manufacturing. Quality control was less accurate and the reputation of the instruments made by California's most famous brand suffered, especially when compared with those built in the past. In the seventies, most popular musicians were using instruments made in the previous decades, but the big companies, as Fender and Gibson, didn't seem yet to be aware of this competition coming from their own past.

In 1969 Gibson also introduced new pickups, the low impedance units used on the Les Paul Professional, later fitted to the Les Paul Personal, Les Paul Recording, Les Paul Jumbo, Les Paul Bass and Les Paul Signature.

Low impedance pickups were Les Paul's favourites for their clean sound and suitability for direct injection to the input of studio mixing boards. However they required a transformer when used with normal high impedance amplifiers. Technically, these pickups had an interesting characteristic, they were humbucking, but instead of side by side, the bobbins were placed one upon the other, a system today popular on many single coil sized humbuckers. The same bobbins layout was also used on the ES 325 guitar and Ripper bass, both high impedance instruments.

In the era of 'Led Zeppelin' and 'Cream' a clean sound was not the most sought after and guitars conceived for the studio but not practical for stage use were not very popular.

In 1973 the SG series was revamped with a new pickup: the Super Humbucking. For the first time the neck and bridge units had different specifications, for a broader tone range and more output. The magnets used were ceramic and the whole unit was soaked in a hard resin to avoid feedback. A traditional metal cover made the Super Humbucking undistinguishable from the standard model with Alnico magnet.

But while Gibson experimented with low impedance pickups or tried to fly on high frequencies with the Super Humbucking, and Fender had big hopes for the new Telecaster models, music was changing thanks to the union of hard rock and jazz.

From Cream to Mountain, from Colosseum to Al DiMeola, the typical set up consisted in a Les Paul through a Marshall amp.

This produced a full, heavy, saturated tone, the opposite of that offered by the classic brands. Musician's requirements will later be met by newcomers, owners of small companies, such as Larry DiMarzio.

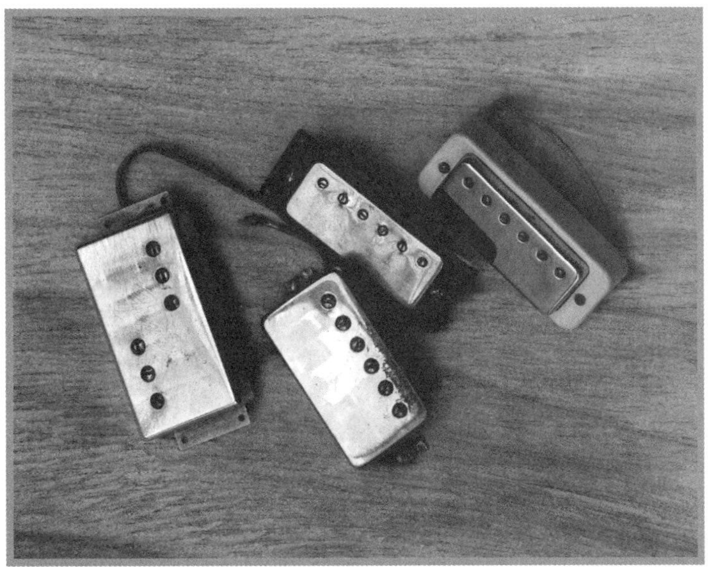

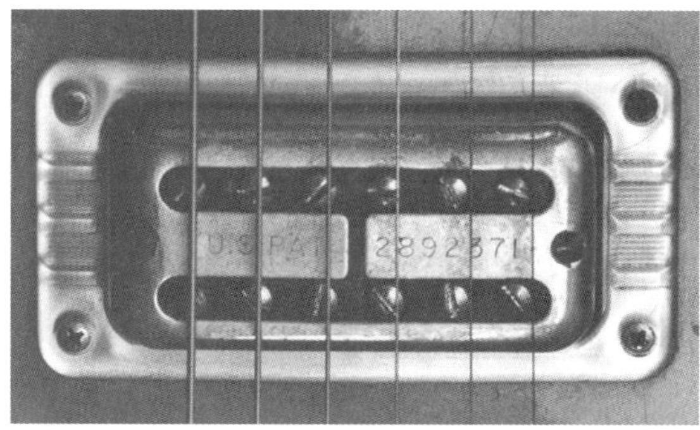

Note

(*) The most sought after Gretsch Filter'Trons were the very early ones, without engraving, or with the words "Patent Applied For" on the cover, even though it seemed that later units, that had the patent number engraving, differed only by having slightly shorter polepieces and later stronger magnets.

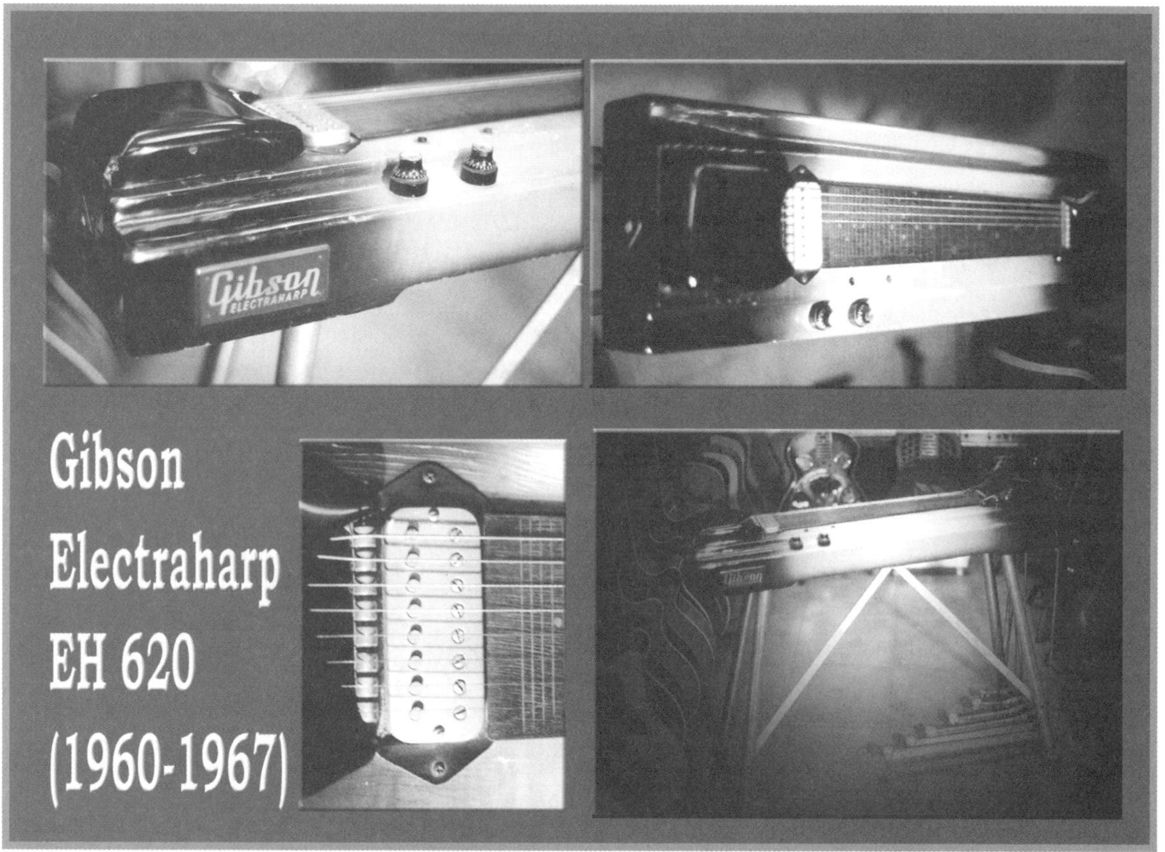

The humbucking pickup on this Gibson pedal steel looks very similar to the prototype conceived by Seth Lover in 1955, the only difference being the presence of a row of adjustable screw-type polepieces. The Electraharp and Console Grand pedal steels were the first Gibson instruments to be fitted with the humbucking pickup during 1956, while the guitars started to be equipped with the new unit only in 1957 (Instrument courtesy of Franco Bandiera; photographs by Claudio Prosperini).

4) A new freedom

Today it may be difficult to understand why most guitar makers seemed insensitive to the new trend in rock music, but in the seventies their customers were still mostly jazz and country musicians, professional orchestra players, plus the unprecedented increase in production brought financial and organizational problems. Some individuals, however had enthusiastic expectations.

Records as Cream's "Wheels Of Fire" ('68) and Allman Brothers' "At Fillmore East" ('71), represented new standards about music and tone for the guitar players, breaking the line between rock and jazz, giving them an appetite for warmer and fuller sounds. The distortion that instrument makers tried to avoid, became sought after by most musicians.

One of the first to propose new solutions was Dan Armstrong, famous designer of guitar effects (very popular in the seventies, was his "Orange Squeezer"), amplifiers and the see-through clear plastic Ampeg guitar made famous by Keith Richards.

These guitars had only one pickup, but it was mounted on a slot running under the strings, with electric connections on the treble side.
The pickup could simply be plugged in or out of the slot, allowing easy replacement with another unit, if so desired. The clever mounting system was conceived by Armstrong, and the pickups were designed by Bill Lawrence. Each guitar was sold with a high output pickup for rock playing, and an extra brighter sounding model, aimed at country musicians. Four other models, with different tone and output characteristics, were available for $55 each.

It was the start of a new wave of thought, which attempted to expand the versatility of the instrument. Fender, in 1974, finally made a five position switch, allowing neck/middle and middle/bridge pickup connections, for that so called "out of phase" sound that players used to obtain carefully positioning the old switch in intermediate position. Up to this moment, to buy a guitar entailed accepting the builder's choice for pickups and electronic features, only a few professionals were able to get the pickups rewound or the circuit modified for different sounds, however the situation was about to change with the arrival of a new pickup builder, of Italian origin, Larry DiMarzio.

Now it was finally possible to mount various hardware and especially different pickups on a guitar. With the new replacement models it was possible to distort almost any amplifier. This was much sought after not only by rock players but also by some jazz players.

The first model produced was the Super Distortion (1972), a humbucker differing from Gibson's design which had a powerful ceramic magnet, twelve Allen screws polepieces and overwound coils, for a D. C. resistance slightly exceeding 13 kOhms. The sound was full and a resonant peak at 6850 Hz gave sufficient clarity to the high frequencies. DiMarzio claimed, in his catalogues of the time, to be the first to use ceramic magnets on pickups. He was surely the first to use them so efficiently.

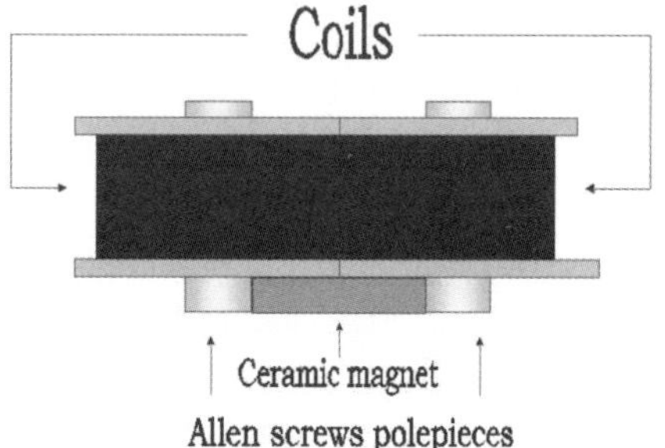

In 1974 the PAF was added, not a faithful reproduction of the classic Gibson model, but a version more powerful and clearer sounding than the contemporary Gibson standard humbucker, due to a very tight winding and a powerful Alnico 5 magnet with M55 dimensions.
On offer for the Stratocaster there was the FS-1 Fat Strat (1974), louder and fuller sounding than the Fender original. In 1977 the Super 2 appeared, a brighter version of the Super Distortion, and in 1978 the X2N, which was the most powerful, and had three ceramic magnets and large bar polepieces. That same year the SDS-1 was introduced, a model made to fit into a Stratocaster pickguard but with a structure similar to a P 90, with two ceramic magnets under the coil and six Allen screws polepieces, for a timbre similar to the Super Distortion. This was so that Strat players could obtain more power and a fuller sound. In the same year the Pre B-1 arrived, a pickup for Telecaster style guitars, without a metallic plate on the base, producing a warmer tone and more mids.

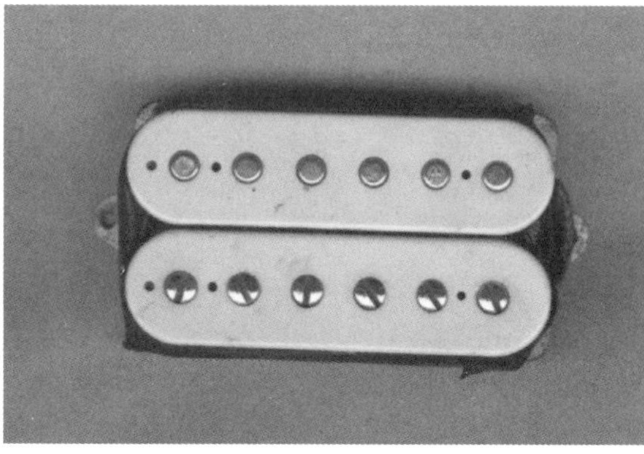

DiMarzio "Paf" model

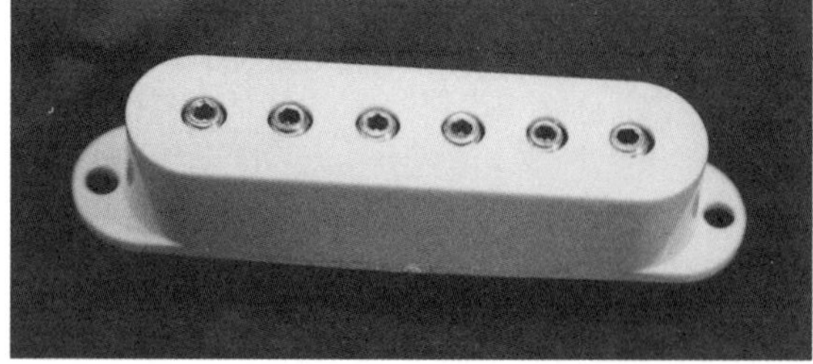

DiMarzio SDS-1

The most unusual tones were those produced by a special version of the Super Distortion, the Dual Sound which, with its four conductor cable (output and ground for each coil), could be wired out of phase with another unit or with the coils in parallel. This created a brighter sound but was nonetheless humbucking, or split, with one bobbin grounded to produce true single coil sounds, (at least in theory).

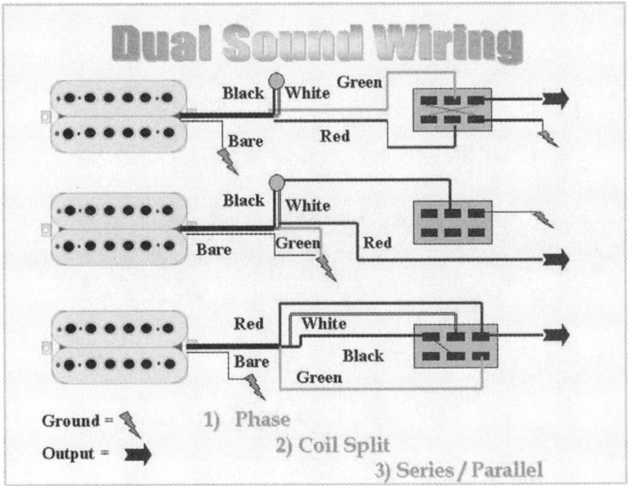

The Super Distortion became an industry standard and many American and Japanese guitar makers such as B. C. Rich, Charvel, Hamer, Kramer, Dean, Guild, Aria, Greco, and even the Italian EKO, used it as standard equipment on high end models.

The DiMarzio pickups were an immediate success and were used by such players as Roy Buchanan, Al DiMeola, Allan Holdsworth, Albert Lee, Steve Hackett and many others.

Soon labels showed the statement "DiMarzio Powered", even on low-end instruments, though sometimes these units were cheaply made, and similar to the real thing only in appearance.

DiMarzio was not the only one to react to the major brands' sluggishness, due to too much bureaucracy and profit minded management (paradoxically often making the correct decision to reduce it!).

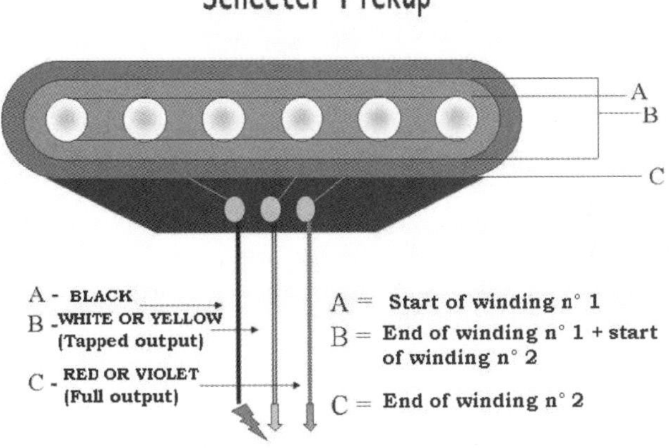

David Schecter who had gained a good reputation for repairing pickups and winding custom units for professional musicians in California was the man of the moment.

In 1976 Schecter started to produce his own model, based on the Fender design, but more versatile. His idea was to wind a coil for an output similar to a normal pickup, connect an output cable, then to continue winding more turns and have another output cable.
When the first output was switched on, the tone was similar to a Fender model, and had a characteristic bright sound, but when the second output was selected the extra winding was added giving a fuller sound with more volume: the tapped pickup was born.

The actually inventor of this technique is not clear, since Seymour Duncan had a patent on this system. As a matter of fact Duncan did some work for Schecter, so it's quite possible that he conceived the idea and Schecter put it into production. All the tapped pickups made since then are based on this design, whatever thc

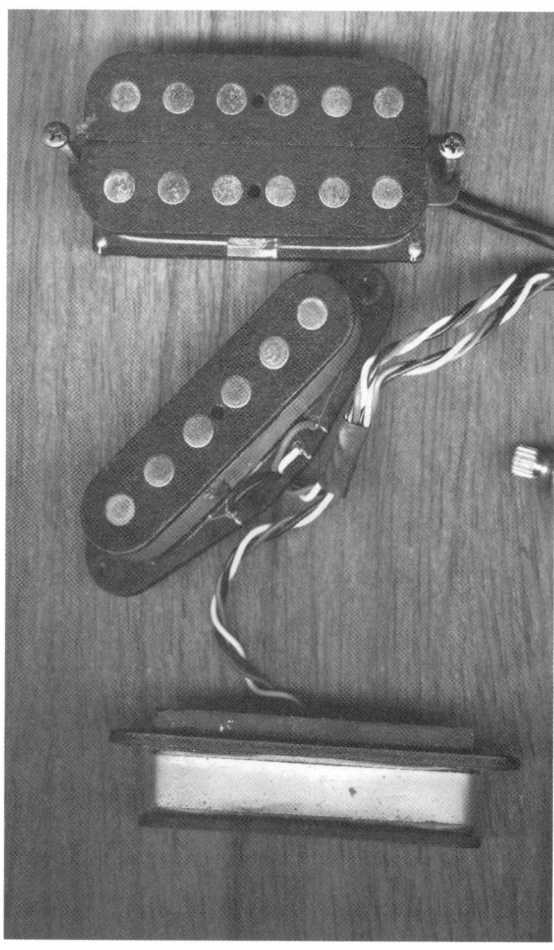

A 1997 Schecter set. The bridge humbucker has Alnico cylindrical magnets directly in the coils, Fender-style, the two single coil pickups have a ceramic bar magnet at the bottom of the winding and ferrous polepieces through the coil. A copper sheet surrounds the bobbins to reduce noise.

Gibson S-1 (Claudio Prosperini).

brand, even though their popularity is now diminishing because of the compromise in tone due to the use of so many turns, more powerful magnets, and the introduction of new designs offering hum cancelling properties.

Another successful model from Schecter was the humbucking Super Rock, loud and clear, offered with three or four conductor output cables and push-pull potentiometers, allowing out of phase and single coil sounds. This replaced the electric harness of the guitar, such as a Les Paul, without other modifications. In 1978 David Schecter offered replacement hardware for all the most popular guitar models and raw Fender-style bodies and necks made from exotic wood.

In the late seventies Gibson seemed to find new vitality and introduced new models, such as the Dirty Fingers and the Velvet Brick, which were high output pickups with ceramic magnets.
Another addiction was the True Blues, with three ceramic magnets and a resistance of only 6 kOhms for a very bright sound, mounted on the L6-S guitar, with a circuit conceived by Bill Lawrence, who also designed the pickups for the S-1 and the Marauder guitars. Other pickup models were the "V" shaped unit for the Flying V II, with ceramic magnets, the Laid Back, a reproduction of the old P 90 with Alnico 5 magnets and the BJB, a minihumbucking for archtop guitars, but players didn't seem very impressed with any of them.

Bill Lawrence, who worked not only for Gibson but also for Gretsch, produced his line of pickups, with blade polepieces and a powerful but clear tone, such as the double coil L 500, with a low magnetic flux for better sustain, the L 250, that had the bobbins one on top of the other to fit into single coil slots. The L350, was a more traditionally looking humbucking with screw polepieces.

Mighty Mite, a brand offering bodies and necks in a wide variety of shapes, produced a line of moderately priced pickups, with an original model, the Motherbucker, with three coils, each with two output cables, creating a variety of connections not possible with normal humbuckers. This was like having three single coil pickups, the centre one with reverse magnetic and electric polarity, in the same ring.

Bill Lawrence L-250 (C. P.)

Some small companies made original pickups for their guitars, with some interesting models, such as Carvin, with eleven poles in each bobbin producing a more balanced magnetic field, or Paul Reed Smith, with Gibson inspired models like the high output HFS, the Vintage and the Deep Dish, a humbucker made to emulate the sound of a P 90.

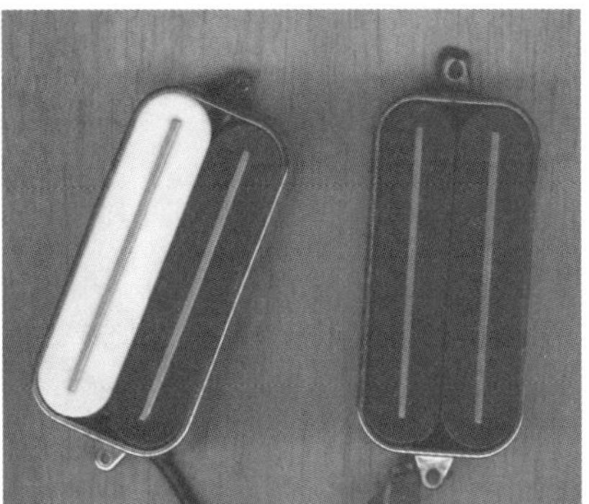

Bill Lawrence XL-500

Leo Fender, after selling the Fender company to CBS, founded Music Man and then G & L with his old friend George Fullerton. He continued his search for brilliant sounds, experimenting with active circuitry at Music man and designing new pickups for G & L that had a more concentrated magnetic field, less winding than on Fender models and ceramic magnets, for more high end.

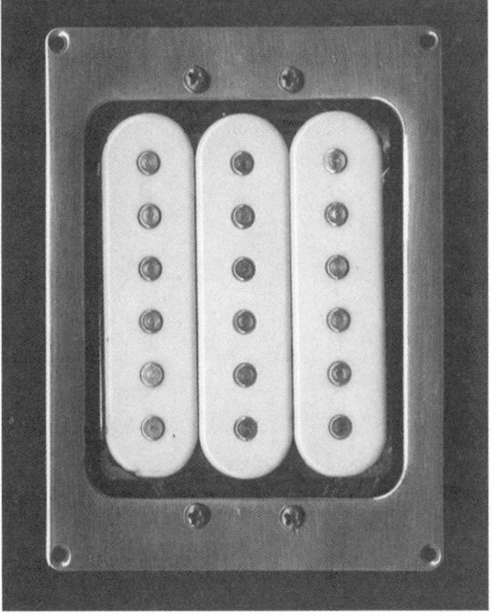

Mighty Mite Motherbucker, with three coils and powerful ceramic magnets.

Active pickups became more popular and the leader was EMG, but other makers had been proposing this kind of design for a long time. One of these was Alembic.

B. C. Rich used active circuitry on top of the line guitars to boost the already high level of the powerful DiMarzio pickups.

Bartolini made active pickups as well as versatile passive units, such as The Beast II, a humbucking model with tapped coils and eight output cables for an impressive series of connections.

G & L Magnetic Field Design

Velvet Hammer built pickups for acoustic and electric guitars with a separate coil for each of the six magnets and stereo output.

Aria, Ibanez, Gibson and Fender, all had some active instruments in their catalogues. Some features, such as active boost and eq, coil split and phase switching were offered on several models.

EMG 85 Model (C. Caldana(.

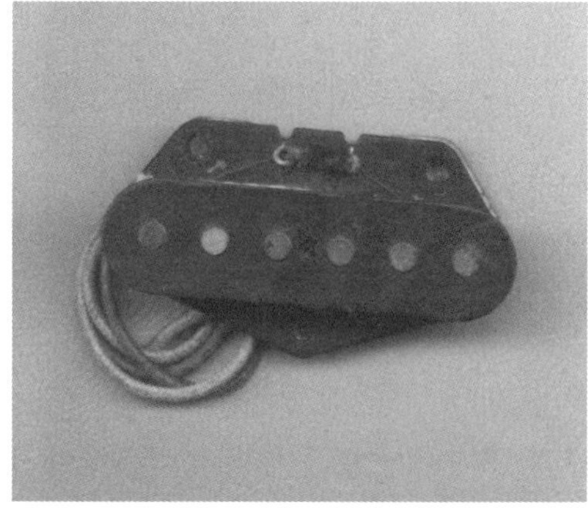

Duncan STL-1b, based on the unit designed by Leo Fender for the Broadcaster

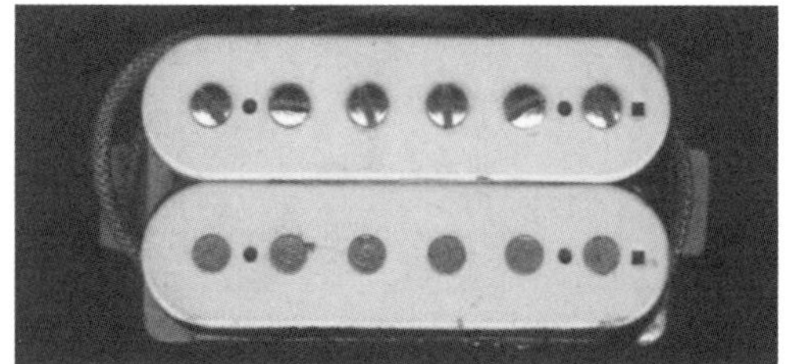

Duncan SH-1 '59 Model. Designed for the neck position this model has fewer turns in the windings for a clearer tone.

Seymour Duncan, who used to work for Schecter, the Fender Soundhouse in London, and wound pickups for Jeff Beck and other famous players, gained a first rate position making a series of models so successful that he became as popular as DiMarzio.

Soon Duncan pickups were standard equipment on guitars built by Hamer, Aria USA, Washburn, Fender (Robben Ford Model), the French Lag and on some Yamaha models.

The first Duncan model to make him so successful was the J. B. Model, based on a Gibson P. A. F. rewound for Jeff Beck and mounted on a Telecaster used to record "Cause We've Ended As Lovers" for the "Blow By Blow" album.

The rocker had a Les Paul stolen and Duncan gave him the Telecaster as a present, with two Gibson pickups coming from a Flying V once owned by Lonnie Mack. The bridge unit was rewound with more turns to provide a fuller sound, giving the Tele some Les Paul-like character, the neck unit was wound for a cleaner sound. It then became the Jazz Model.

The production J. B. Model and Jazz Model, chosen for the Jackson "Randy Rhoads", became the classic pair for a rock guitar, the new standard replacing the old one (the popular DiMarzio Super Distortion/PAF couple).

Duncan also offered the best replicas of classic models from the past, such as the SH-1 '59, based on the original Gibson humbucking, the SSL-1, a faithful copy of the first Stratocaster pickups, the STL-1B, which finally offered the sound of the old Broadcaster model.

These were all made with great attention to details, using calibrated magnets, with the same magnetic flux as the old ones, or the square hole on the humbucking's bobbins, present on the original PAF pickups.

For modern rock players there were the Distortion and Custom models as well as the massive and most powerful Invader, that had ceramic magnets and bigger polepieces for maximum energy transfer.

The commercial success of the smaller companies took the big corporations by surprise. Fender and Gibson tried to respond with their Custom Shops, but their leadership in this field seemed to be lost. As DiMarzio once said, 'to produce good pickups is a specialized field, but hopefully the big companies can continue to make good instruments', hopefully indeed!

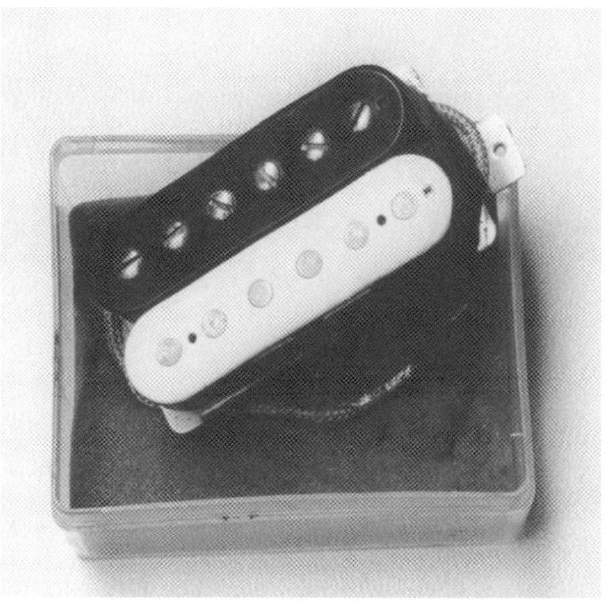

Duncan SH-1b '59 Model for the bridge position (Claudio Caldana)

In the field of amplification the new trend was to use mixed circuits, as on the Musicman models, with transistor preamp and tube power amp. Fender and Gibson, continued to dominate the guitar market, but with the amplifiers they had to face a very strong competition and several well known musicians, as Eric Clapton and Johnny Winter, in the early seventies preferred those made by Musicman. In the early eighties Musicman was sold to Ernie Ball and the amplifiers' production came to an end.

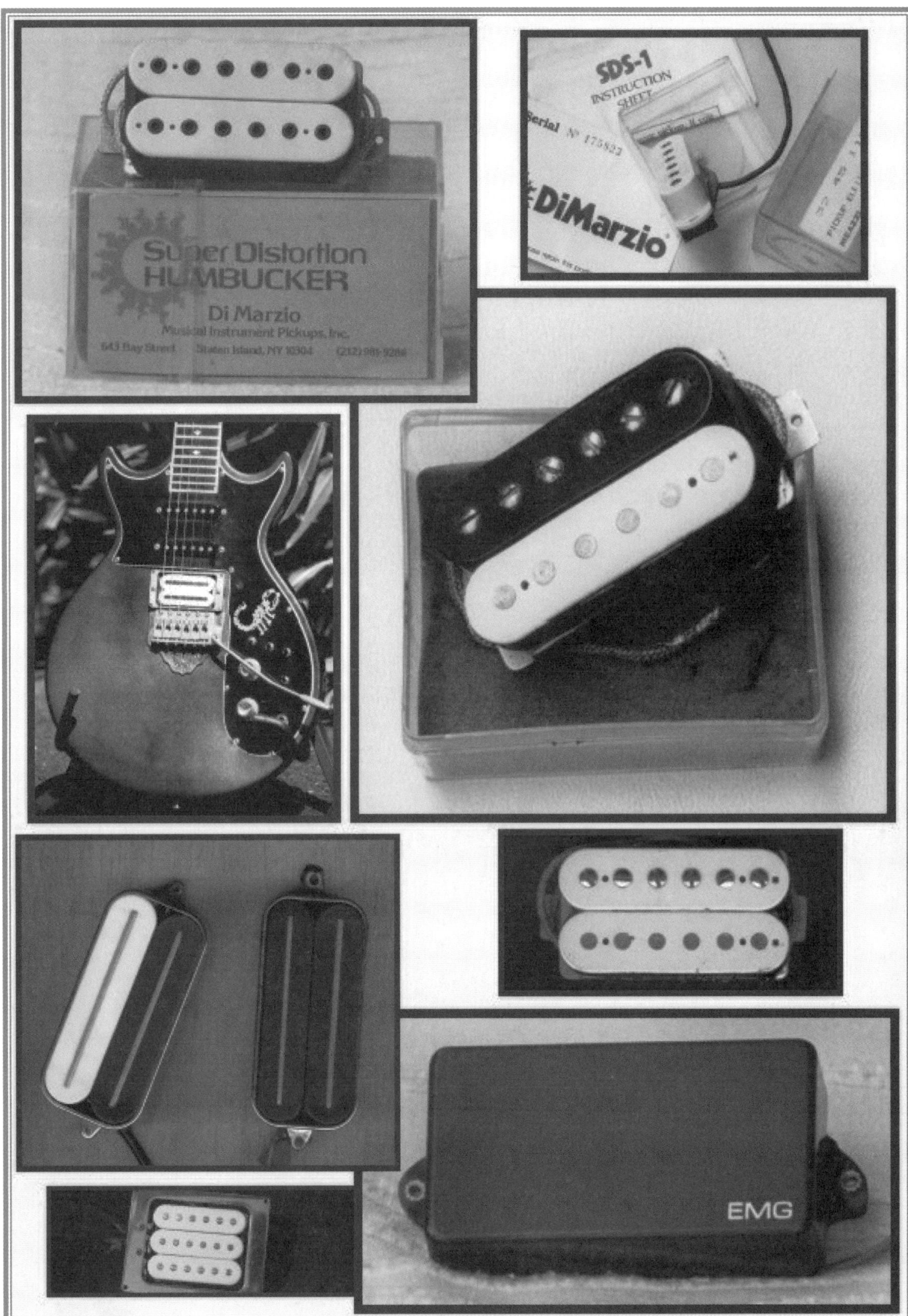
Super Distortion
HUMBUCKER
Di Marzio
Musical Instrument Pickups, Inc.
SDS-1
INSTRUCTION
SHEET
DiMarzio
EMG

5) Reissue time

In the eighties the vintage market continued to grow. Instruments from the major brands made in the classic years, roughly before 1965, were sought after by players as well as collectors and prices were increasing accordingly.

Culture on the subject was growing too, thanks to magazines and books such as "Guitar Player", Tom Wheeler's "The Guitar Book" (1972, revised edition in1978) and "American Guitars", 1982.

Most solutions for customizing a guitar, made available by DiMarzio, Schecter and others, were by now standard features on many factory-fitted instruments incorporating any conceivable optional, as those seen on models from Schecter, Carvin, Yamaha, Ibanez, Aria.

Gibson introduced the Heritage Standard and Heritage Elite Les Pauls in 1980, with pickups called "Pat. Appl. For" with Alnico 2 M56 style magnets. Fender produced the Reissue Stratocaster and Telecaster models in 1984, with matching reissue pickups.

The competition from their own older models and from new companies offering instruments inspired by the past, such as Hamer, Paul Reed Smith and Heritage, pushed Fender and Gibson to make a serious effort to re-launch the qualities of the old models, including pickups.

Heritage H 535. The Fralin pickups, knobs and Tune-O-Matic are not original (C. C.).

In 1985 Gibson transferred their electrical production to Nashville, Tennessee and acoustic production in a new factory in Montana.
Part of the personnel, preferring to remain at Kalamazoo, took over part of the original factory and founded Heritage. Here they produced instruments which were clearly inspired by the Gibson tradition and maintained the characteristics of their most popular older models, including pickup specifications.

During the eighties Gibson continued to carry out research on old models improving their reissue models with the especially fine Les Paul 1959 Reissues.

Complying with the interest for older instruments, several “vintage” amplifiers and instruments appeared on the market. Shown is a Limited Edition Marshall “Bluesbreakers” combo, with special white finish, with a flame top ’59 Reissue Les Paul with ’57 Classic pickups.

In the course of the nineties, the most exact replicas were those achieved in the high class Historic Collection Series, introducing uncompromised versions of all the fifties models, made in the Custom Shop.

The result of such accurate research was the ‘57 Classic pickup, a very good copy of the original humbucking, with Alnico 2 M55 size magnet, AWG 42 wire, differing from the real thing by a double waxing process to avoid feedback in high output applications (the originals were not potted).

With the clear but smooth ’57 Classic, Gibson produced his best pickup since the sixties, with a quality often lacking in previous attempts.
Soon a slightly more powerful version, the ’57 Classic Plus, was added.

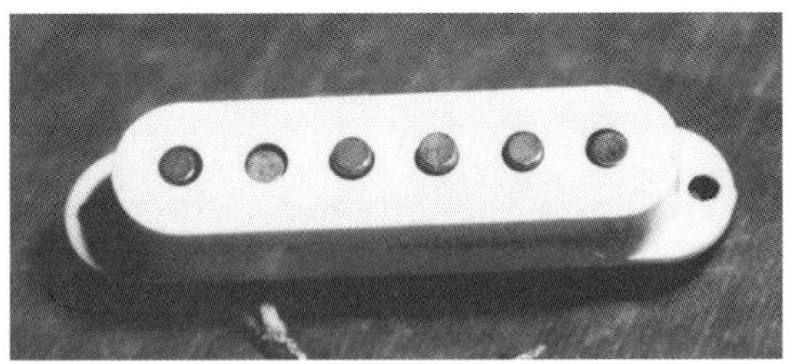
Fender “57/’62 Stratocaster Reissue” (C. P.).

Fender too paid more attention to the magnets used, improving the already good reissues (some players, however, contend that the latest versions were a bit thinner sounding than the first ones).

Gretsch offered Filter'Tron and Dynasonic reissues made in Japan(*), Rickenbacker, proud of his old style manufacturing methods, produced a very good copy of the original "Toaster" single coil.

DiMarzio Air Norton

But to recreate exact versions of the old pickups required time and expense, two things that big corporations could not afford, so the major brands gave the job to smaller structures such as their Custom Shop, in the attempt to compete with an increasing number of small companies which were more suitable for the production of high quality handcrafted items.

In the meantime, more and more models were being added to the Duncan and DiMarzio catalogues.

DiMarzio had an impressive number of

models, such as the Tone Zone, the Cruiser, the PAF Pro and the Air series, with reduced magnetic flux for more sustain.
He also expanded the "Signature" series with models for Steve Vai (Steve's Special and The Breed), Ingwie Malmsteen and the Steve Blucher designed pickups for the "Eddie Van Halen" guitar made by Music Man.

By the end of the seventies, big changes occurred in the field of amplification. Mesa Boogie led the way with multi-stage preamps and soon other makers followed with similar models, as this beautiful Kitty Hawk (Claudio Prosperini).

Duncan copied almost every model ever produced by Fender and Gibson (except the "Charlie Christian", the first ES 125 model and the Melody Maker). He also added "Hot" versions: the powerful "Quarter Pound" models and high output humbuckers such as the Custom, (with ceramic magnets) and the "Custom Custom", an overwound Alnico 2 model.

While the number of "vintage" models continued to increase, new designs were aimed at overcoming one of the problems of Fender-style pickups, the hum.
One solution was to make pickups with two coils, one on top of the other, in humbucking configuration, with the same dimensions and look as standard single coil units. Pickups of this kind were the Duncan Classic Stack, the Hot Stack (with ceramic magnet and blade polepiece) and the DiMarzio HS models. With this system the pickups could be mounted on Fender style instruments without modifications, and the magnetic window was narrower as on the originals, producing a more authentic sound.

The system was not really new, a patent on a humbucking pickup with superimposed bobbins was applied for in 1938 and Gibson used a similar configuration for several low impedance and high impedance models in the early seventies.
The design however was effective and the sound was sufficiently similar to the originals for many players, but without the noise. The only limitation was that, in direct comparison to true single coils, the brightness was reduced, although for some hum-obsessed musicians the result was good enough and those models enjoyed a certain success.

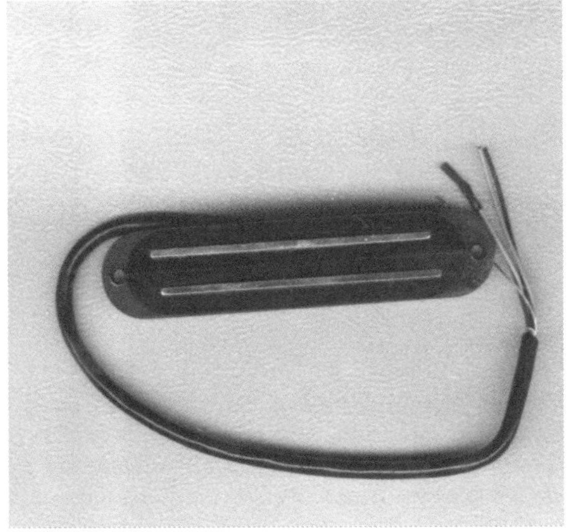
Joe Barden pickup for Stratocaster

Joe Barden, famous for making special pickups for Danny Gatton, used a different method, winding the coil around two thin blade polepieces, in the same space used on a normal single coil, so that the short distance between the blades provided a narrow magnetic window. This

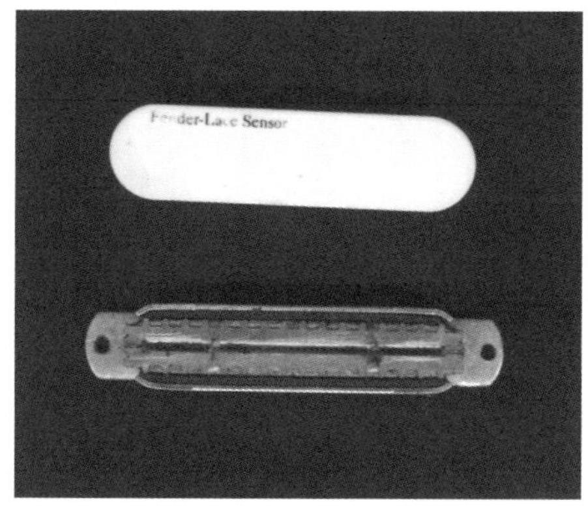

Fender Lace Sensor, designed by Don Lace of Actodyne General Inc.

way it was possible to produce a sound close to that of a single coil but without the hum, which could be altered depending on the kind of wire, number of turns and magnets used.
Barden used ceramic magnets for great brilliance and a very clean tone, almost high fidelity. Joe Barden didn't apply for a patent and soon other manufacturers were producing similar models, albeit for different purposes, in the field of tone.

Models using the twin blades concept were the DiMarzio Fast Track, Chopper, Cruiser, the Duncan Hot Rails, Cool Rails and Duckbucker.

A truly new design was the Lace Sensor, completely different from traditional pickups. A sheet of small magnets at the bottom of the coil provided a low density magnetic field, concentrated towards the strings by a notched metallic structure, without dispersion at the base. A very efficient shielding system made the pickup quiet almost like an humbucker and the output level was comparable to traditional single coil units and, on some models, much higher. Don Lace showed his design to the Fender company and four models were produced, distinguished by the colour of the mark on the plastic cover: gold for normal single coil output and tone, silver for a warmer and hotter sound, blue for a standard humbucking-style sound and red was the high output model.

Sixties' dream gig set (C. C.)

Don Lace's design was wonderful from a technical point of view, but while doing a good job at imitating a single coil tone and delivering the different output characteristics devised for all models, for many players the sound was a bit too clean and flat sounding, almost the same as with active pickups. The Lace Sensor pickups were successful enough, however, to be used as standard equipment on several Fender guitar models.

In the meantime the value of older Fender and Gibson models continued to increase, thereby pushing up the price of other maker's pickups from the same era, such as the DeArmond Dynasonic and the Gretsch Filter'Tron.

Notes

(*) The first Gretsch Filter'Tron replicas had a D. C. resistance of 7,5 kOhms instead of 4 kOhms as on the originals and a ceramic magnet. Recently more accurate "vintage" versions with Alnico magnets and original specs are offered on some guitars and selected models come stock with TV Jones Classic units. The Dynasonic reissue has Alnico magnets although the wire seems to be not exactly the same as on the original model.

6) Archaeology and technology

For a big corporation it was difficult to manufacture products using methods from forty or fifty years before, yet it was relatively easy for limited high quality productions. This situation left room, on a blossoming market, for small and specialized companies, and the "Custom Shops", producing a relatively low number of items, made with hand guided winding machines using high quality materials and specifications based on a patient scrutiny of the characteristics which made the old pickups so desirable.

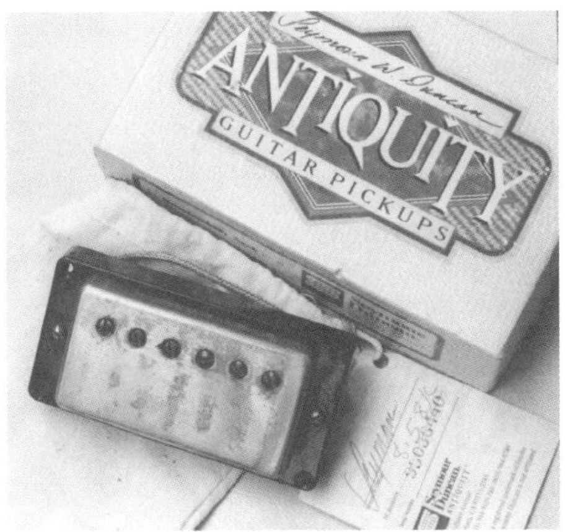

Duncan Antiquity humbucker (Claudio Caldana)

These handcrafted products were sold at a proportionally high price, compared to mass produced models, but were able to give to the discerning player those subtle nuances often lost in intensively produced items. To make these models requires the passion and the accuracy of an archaeologist.

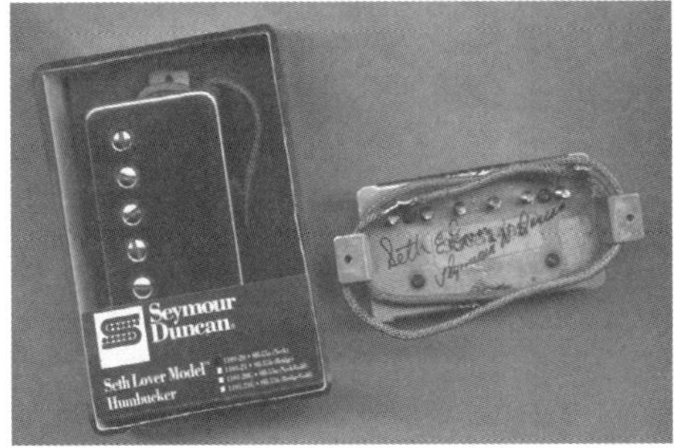

Duncan SH-55 "Seth Lover". On the bottom are Duncan and Lover's signatures.

The most appreciated makers were Tom Holmes and TV Jones, the only ones to offer "boutique" versions of the Filter'Tron, Lindy Fralin, with fine models for Telecaster, Stratocaster, humbucking and P 90 replacements. W. L. Van Zandt*, with good versions of the most popular vintage models, Seymour Duncan, with the Antiquity series and the "Seth Lover", with which the popular pickup maker paid homage to the humbucker's inventor.

Fralin Humbucker

Gibson issued the Burstbucker, designed to replicate those P. A. F. pickups having slightly uneven coils, offered in three versions differing slightly in output. Similar is the "Legend" by Wolfetone, available with "new" or "aged" look. A good PAF version is also the "Imperial" from Lollar, who also offers good replacements for Stratocaster, Telecaster and lap steel, including copies of the most ancient models. Fender offers selected models from the Custom Shop, the most popular being the Fat '50s set.

Other times, makers used the old models as an inspiration for tone, but instead of recreating them exactly, took liberty as far as techniques and materials were concerned. With specifications often based on those few pickups which had more output than normal, such as some overwound PAFs, or altering the

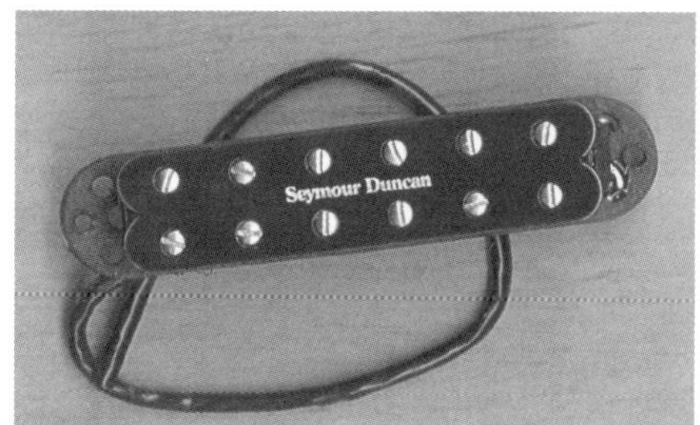

Duncan J. B. Junior

Rio Grande "Bastard". P 90's structure and specs, but in a format allowing to mount it on a standard humbucking's ring. Available with nickel cover.

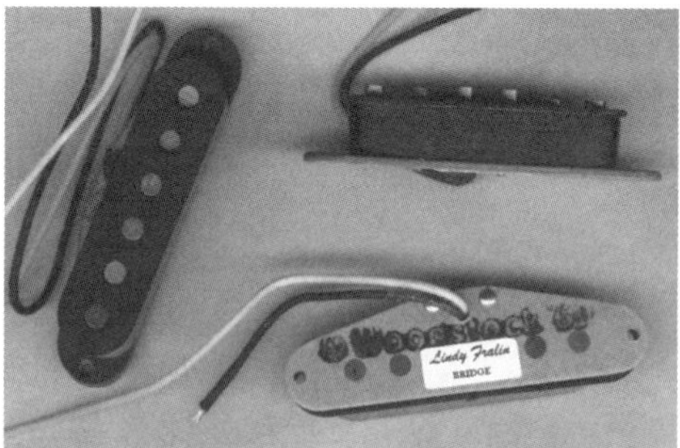

Fralin "Woodstock '69" set, with reverse staggered magnets for "lefty" sounds.

Rio grande "Tallboy" for Telecaster

characteristics to pursue a more personal tone, although applying the same attention to details and quality of materials as on their more historically correct replicas.

Some examples of this kind of high quality productions not aimed at exact "vintage" copies came from Wolfetone, Joe Barden, Rio Grande, Harmonic Design and the Italian Red Push. Today the purpose of many pickup makers seems to be to free the player of some of the physical limitations of older designs, producing models with tone characteristics normally associated with pickups of different dimensions or structure.

DiMarzio offered the 'Humbucker From Hell', a humbucking pickup promising single coil tones, or the Pro Track, which went the opposite way, a single coil sized humbucker with a PAF-like sound.

The Duncan Little 59 and the J. B. Jr were based on a similar concept, with single coil dimensions but actually humbucking, and with miniaturized screw polepieces. Very recent additions are more hybrid models, such as the Rio Grande "Stelly" and the Seymour Duncan "Twangbanger", models with Telecaster's lead model's specs but designed to be mounted on Stratocasters. Also from Duncan the "Phat Cat", P90 tone but fitting humbucking rings.

TV Jones, known for his excellent reproductions of the Filter'Tron models, used also by Brian Setzer on some of his guitars, also made the TV'Tron, a version made with a nickel or gold plated cover with the same dimension of standard Gibson-style humbuckers to bring some Gretsch-like clarity to guitars from other brands. Added to the line was also a version of the single coil Hi-Lo'Tron (HT-1), made to fit into Filter'Tron slots in order to adapt to recent Gretsch guitars. Also on offer, for those seeking the classic twang with more power, the choice is between the Classic Plus, the Power'Tron, the Power'Tron Plus and the Magna'Tron, this one made with 12 adjustable cylindrical alnico magnets for more sensitivity. Most models available in formats allowing to fit them in standard humbucking rings (TV'Tron size) or P 90 cavities (P'Tron size), to add the inimitable twang to most guitars from any popular brand.

In order to improve harmonics, especially on high frequencies, DiMarzio produced some humbucking models with uneven coils, each with a different resonant peak, described as similar in concept to an amplifier with two cones of different diameter. DiMarzio used this system the first time on the FRED model (1993), then in others such as the Norton, Tone Zone, Cruiser, Minibucker, DLX 90, just to name a few.

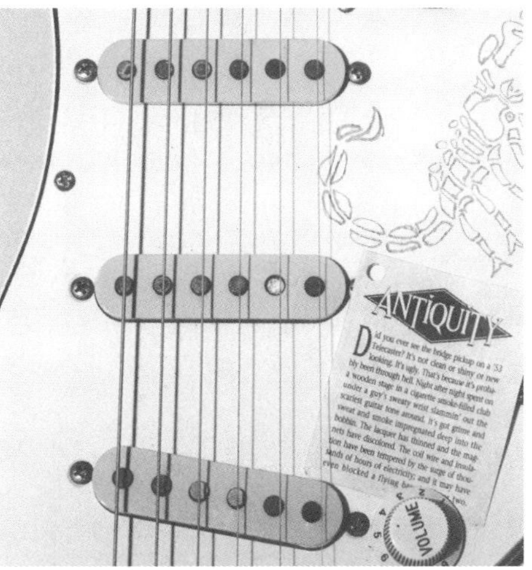

Duncan Antiquity "Texas Hot" set (Claudio Prosperini)

The improvements in winding machine technology made it possible to realize complex pickup designs and the result was a new generation of single coil sized humbucking pickups, basically an evolution of the models, with superimposed coils from the previous decade, presumed to have a truer, single coil type tone. Models of this kind were offered by DiMarzio (Virtual Vintage), Kinman and Fender (Noiseless).

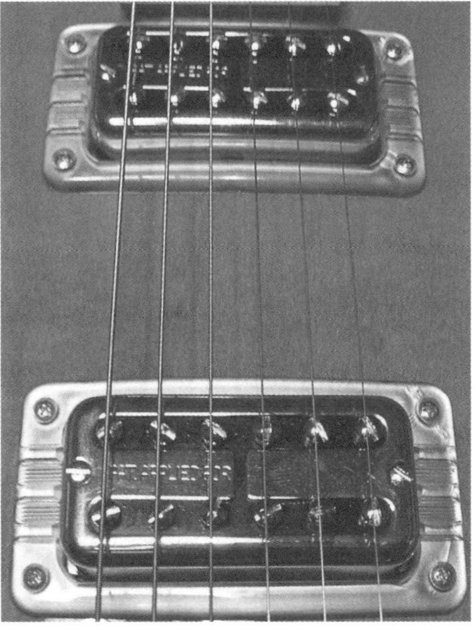
TV Jones Classic (Attilio Giacomini)

Seymour Duncan made good use of his great experience in magnets, and introduced the Nashville series, single coil models with Alnico 5 rod magnets under the three low strings for more clarity, Alnico 2 for the top strings for warmer highs. Fralin offered similar models using Alnico 3 and Alnico 5. Real or presumed innovations were always being introduced, most of them promising to eliminate some of the defects, (or so reputed), of the classic designs, such as noise and production inconsistencies, while keeping the sought after tone quality. As a matter of fact, even the most accurate "vintage" model pickups of today, are more consistently built than fifty years ago, with less than 10% tolerance instead of 20% as in the past.

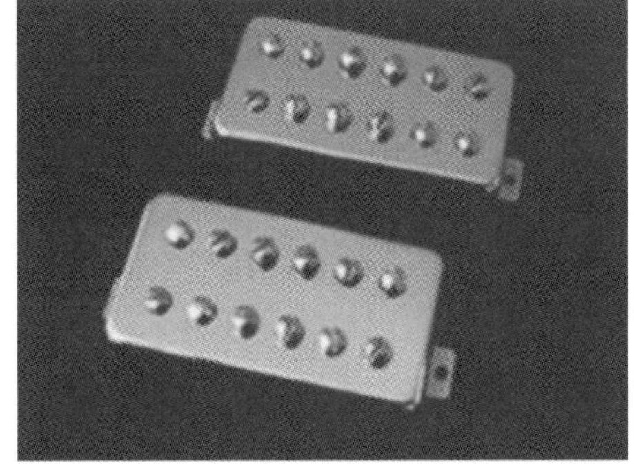
TV Jones TV'Tron, classic twang for guitars with standard humbucking cavities (courtesy of TV Jones).

The good news for guitar players is that average quality is pretty fine, and today even on cheap instruments is possible to find at least decent pickups. The range of the available replacement pickups is really impressive, from the low priced models designed by Kent Armstrong (son of the famous Dan), made in Korea with the Sky brand, to the always popular DiMarzio, Duncan, EMG, Fender, Gibson, up to the specialized and top quality Duncan Antiquity, Fralin, Tom Holmes, Van Zandt, Harmonic Design and others.

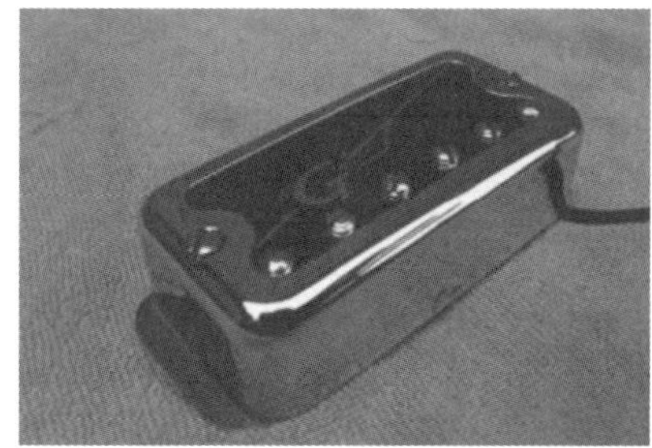
TV Jones HT-1 (courtesy of TV Jones).

The number of small companies building custom pickups was still growing. Among these were, Jason Lollar, (a guitar maker who also made his line of pickups with many special models for Lap Steel), Lynn Collins, J. M. Rolph, Wolfetone Pickups which was founded in 1996 by Wolfe McLeod, and Peter Florance's Voodoo Pickups.
These small companies were important not only for demonstrating the great vitality of this market, but also because they could offer a kind of service unavailable from bigger companies.

These included pickup rewind, repair and the making of personalized units designed specifically for the customer's guitar, amplifier, playing style and tone preferences. Some of these makers progressed to the point of winding a pickup several times until the desired sound was achieved. This was the only way to obtain a really personal sound but unfortunately this kind of service was possible only through direct contact with the craftsman.

Never before, in the history of the electric guitar, had the player had such vast possibilities to customize his guitar and surely there is more still to come.

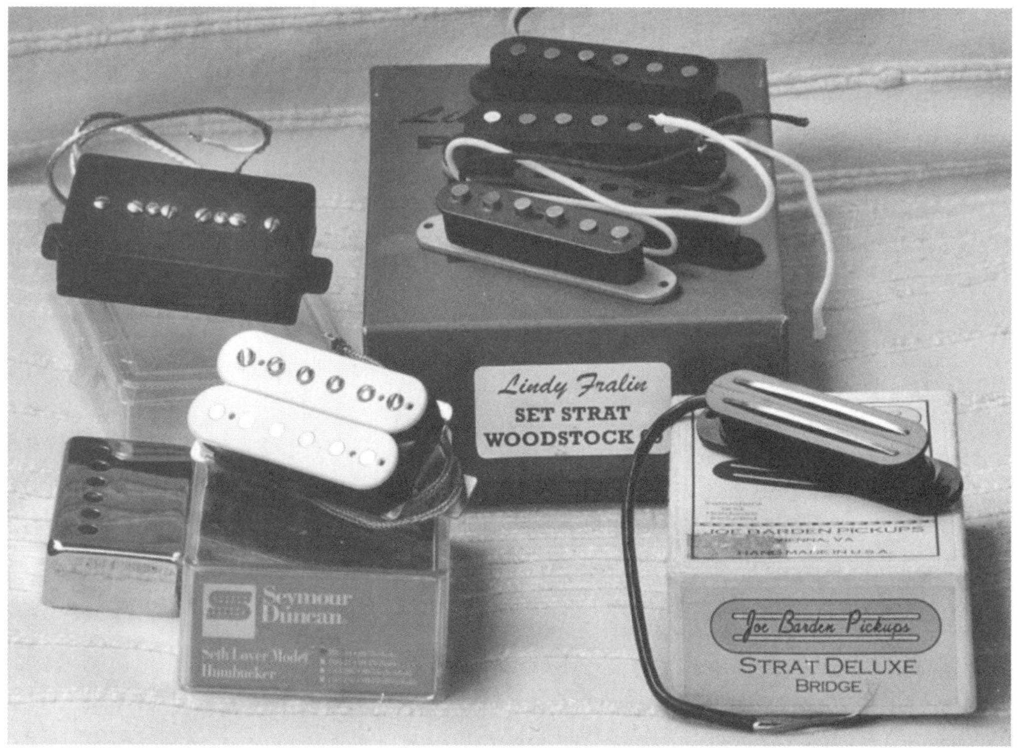

Some "boutique" models: Seymour Duncan SH-55 "Seth Lover", Rio Grande "Bastard", Lindy Fralin "Woodstock '69" and Joe Barden "Strat Deluxe" (Claudio Caldana).

Collecting pickups

A '65 Fender Stratocaster with fiesta red finish, truly a classic on the "vintage" market (Claudio Caldana).

Some instruments, built in the so called classic years, which varied according to maker and model, have become collector's items. Today, some parts, including pickups have a value which reflects the price of the instruments to which they are connected. The first reason to look for such pickups, is the need to replace a broken unit, however musicians soon discovered that they could get closer to the original sounds by fitting them to new instruments, while others started to collect old models as examples of craftsmanship from the past. Even if collecting pickups is not as popular as collecting the whole instrument, some models have reached a very high value on the market.

The Gibson humbuckers produced between 1957 and 1962 with the "Patent Applied For" label, in particular those with both cream coloured bobbins, are much more valued than the black or zebra ones.

Other valuable models are the DeArmond Dynasonic, the first Gretsch Filter'Tron, those made by Fender for the Telecaster and Stratocaster guitars before 1964 and the Gibson P90.

Less popular, but nonetheless of great historical interest are the Gibson "Charlie Christian" bar pickup, the "Alnico" model, the Rickenbacker "Horse-shoe" the Epiphone "New York" Model and the Fender units for the Jaguar and the Jazzmaster.

Other models, although not exactly collector's items, are much in demand by musicians for their good tone, for example, the Gibson humbucker made between 1962 and 1968, the Minihumbucking built for Epiphone guitars of the sixties, the Les Paul Deluxe, the Gibson Melody Maker and the Lap Steel models made by Fender. Less sought after are the Guild humbuckers and the Rickenbacker "Toaster".

Even some modern models, such as the first version of the DiMarzio Super Distortion earn their place in a collection.

Collecting instruments is often financially beyond reach for most people, but the collection of pickups is relatively affordable and represents an interesting historical insight into some of the technological achievements concerning the development of the electric guitar through the decades.

Notes

*W.L. Van Zandt passed away in February 1997 at 66 years old. The pickups he designed continue to be produced by his family.

7) Out of the USA

Japan

The invention, development and diffusion of the electric guitar and the pickup, was typically a North American phenomenon, and as with Coca-Cola and television, the whole world was rapidly involved.

In the early decades of the 20th century, Edison opened some factories in Japan and was the first to offer cylinders and records of traditional Japanese music to American tourists (courtesy of Peter Liebert).

日本では、ギターに対しての興味は、19世紀初めに始まった。

けんぱち　ひるま

In Japan interest in the guitar started in the early years of the nineteenth century, and the first guitar teacher was Kenpachi Hiruma, who studied guitar and mandolin in Italy and Germany in 1899.
The first foreign teacher was Adolfo Sarcoli from Siena, Italy, who moved to Japan in 1911 and taught singing, guitar and mandolin. The craze for Hawaiian music and electric guitar increased in the early 1930s and the first experiments carried out were based on the production of lap steels.

World War Two forced the interruption of these experiments, but they started again with renewed enthusiasm once the war was over. The new vitality gave birth to a production of instruments which immediately copied any innovation coming from the USA, even if quality was poor due to lack of experience and limited material resources.

あつお　金子

どうりゅう　松田

Near Tokyo, in 1946, the guitar player Atsuo Kaneko and the engineer Dohryu Matsuda founded the Awoi Sound Research, in order to build electric guitars and amplifiers. In 1948 Mitsuo Matsuki founded Guyatone, while Awoi was renamed Teisco.

In 1954 Teisco built the electric guitar TG 54, and in 1955 Matsuki created a entire line of solid body inspired by the Les Paul with the models LG 30, LG 50 and LG 60.

日本のメーカーは、生き残る為に、輸出に頼らなければならなかった。

After the war the financial situation, in Japan, was very difficult, but the internal market, however, seemed to be interested only in American

Teisco EP 200-L, 1966
(Claudio Prosperini)

instruments, thereby ignoring national production. Japanese makers had to rely on export, to survive. At the same time most distributors, in the USA and Europe, had the problem of an ever increasing demand for cheaper instruments, and so they became very interested in Japanese production.

Soon oriental models were distributed alongside European products, such as those made by Neoton in Czechoslovakia, with the brand name Grazioso which were imported into the UK under the name of Futurama. Also the Höfner and Framus made in Germany, and the Goya built by Hagstrom in Sweden, thus gradually conquering the lower end of the market. Japanese production grew and non authorized copies of American models appeared under the Aria Diamond, Tokai, Univox and Electra brands. The big American companies didn't seem to worry as these instruments were filling the market left empty by Harmony, Sears and other distributors of cheap models.

In time the Japanese makers made good use of the experience gained and even though they were not yet able to compete with high level instruments, they were, however, capable of offering products with a good performance / price ratio for low and medium grade models. The 1974 Ibanez catalogue showed 13 SG models, 21 various Les Pauls, one Firebird, an ES 175 and four Stratocasters, the quality of which was not bad at all. In 1975, the extremely accurate Explorer and Flying V copies were added, whilst from Korea, Hondo was producing even more copies.

日本の会社は原作以上のデザインを作る準備が出来ていた。

Ibanez Concord, a copy of the Gibson J 160 E. The copy is based on a '970s version, not the Southern Jumbo style made famous by the Beatles. The pickup on both versions was a P 90 (C. P.).

In 1976 Gibson and Fender decided to sue the copy makers, but by now the Japanese companies were ready to compete with original designs. Since 1973 Yamaha had already had the successful SG 2000 on the market, which had been used for a long time by Carlos Santana. Ibanez introduced the AR 300, AR 500 with active equalizer and, in 1977, the "George Benson" archtop and the semi solid LR 10, designed for Lee Ritenour, both with pickups conceived exclusively for those models. In 1979 Ibanez built the

Iceman, which had an appearance and sound aimed at the hard rock crowd, the JP 20, dedicated to Joe Pass and aimed at the Jazz player, whilst Arai proposed the Aria PE-1000. The great variety of guitar models offered by Japanese makers reflected the wide range of pickup models available, some really unusual, with a coil for each string.

Documents about these first experiments are scarce and most pickup models on imported instruments were imitations of those made by Fender, Gibson, Gretsch and other American makers. Most of the time the imitation of appearance was better than that of sound and often, there was actually only one coil under the cover of many humbuckers, revealing the fact that they were single coil units disguised as humbucking models.

Although varying in a great number of shapes and used by different companies, most pickups had a common origin, due to the fact that they were generally built by Maxon, a company specialized in the manufacture of electronic components.

The pickups on a '65 Teisco WG 4-L (Claudio Prosperini).

Maxon also produced effects for the guitar, the most famous being the TS 808 designed for Ibanez.

Experience and improved components resulted in production of better products and by the end of the seventies Ibanez offered a series of good sounding models, such as the clear and powerful Super 80, the bright toned Super 70, and the special models designed for the "Signature" series guitars dedicated to George Benson and Lee Ritenour.

In the early 1980s the Super 70 was substituted by the Super 58, a humbucking model with medium output and an Alnico 3 magnet. It had a warm sound, good presence on middle frequency and a sweet top end, though perhaps rather too sugary, but proved very successful and is still in use.

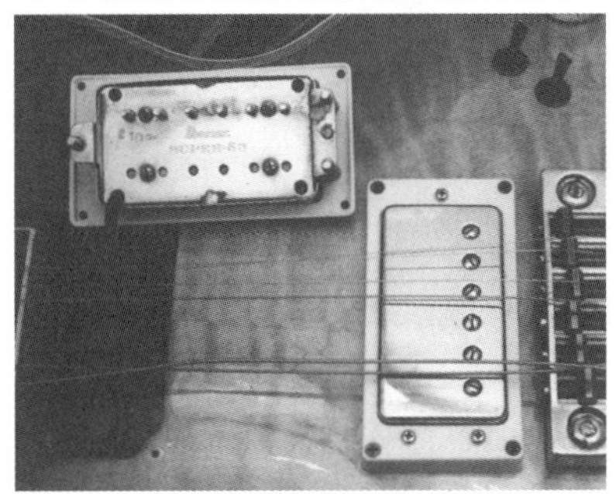

Super 58 pickups on a Ibanez Artist 300 (Claudio Prosperini).

Yamaha used an Alnico 5 pickup on most models, which was as good as those made by Gibson at the time. In the eighties, for the top of the range of the solid body line the SG 3000, they introduced a new, brighter model with a magnet made from a new alloy which in the catalogues was called Spinex.

The unusual pickups of a Yamaha SG-80, made in 1976 (Claudio Prosperini).

These developments, which involved all brands, reduced the gap between Japanese and American products, but the increasing popularity of DiMarzio and Duncan models forced the major oriental brands to offer pickups made by these two companies on their top of the line instruments. On their lower grade guitars, however, they used pickups designed by the two specialists and produced under licence in Korea.

日本の製作所は. アメリカの
モデルでない物で日本の市場を占めた.

Quickly instruments produced in Korea and Taiwan became the best sellers in the low end market superseding American and European models previously sharing that space.

Then, even though some producers, such as Yamaha and Ibanez, still offered their own pickups on some instruments, research seemed to have come to a standstill.

Ibanez "Steve Lukater" SL 10. Joe Pass, George Benson, Pat Metheny, Lee Ritenour, Joe Satriani, Steve Vai, Paul Gilbert, are other well known players connected to Ibanez models (Claudio Prosperini).

Europe

In Europe, though very desirable, the US made instruments were out of reach for the majority of players due to their high cost, therefore, the fifties and sixties, were inundated with Japanese and European models.

Wandré Scarabeo (C. P.)

In Italy, in the early sixties, guitars were made by Bartolini, Crucianelli, Gemelli Cingolani and EKO, who was the most popular, and also later made instruments for the Vox brand.

The most original instruments, (today avidly collected), were those designed by Wandré Antonio Pioli, produced in his factory in Cavriago and sold with various name brands, such as Davoli, Wandré, Noble, Meazzi, Framez. Pioli even made for a short time some models for Jennings, a Vox distributor. Some confusion was created by the fact that on many instruments several names were present and these could refer either to the model or the brand.
The sole certainty being that the pickups were made by Athos Davoli, leader of a company which produced amplifiers and other electronic items.
Wandré's guitars were extravagant creations, which were a mixture of plastic and aluminium, with shapes no less than bizarre, inspired by the motorcycle and the world of art, such as the Oval Rock, the B. B., dedicated to Brigitte Bardot, and the Scarabeo. The pickups were not very powerful and their structure was unnecessarily complicated, but the sound was personal enough to contribute to the appeal of the instrument.

Wandré Tigre (C. P.)

In Europe, in the sixties, the German Höfner gained popularity, after Paul McCartney used one of their basses. The London based Burns made the interesting TR 2, with active electronics, and two models later became collector's items, the "Hank Marvin" and the "Bison".
Unusual sounds were offered by the Vox Guitar-Organ and the Italian Godwin Guitar-Organ. The Swedish factory Hagstrom, known in the sixties for their Goya guitars, in the following decade made their own higher level instruments and were for a while sponsored by jazz player Larry Coryell.

The best known out of the many pickups produced in Europe were the Schaller models, which for a long time were the only ones available as after-market items.

Japanese and European guitars with four pickups, as this Eko 700 4 –V, were very common, in the sixties (C. P.).

In Italy the major producer was EKO, with some original models, such as a single coil with small blade polepieces under each string, recalling a transformer core, with an Alnico magnet on the base, partially inserted into the bobbin. The magnet was not very powerful, but the polepieces were very efficient in transferring the magnetic flux. Having a D. C. resistance of nearly 6 kOhms, the pickup was pretty loud and clear sounding. Unfortunately the use of complicated circuits with too many resistors and capacitors filtering the signal didn't give the pickup the recognition it deserved. It was a good design on the wrong guitar.

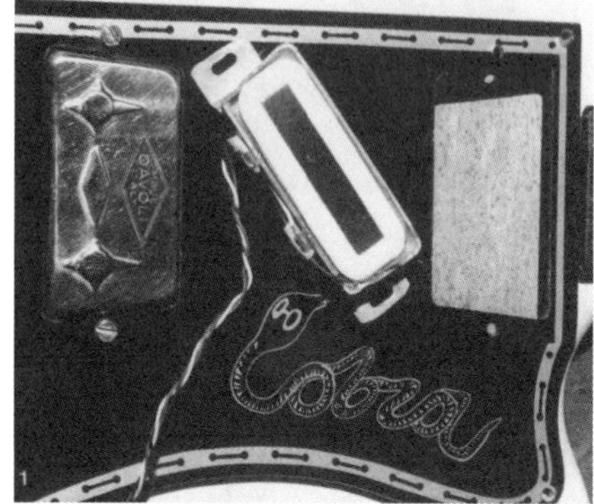

Davoli pickup on a Cobra guitar (Claudio Prosperini)

European makers, especially from Italy, seemed more concerned in designing complicated circuits, with lots of switches and up to four pickups on a guitar, than improving the quality of the pickups.

The models made by Jim Burns were single coil, with Alnico or ceramic magnets. These pickups had a metallic frame extending on the sides of the coil, bent around the base of the cover, thereby concentrating the magnetic field toward the strings, much as the frame of the Jaguar pickup (it seems that Burns achieved this before Leo Fender). The same principle, though applied in a different way, was used on the Lace Sensor models used by Fender in the late eighties.

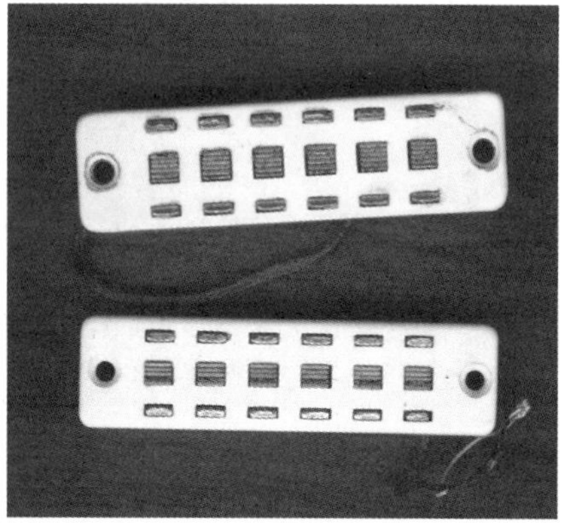

Eko SB-1. Two version were made, with the same specs but slightly different sizes (C. Prosperini).

The Burns pickups renewed their popularity when Brian May used ceramic models to power his home-made guitar, which coupled with Vox AC 30 amplifiers, produced one of the most distinctive sounds in rock music, so much so, that copies were made by DiMarzio, Duncan and Kent Armstrong.

During the 1990s two pickup makers from the UK, David White and Jim Carnes, became reputed for their models inspired by Fender and Gibson classics, although they were relatively unknown abroad.

In the sixties, the Höfner guitars, in particular the solid body models 175 and 176, were well known to many as the poor man's Fenders. They had a singular finish which was made by applying vinyl sheets to the body, and both had pickups similar to the Gibson mini-humbucking. They often had a single coil under the cover but when two coils were present they had different wire gauges on each bobbin. Because of the use of light wood and weak magnets, these pickups didn't give much voice to the guitars, but they had a sweet tone which, though not appreciated at the time (as everybody was seeking the bright sound of Fender guitars or the full sound of Gibson humbuckers), in retrospect had its particular appeal.

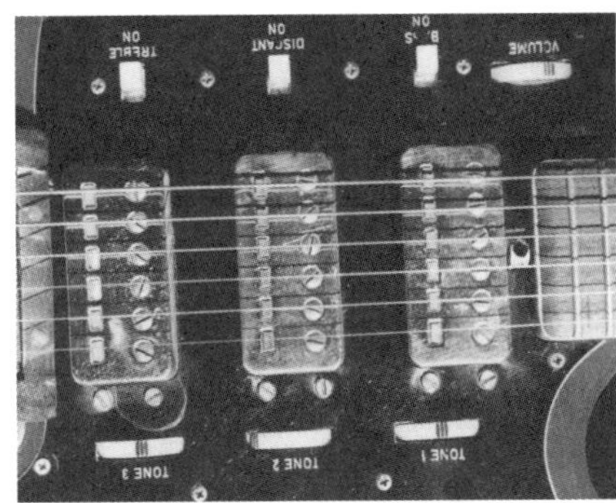
The pickups of a Höfner 175 (Claudio Prosperini)

Schaller, in the past the only European maker offering pickups to electrify an acoustic guitar, similar to the DeArmond units of the same kind, later made models for other brands and offered his own line of copies of American models with a good price / performance ratio. The humbucking Golden 50 is still standard equipment on the Kalamazoo built Heritage guitars (Duncan models are available as an option).

Other German producers were Framus and Shadow, the latter with a wide range of models for acoustic guitar amplification and for electric guitars.

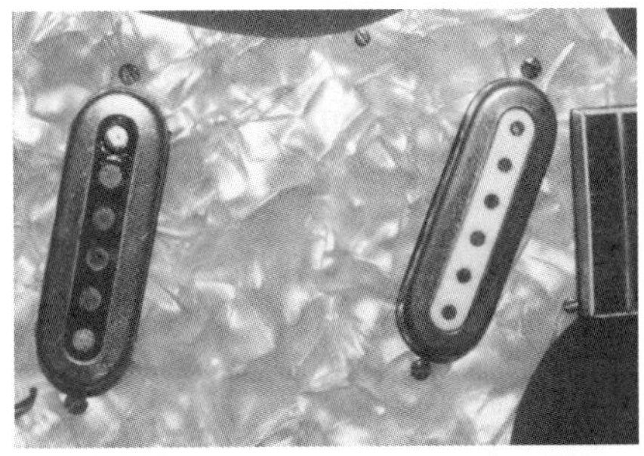

The pickups on two Ellisound guitars (Claudio Prosperini).

When DiMarzio pickups conquered the market, most brands started to offer them as standard equipment on their high quality instruments and even EKO guitars became "DiMarzio Powered", while on cheaper models copies of the original items were used.

Gradually most of the European guitar makers disappeared, to be replaced by Japanese and Korean models. Pickup production was also reduced.

In Italy there were only occasional bursts of activity, as shown by Magnetics, who made active and passive models designed and built by Piero Terracina. For a while these were used by various Italian and foreign guitar makers, even if not always credited, and were relatively successful.

Schaller pickguard-pickup set for archtop guitars (C. P.).

Today, the Red Push Pickups are original models designed and hand built by Giovanni Gaglio, a well known luthier from Rome, who retired to concentrate exclusively in the repair of pickups.
The single coil models have two alnico cylindrical magnets posed diagonally under each string (diagonal pole system), for a wide magnetic field giving a fatter sound.

A Framus model, similar to a P 90, but with two ceramic magnets on the outer sides of the coil (C. Prosperini).

The coil is wound directly around the magnets, Fender-style. The humbucking model is made using the same structure and has a very big sound.

The Red Push pickups are not copies of vintage models, they have their own voice and are aimed at the player seeking a personal sound, but are completely hand made, the way old time craftsmen used to do, just like the first vintage models.

Now a new model is announced, the Fantasma, made using an unusual winding configuration, patented, with zero resistance, conceived to give a more airy sound while keeping the full tone of previous Red Push models.

Available in single coil and humbucking models, the new design can be used without capacitors for the tone controls, so the sound is not dampened resulting more open than with traditional systems (the Fantasma single coil can be ordered with diagonal pole system or with a more traditional single pole line, for a more classic appearance).

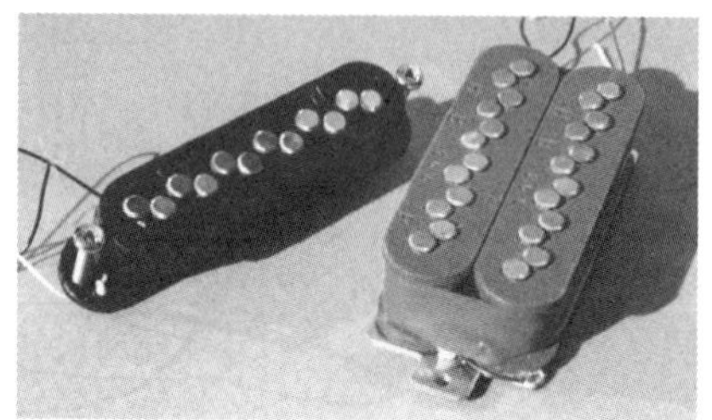

Red Push pickups
(Vincenzo Tabacco).

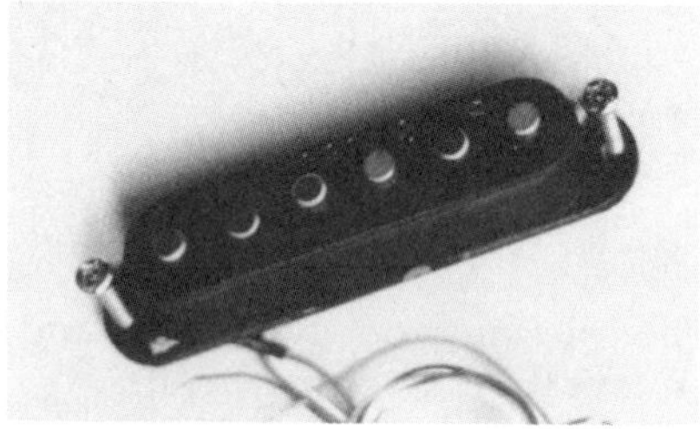

Red Push "Fantasma" in the optional single pole version (Vincenzo Tabacco).

Shadow makes almost any kind of pickups, but the most popular models from this brand, are those for acoustic guitar's amplification (C. P.).

EKO Master 4-V

EKO Kadett

EKO M-24

EKO Master 2-V, champagne sparkle finish

Ellisound pickups

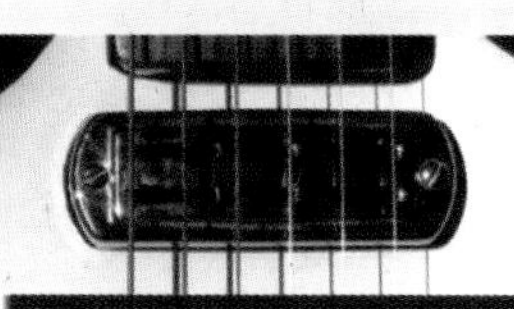

Ellisound pickup

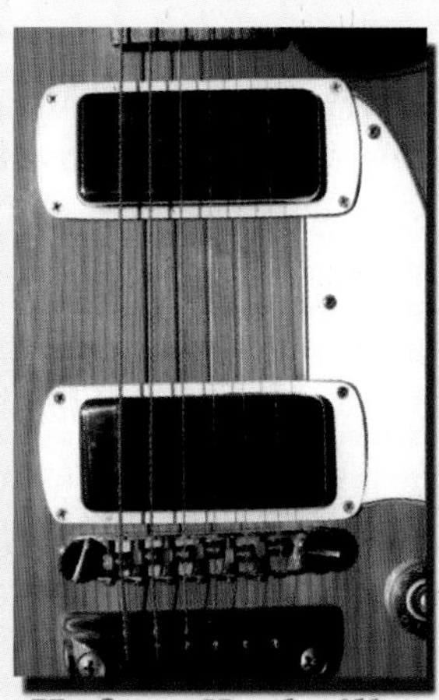

Hofner Nashville

Hofner Archtop

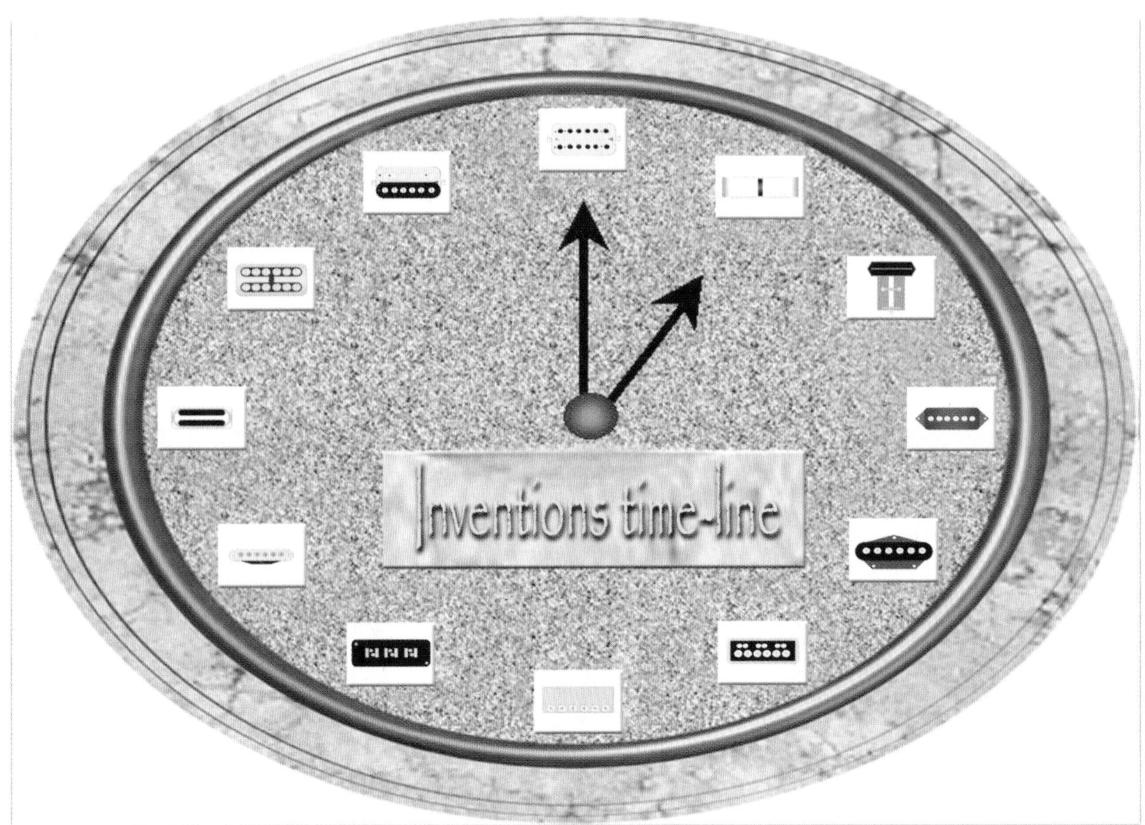

1850

In the early years of the decade Antonio De Torres develops the Spanish guitar and the lighter flamenco guitar. At the same time, in USA, C. F. Martin standardizes the sizes and specifications of his flat top guitars with scalloped X-bracing, developing the modern American-style acoustic guitar.

1851 - In London is held the first World's Fair exhibiting industrial and technological achievements.

1864 - James Maxwell develops the theory about the electromagnetic wave. It will be the basis for radiowave propagation.

1876

In Hawaii is evolving an original style of guitar playing using open tunings and slide techniques. According to some stories James Hoa invented it in 1876, others credit Gabriel Davion.

1878 - Thomas Alva Edison patents the recording of sound on cylinders, experimented one year before, at the same time as Charles Cros carried out similar experiments in France.

1879 - Edison announces the invention of the incandescent light bulb. The modern electric era begins.

1887 - Edison announced an improved cylinder phonograph.
Heinrich Hertz proves that radio waves can be transmitted and received from short distances.
Emile Berliner registers his invention of the gramophone and the record disc.

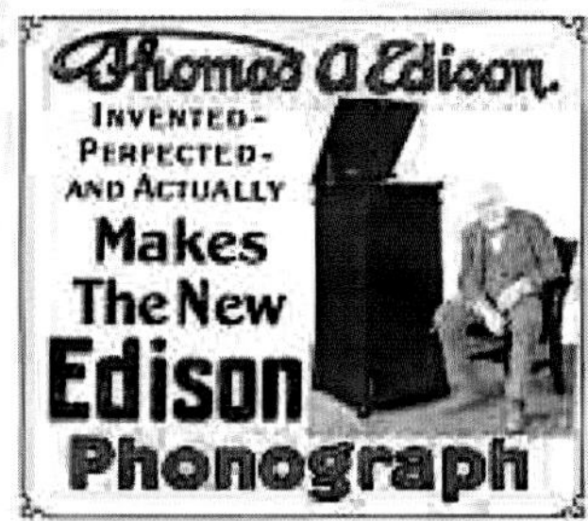

1888 - Emile Berliner realizes a flat 7" disc with a recording capacity of two minutes, Oberlin Smith develops the basics of magnetic recordings.

1894

Orville Gibson starts making his original guitars built to be strung with steel strings.

1895 - Guglielmo Marconi develops the wireless telegraph system.

1898

Orville Gibson patents the one-piece neck and sides mandolin. On the market appears the six strings guitar-banjo, the loudest six strings instrument of the time.

Valdemar Poulsen patents the magnetic wire recorder, called Telegraphone.
1901 - The paper label is for the first time applied on record discs.

1902

The Gibson Mandolin & Guitar Manufacturing Company Ltd is founded. Martin introduces the first OOO size models (15" wide).

Ademor Petit patents a 10" disc with a capacity of ten minutes.

1904

Harmony opens a 30.000,00 square feet plant in Chicago.

Odeon introduces discs recorded on both sides.
1905 - Sir Ambrose Fleming develops the electron tube.

1908

The Regal Musical Instruments Co. is founded.

1912 - Lee De Forest develops the Audion vacuum tube amplifier.
1915 - Carbon microphones are used for telephone, but are too noisy and limited in range to be suitable for music's recording.
1916 - AT&T develops public address amplifiers and speakers.
At Bell Labs E. C. Wente develops the condenser microphone.

1917

George D. Laurian at Gibson invents the suspended pickguard.

Music is still recorded through a large acoustical horn directing the soundwaves to the vibrating diaphragm of a phonograph.

1919

Lloyd Alayre Loar is hired by Gibson. He will develop the Style 5 Series, including the L-5 guitar, issued in '23.

The KDKA of Pittsburgh, Pennsylvania, is the first radio station.

1920

The truss-rod is invented by Gibson's Ted McHugh. A patent is applied for in '21 and granted in '23.

The first radio station broadcasting music, news, weather informations and commercial announcements is the XGA in Montreal, Canada, for a while owned by Guglielmo Marconi.

1925 - Realized the first recordings using a microphone. The system, consists in a Western Electric 1-B microphone and a vacuum tube amplifier.

1926 - The condenser microphone, perfected as the Western Electric 394-W, is used for sound motion pictures.

1927

John Dopyera patents the resophonic guitar.

1928 - Georg Neuman, in Berlin, introduces the condenser microphone CMV-3

1930 - Albert L. Thuras patents the bass-reflex principle for loudspeakers.

1931

Martin introduces the Dreadnought D-1 and D-2, then evolving in the D-18 and D-28 a few years later.
George Beauchamp invents the magnetic pickup helped by Paul Barth and Adolph Rickenbacker produces the first electric lap steels.
The Kay Musical Instruments is founded by Henry Kay Kuhrmeyer.

The Bell Telephone Laboratories are experimenting with stereo recordings and two way speakers.
The dynamic microphone, developed by W. C. Wente and A. C. Thuras at Bell Labs, is patented.
The RCA introduces the ribbon microphone 44A. In UK Alan Blumlein patents the binaural (stereo) recording.

1932

Selmer builds guitars designed by Mario Maccaferri.

Invention of the juke box in USA.

1933

Lloyd A. Loar founds the innovative but short lived Vivitone Company.

Edwin Armstrong develops the theory of frequency modulation (FM) for radio broadcasting.
RCA introduces the cardioid ribbon microphone 77-A.

Gibson makes electric lap steels with the bar pickup designed by Walter Fuller.

Development of separate tweeter and woofer loudspeakers to reduce distortion.
AEG/Telefunken, in Germany, develops the magnetic tape recording.

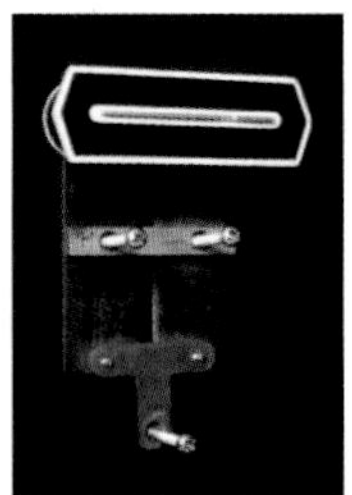

1936

Gibson introduces the ES-150 electric guitar with the bar pickup.

1937 - RCA introduces a smaller and more sensitive ribbon microphone: the 77-B.

1938

The Gibson Super Jumbo is on the market. It will be renamed SJ 200 in '39.

1939

G. B. Jonas invents the AlNiCo magnet, an alloy of alluminium, nickel and cobalt. Walter Fuller designs the first nickel covered Alnico pickup for Gibson on which the P 90 will later be based.

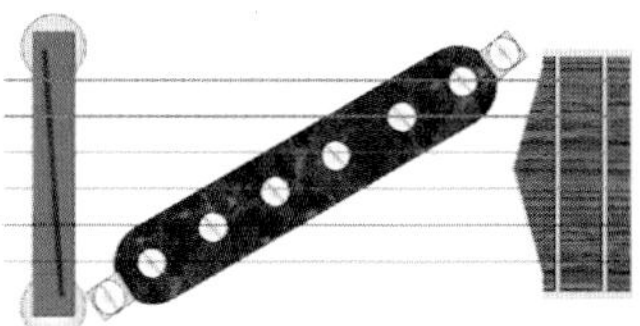

1940

Introduced by Gibson the long diagonal pickup, soon replaced by the short diagonal pickup.

1941 - Shure develops the Unidyne microphone.

1944

Fender & Kauffman make lap steels equipped with Leo's "Direct Strings" pickup.

1945 - Paul Klipsch patents the Klipschorn speaker.

1946

Gibson introduces the P 90 designed by Walter Fuller, the most famous single coil since the Bar Pickup from this brand.

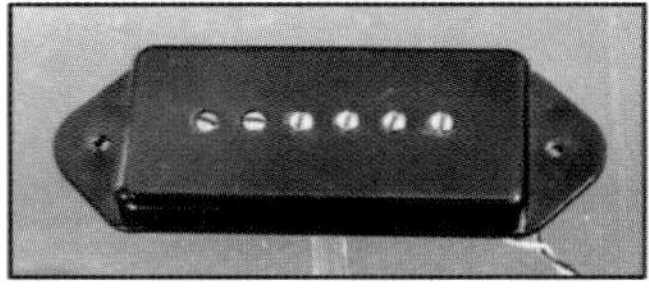

1947

Albert Augustine, prompted by Andres Segovia, unhappy with gut strings, develops the nylon strings.

1948 -Columbia introduces the first 33" ½ long playing records, developed by Peter Goldmark, that same year the transistor appears.

1949

Gibson introduces the ES 5 with three P 90s, the ES 175 and the McCarty Unit, a pickguard-pickups assembly for acoustic archtop's amplification.
Introduced the De Armond Model 200, standard feature on Gretsch guitars and later famous as the Dynasonic pickup.

The RCA issues the first 45 rpm, 7" records and Harry Olsen develops the acoustic suspension speakers.
Neuman introduces the U-47 microphone, Frank Sinatra's favourite.
Introduced the MacIntosh 50W1 amplifier, 50watt with 1% distortion over a frequency range of 20-20000 Hz.

1950

Leo Fender announces the Broadcaster; the pickups have different specs for neck and bridge positions.

1951

Epiphone guitars are equipped with the new "New York" pickup.

Introduced the Nagra portable recorder.

1952

Introduced the Gibson Les Paul.

1954

Introduced by Gibson the Tune-O-Matic adjustable bridge, designed by Ted McCarty.
Announced in september the Gibson "Alnico" Pickup, designed by Seth Lover.
Leo Fender introduces the Stratocaster.

Acoustic Research introduces the AR-1 bookshelf loudspeaker.
The transistor portable radio appears on the market.

1955

Seth Lover designs the humbucking pickup. The model, however, will be introduced only in 1957. Nat Daniel designs the first Danelectro guitar.

1956

Vox introduces the AC 15, designed by Dick Denney, on which the more famous AC 30 will be based.

1957

Gretsch introduces the humbucking Filter'tron pickup. Rickenbacker replaces the "Horseshoe" pickup with the new "Toaster".

1958 - The first stereo long playing records are introduced (stereo tapes were available since '54). The first stereo headphones are introduced by Koss.

1959

Gretsch uses a stereo pickups configuration, called Project-O-Sonic, on the White Falcon.
Gibson issues the stereo ES 345 TD with Varitone.
The system is also offered on the ES 355 TD-SV. The guitar is still available in a mono version as the ES 355 TD. The patent for the humbucking pickup is granted, but Gibson still uses the "Patent Applied For" label.

1960

Gibson introduces the CE-1, a classical guitar with a piezoelectric pickup.

1962

A label with the number "2.737.842" gradually replaces the "Patent Applied For" label on Gibson humbuckers.

First stereo radio broadcasts.

1963

Gibson introduces the Firebird Series with Minihumbucking pickups. Guild makes his own humbucking model, slightly less wide than Gibson's standard model.

Philips develops the compact audio cassette, with BASF polyester 1/8" tape.

1965

On January 5 the acquisition of Fender by CBS is legalized.
Introduced the Marshall Combo 1962, better known as the "Bluesbreaker".

1967

The Ovation line of guitars is introduced.

1969

Gibson introduces the Les Paul Professional with low impedance pickups.
Norlin Industries acquires Gibson.

The Dolby noise reduction system is introduced.

1970

Guild replaces the '63 humbucking pickup with a new, larger model called the HB-1, similar in dimensions to the Gibson unit but brighter sounding and with three adjusting screws securing it to the mounting ring.

Introduction of the electret microphone.

1972

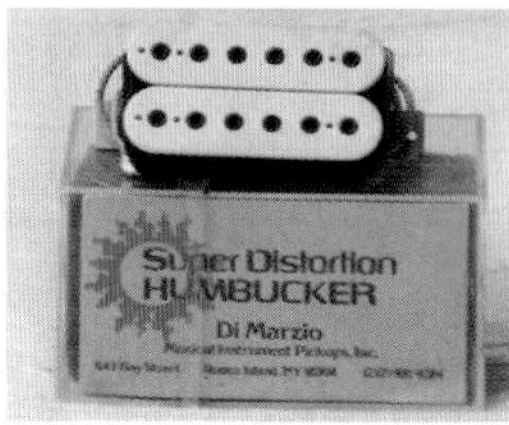

Larry DiMarzio announces the Super Distortion pickup.
The Music Man Company is founded by a restless Leo Fender.

1974

Introduced the EMG-SA active pickups set for Stratocaster from Overland-EMG, soon becoming a leader in this field.
Other high tech builders will be Bartolini and Alembic.

1976

Seymour Duncan introduces faithful replicas of the most popular vintage models.

1979

Leo Fender founds a new Company, the "G & L", with his old mate George Fullerton, introducing new guitar models and the "Magnetic Field Design" pickups.

1980

Gibson attempts to reproduce some "vintage" characteristics on the Les Paul Heritage Standard '80 and Heritage Elite '80 models.

Sony introduces the Walkman.

1982

Announced the Vintage Reissue Series by Fender. Vintage-style models, competitively priced, are also produced in Japan, by Fuji Gen-Gakki for Fender Japan and marketed with the Squier brand.
Introduced the Gibson CEC, a solid body classical-electric guitar designed with Chet Atkins.

1983 - The first CD players, based on a digital recording technology developed between '75 and '78, are introduced by Sony and Philips.

1983

Joe Barden introduces the first dual blades pickups, noise-free but with a clear, single coil-like tone, designed for the great Danny Gatton.

1986

Norlin Industries sells Gibson to Henry Juskiewicz, David Barryman and Gary Zebrowski.
The new owners do their best to resume quality and in 1993 the Custom, Historic & Art Division is created.

Magnets
North = N
South = S
North
Pickups on Tour
Pole orientation on some
K&F Direct
Direct strings Pickup
North
Rickenbacker pickups for richer and more brilliant tone response
The "Horse-shoe"
The "Toaster"
Gibson P90
Late fifties' Combo 800
Cover
Coil
RICKENBACKER'S
MAGNETS
S
N
Alnico magne
Gibs

Gibson late seventies reissue bar pickup "Charlie Christian"

Early fifties' Gibson ES 5

(This guitar had humbuckings fitted, when restored, a larger base was placed under the original P 90s)

P 90
'53 Ultratone
Lap Steel
'63 SG TV
'68 Les Paul Standard
Late sixties'
Epiphone Coronet
'66 ES 330 TD
1954
Les Paul Junior
ES 295 Reissue

Fender 1949's lap steels
and sixties' Supro 1696T

Fender 1950's Broadcaster
and 1953's Deluxe Amp
Top left: late '60s
Telecaster pickup
FENDER
PAT. PEND.

Fender

'55 Stratocaster and Deluxe Amp

'59 Jazzmaster

'62 Jaguar

Early sixties' Stratocasters

Fifties' Epiphone Zephyr Deluxe Regent's pickup

Fifties' Epiphone Zephyr Emperor Regent and sixties' Epiphone Electra amp

1967's ES345 TD Stereo

1961's Patent Applied For

1969's Mini-Humbucking

1961's ES 335 TD

'61 Les Paul Standard
PATENT
APPLIED FOR
Gibson
KALAMAZOO, MICHIGAN
ECHOREC
VOX
BUONA DOMENICA
CENTOCITTA
ONDINA
ANTONELLO VENDITTI
'63 Firebird V
Les Paul models:
Standard, Custom and Deluxe

HUMBUCKERS

GIBSON "PATENT APPLIED FOR"

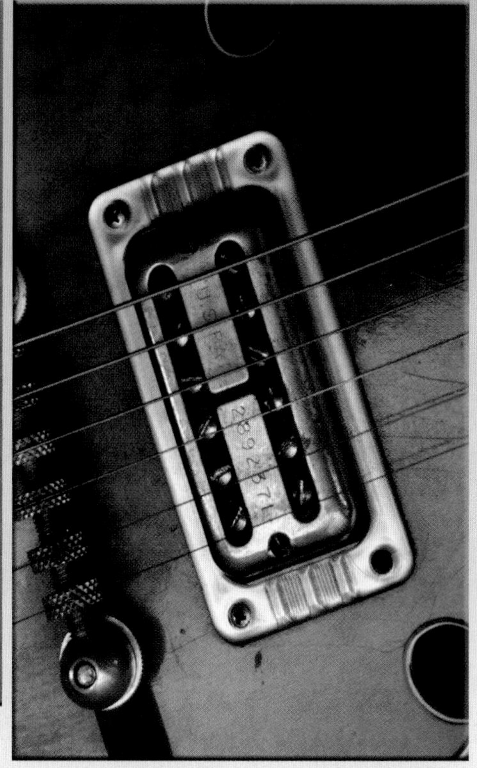

GRETSCH FILTER'TRON

PAF COPIES FROM FRALIN, DUNCAN ANTIQUITY (right) AND VOODOO PICKUPS

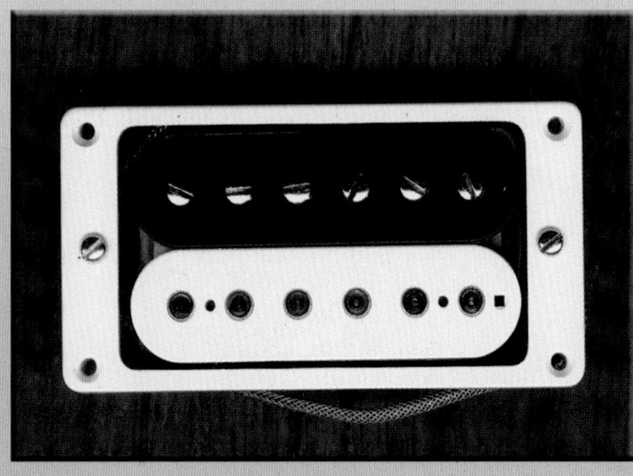

Sixties' Teisco
SMILE
日本製
"THANKS TO THE WORLD"
BOSS
Roland
Sonny
TOKYO

Ibanez
AR 300

MADE
IN JAPAN

Yamaha SG 80

Eko
from the sixties
K
a
d
e
t
t
Pickups from a Master 2 V
(inset: 700 - 4V Alnico)
Rokes 12
(DeArmond pickup)
Master 4 V

Scarabeo and Tigre,
Wandré guitars from the sixties

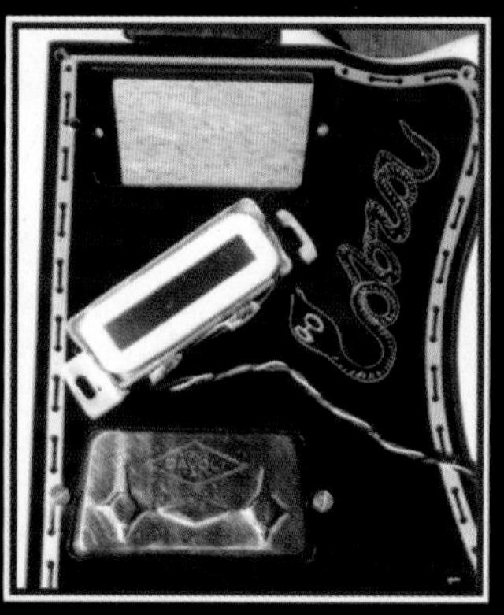

Close view of the pickups on a Cobra

Davoli amps

Euro-style
Goya
FULL
1+2
1+4
2+3
3+4
OFF
Schaller
electronic

Hoyer Special
Fender
Deluxe Amp

Hofner
VOLUME
BASS ON
DISCANT ON
TREBLE ON
TONE 1
TONE 2
TONE 3

Höfner

SOMETHING A BIT LESS USUAL...

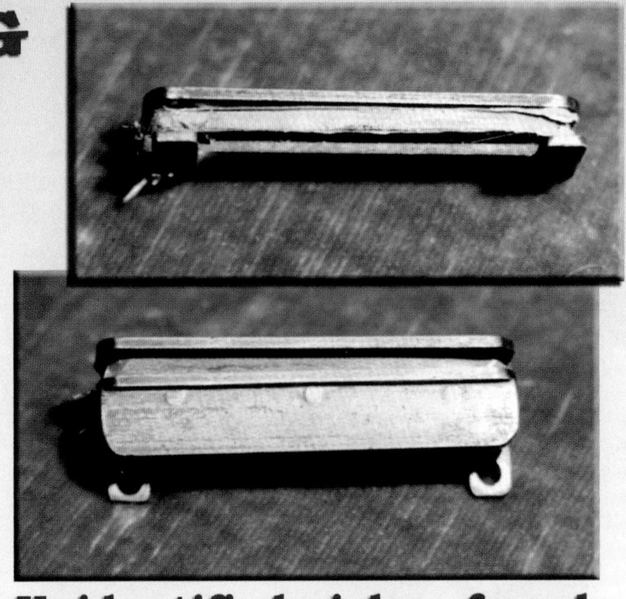

Unidentified pickup found on a Gretsch archtop from the forties

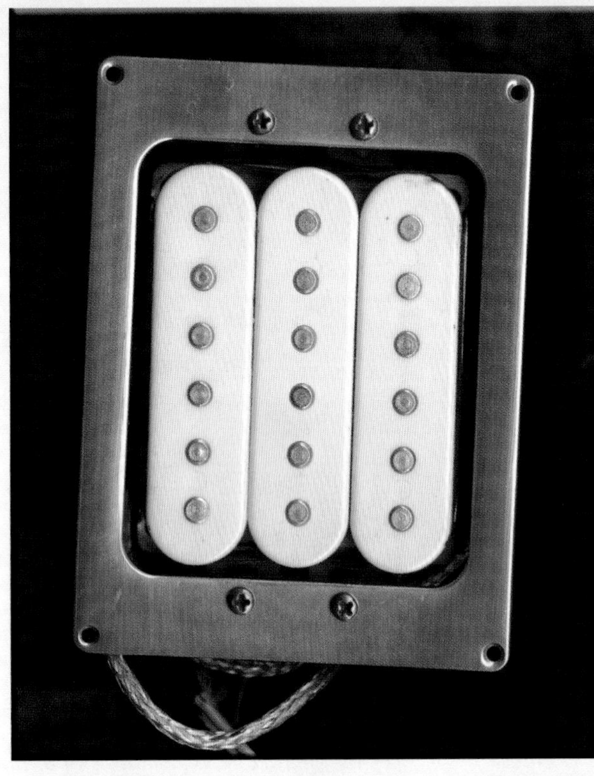

The Mighty Mite Motherbucker model is one of the most famous triple coil pickups, used on some Hamer guitars, other triple coil models were also made by other bulders, one of them being Yamaha.

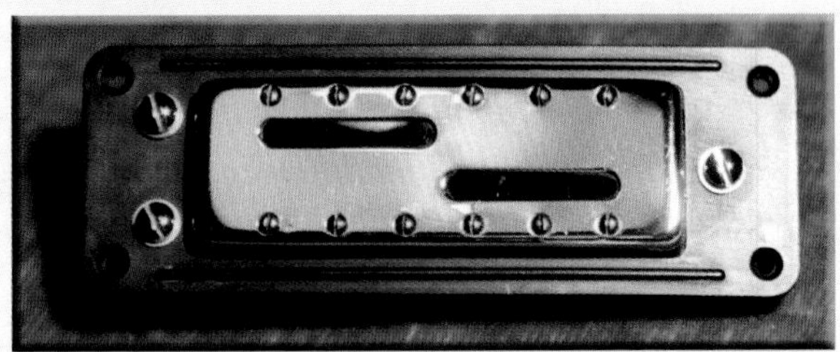

A fine sounding '60s pickup from un unidentified manufacturer.

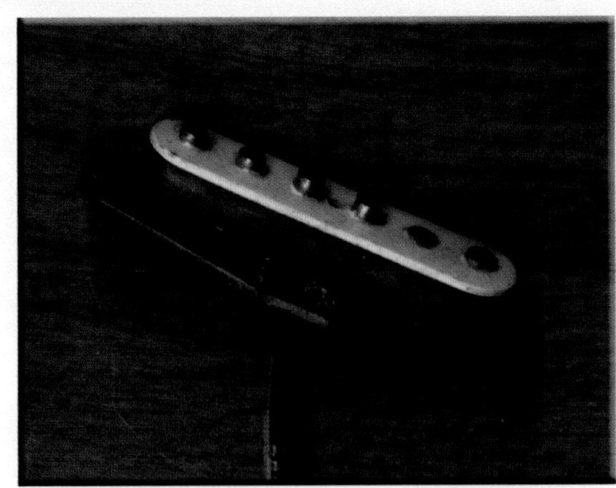

An uncommon Fender Stratocaster pickup made with a cream top.

REPLACEMENT PICKUPS

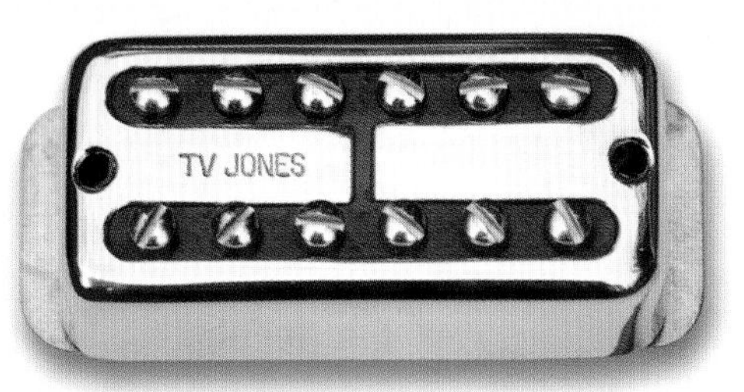

TV Jones Classic - Gold

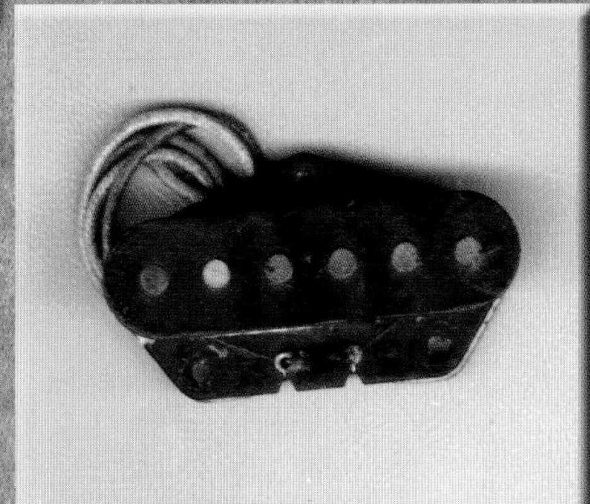
Duncan STL-1B

Duncan SH-1 '59 Model

Rio Grande Tall Boy for Telecaster

Duncan Antiquity P 90 Set

DiMarzio Paf Model

MORE REPLACEMENT PICKUPS

DiMarzio Air Norton

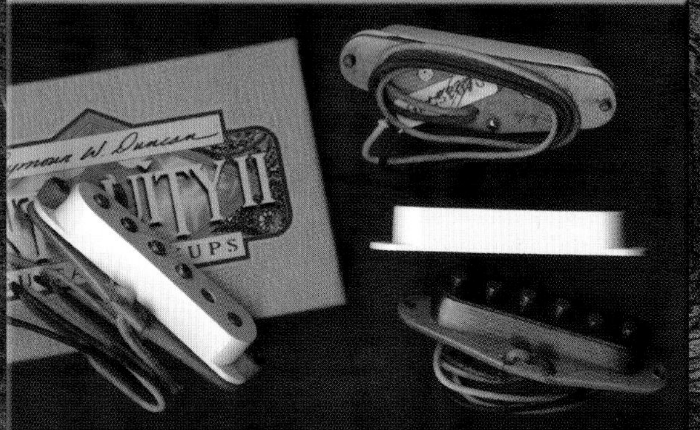

Duncan Antiquity II Set

Duncan Antiquity set

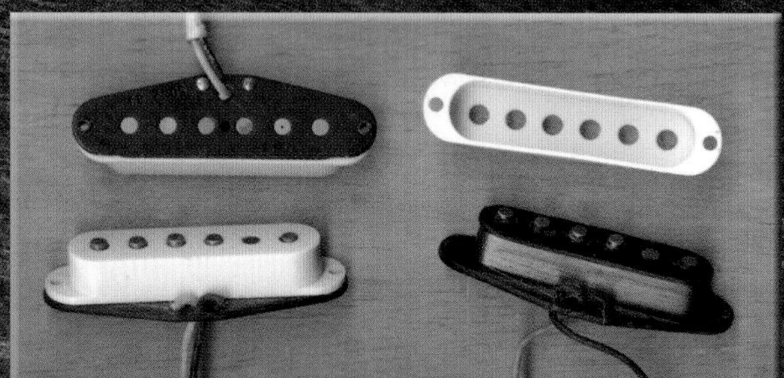

Duncan Alnico Pro set

DiMarzio Mega Drive

Duncan Allan Holdsworth

EVEN MORE REPLACEMENT PICKUPS

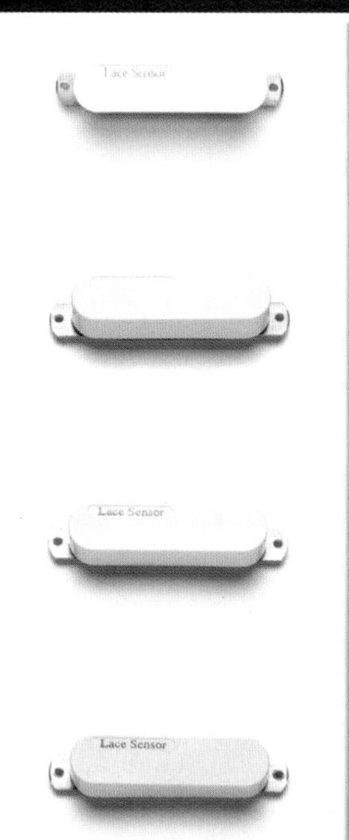

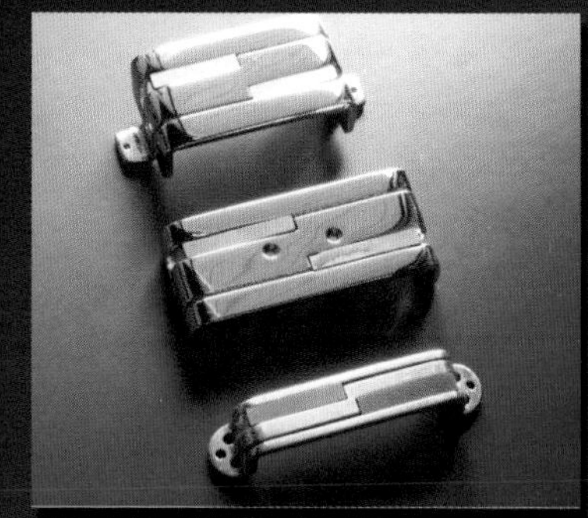

Joe Barden

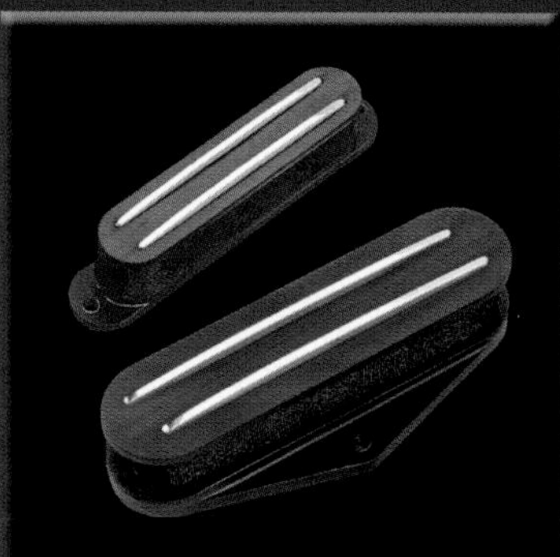

Danny Gatton Tele Set

Lace Holy Grail

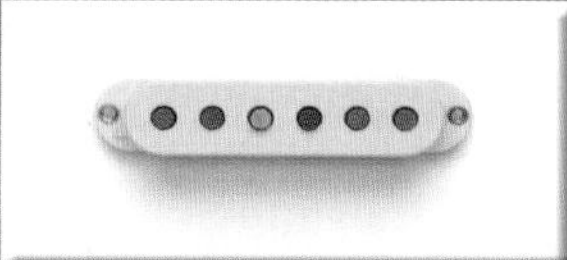

Lace

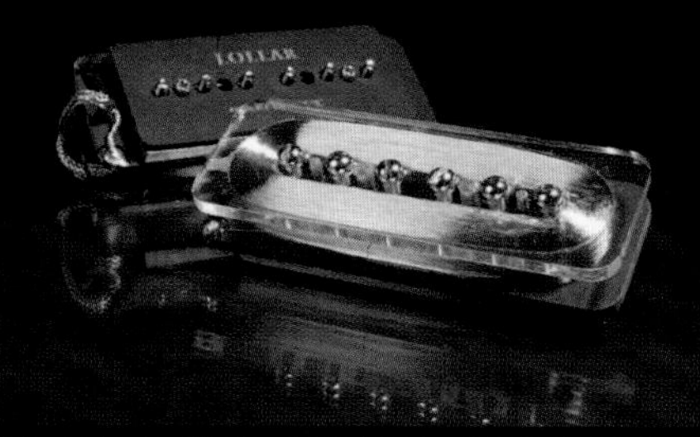

Vintage style pickups for lap steel and guitar

Modern strategies

DiMarzio SDS-1

EMG-SA active set

Duncan SSL 52-1

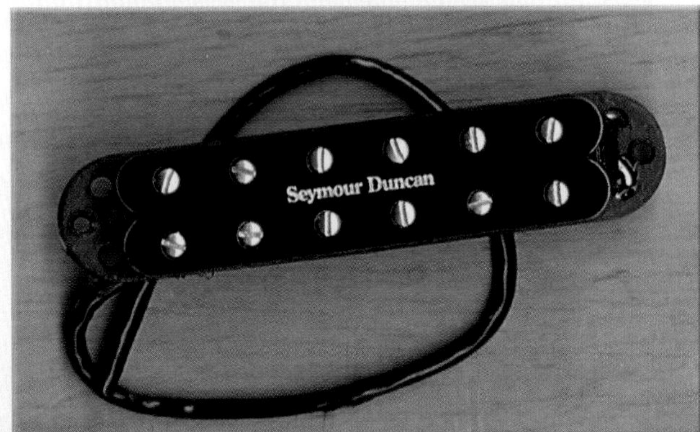

Duncan APST-1

Duncan SJBJ-1

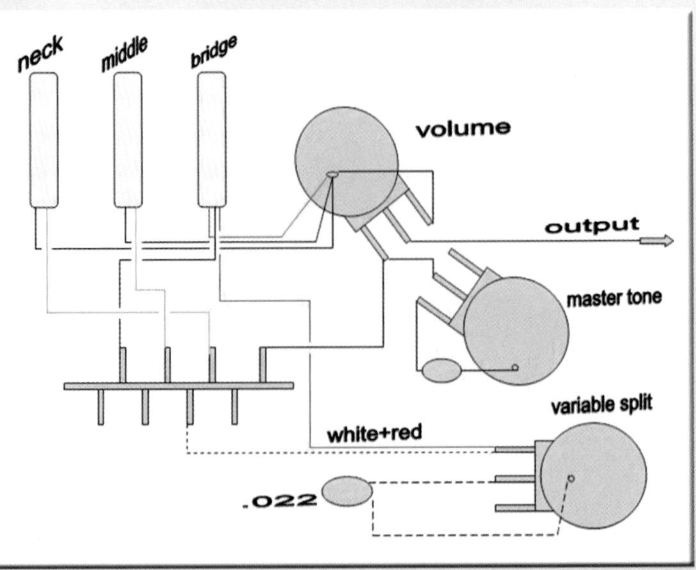

Variable split on bridge dual coil pickup, to clean up the tone while retaining fullness

Models for acoustic guitars

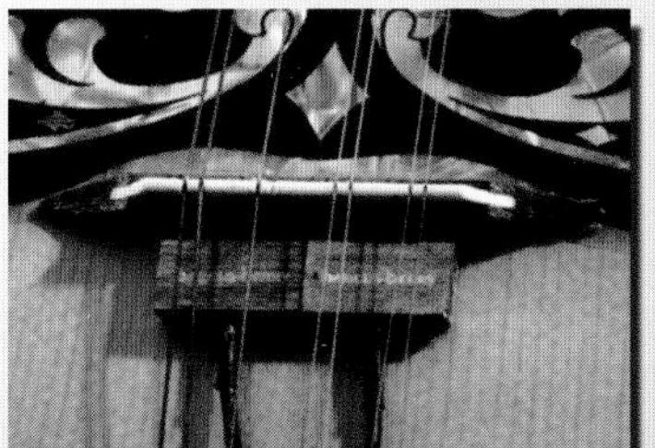

Barcus-Berry Contact Pickup

Shadow Pickups

Bartolini TXE

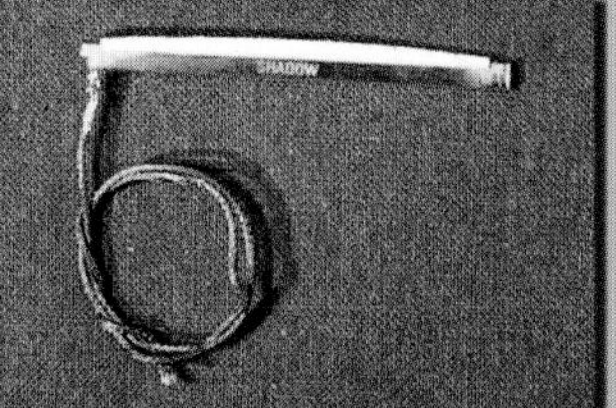

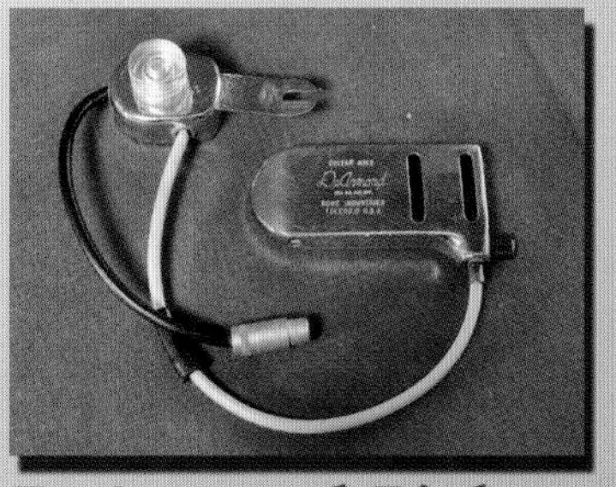

DeArmond Pickup

Schaller Pickup

L. R. Baggs M-1

Gibson McCarthy Unit on a 1937 Gibson L 7

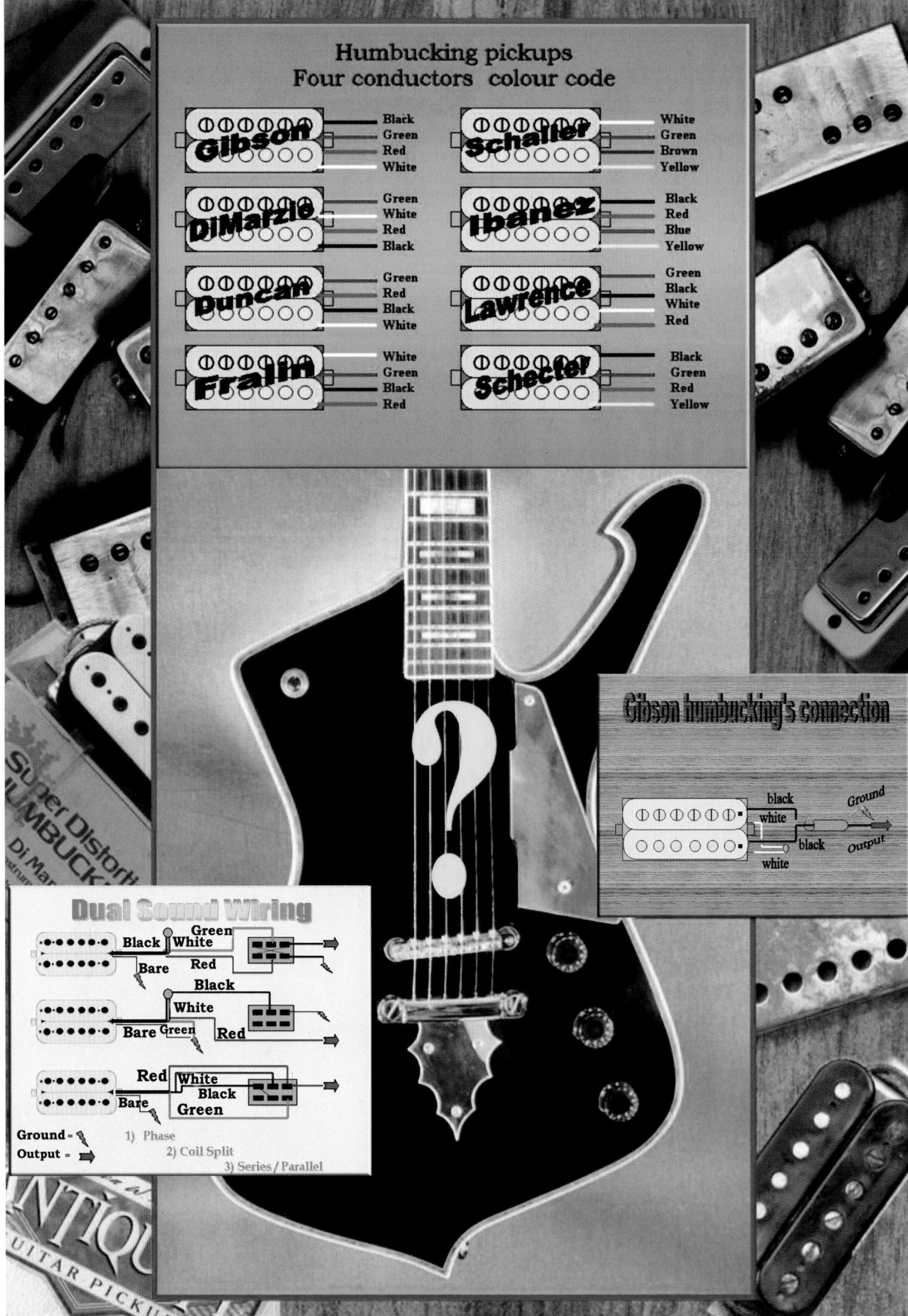
Humbucking pickups
Four conductors colour code
Gibson
Black
Green
Red
White
Schaller
White
Green
Brown
Yellow
DiMarzio
Green
White
Red
Black
Ibanez
Black
Red
Blue
Yellow
Duncan
Green
Red
Black
White
Lawrence
Green
Black
White
Red
Fralin
White
Green
Black
Red
Schecter
Black
Green
Red
Yellow
Gibson humbucking's connection
black
white
black
white
Ground
Output
Dual Sound Wiring
Black
White
Green
Bare
Red
Black
White
Bare
Green
Red
Red
White
Black
Bare
Green
Ground =
Output =
1) Phase
2) Coil Split
3) Series / Parallel
Super Distortion
Humbucker
Di Marzio
Antique
Guitar Pickups

Part 2 - The pickup under the magnifying glass

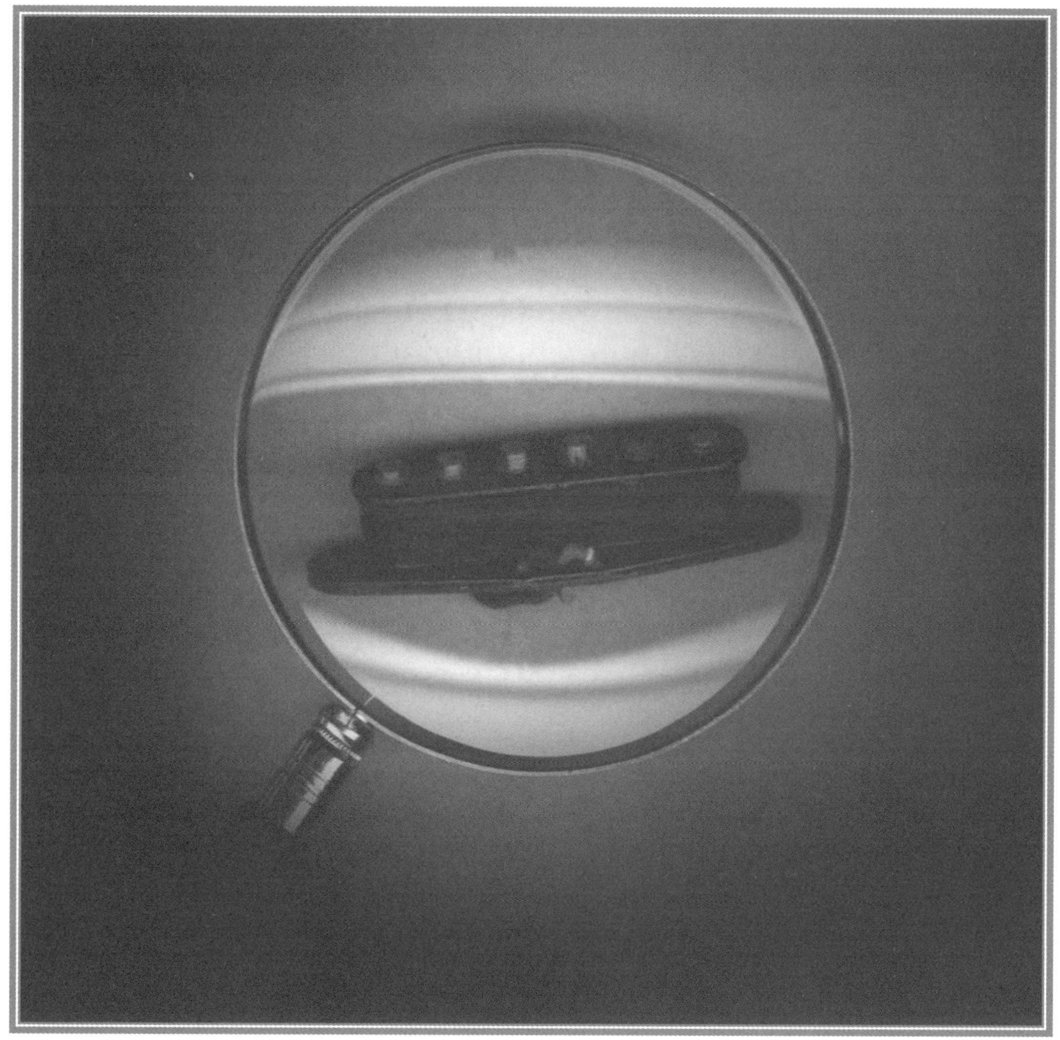

A magnetic pickup for the electric guitar appears to be a very simple device, especially if compared to other components in the field of musical instruments. It is after all made only with copper wire, insulated to avoid short circuits, wound around one or more magnets in a variety of formats.

Several details, however, such as the gauge of the wire, slight differences in magnetic flux, which are of little importance in other applications, can have noticeable effects on the timbre of the pickup.

In order to obtain a pickup with a good output level, which is also harmonically rich, and has enough sustain, it is necessary to accurately balance all it's components. It is also important to choose the best materials and the appropriate manufacturing methods.
This section will be dedicated to explaining how the structure of the pickup and the characteristics of any single element used to make it, contribute to the final sound.

The Magnets

Magnetism is a phenomenon concerning the property of certain materials capable of orientating groups of atoms thereby determining energy fluxes aligned in opposite directions. Most of the time these energy fluxes, are fortuitous and tend to cancel each other unless an external force compels them to align. However in some materials they can line up naturally as in natural magnets. In most materials the flux can be forced to align by a stronger magnetic flux, but when this influence is not applied, the alignment ends. In others, once the force is applied the alignment remains: these are called "permanent magnets".

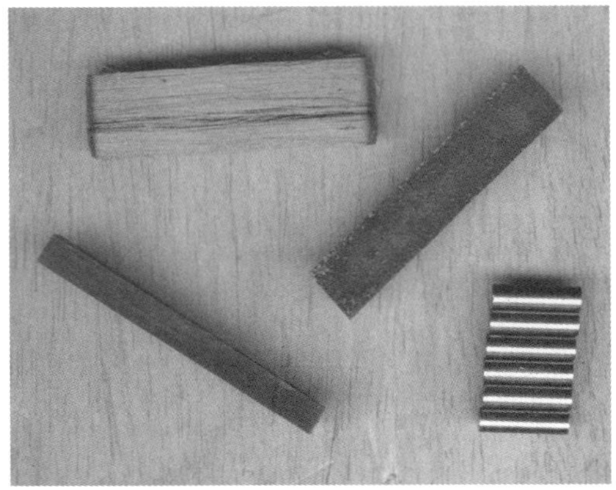

The basic elements to build a pickup (Clockwise): the coil, an Alnico bar, six Alnico cylinders and a ceramic bar.

The magnets used to make pickups are all permanent magnets.

Various magnetic materials used together, tend to strengthen each other, therefore the magnets are made from alloys of various magnetic metals. The alloy is then cut to the desired dimension and shape and exposed to the alignment process which determines the flux running from one side to the other, called respectively north and south poles. Any pole is attracted by that of the opposite polarity and rejects those having the same polarity.

The name of the poles is due to the attraction they have for the opposite poles of the Earth (North toward the South Pole, South toward the North Pole), which is actually a big natural magnet.

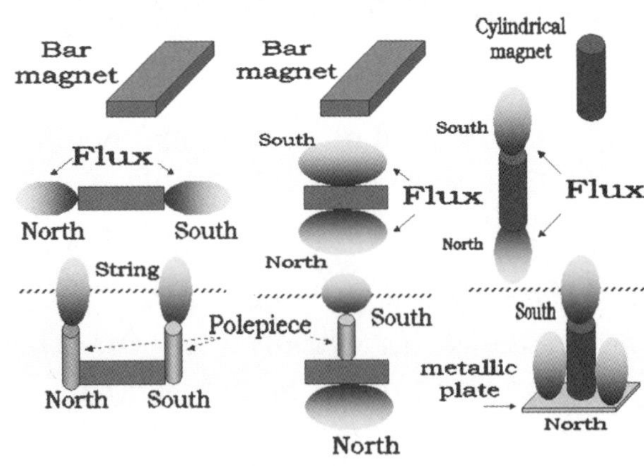

The magnetic field can be forced to the desired direction using polepieces or metallic plates.

The magnetism emanating from a pole tends to go towards the opposite pole, creating an invisible flux around the magnet, which can be modified by the presence of polepieces or other metallic objects which widen or change its shape.

The manner in which the magnets are placed under the strings, whether directly in the winding or on the bottom, with the magnetic field extended through polepieces, and the dimension and shape of the components are all very important to the wideness and intensity of the magnetic flux.

Pickup makers have used many different solutions depending on the pickup's model and the materials available at the time.

The wideness of the magnetic window and the length of the strings affected by the magnetic field, is strictly related to the physical dimensions of the pickup. Therefore a humbucking will have a wider magnetic window than a minihumbucking and a fuller sound, while a typical single coil will have a thinner sound than a minihumbucking.

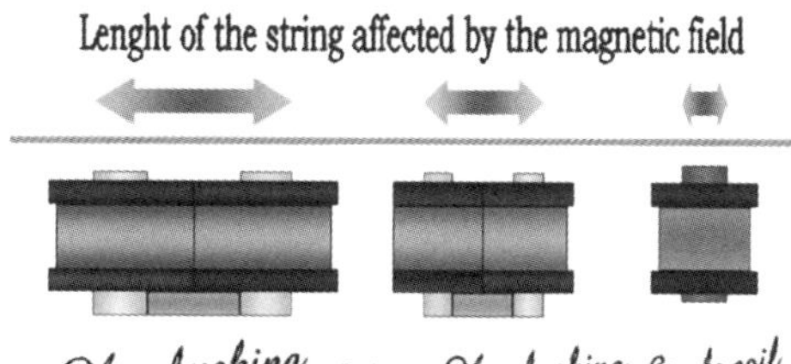

Sometimes an invisible element can affect this parameter, as is the case on the Telecaster bridge unit, on which a thin copper coated metallic plate, under the winding and magnets, strengthens and enlarges the magnetic field creating a wider magnetic window. To generate the sound a string is struck and the resulting vibrations are transmitted to the instrument. The wood, thus stimulated, vibrates and so contributes its own harmonics which are added to those generated by the string. It is during this dynamic process, in which the neck, body and other components, each contribute with their particular resonance, that the harmonics we call timbre are created.

The metallic plate at the bottom of the lead pickup on Broadcaster and Telecaster guitars widens the magnetic field and increases efficiency of the high frequencies (Claudio Caldana).

The timbre is the result of a combination of attack, decay and relative loudness of the harmonics which the note is made up of and this permits us to distinguish which instrument the sound is coming from (a piano, a violin, a guitar, etc).

The oscillations of the string disturb the magnetic field which induces the coil to produce a feeble electric current. The voltage of this current is proportional to the number of turns in the coil and can be of about 60 mV in most single coil pickups and up to over 500 mV in the most powerful humbucking models.

If the oscillations had a simple up and down movement, only the fundamental frequency of the note would be produced. The string, however, tends to have a circular motion, the shape of which can be modified according to the angle and velocity of the hit, thereby producing a complex series of harmonics. The addition of harmonics contributed by the wood makes it easy to understand that a simple note can determine a very complex signal.

The way the signal is generated is related to the movement of the string, and that is the reason why the guitar player's touch has a great influence on the kind of sound produced.

For instance, if you try to pluck the string with bare fingers and then with a pick, you will notice how much the tone changes.

As explained, there are materials which, albeit not magnetic in nature, can become magnetized if exposed to the magnetic flux of a permanent magnet. The strings of an electric guitar, in order to be effective, have to be made from the above mentioned materials. With this kind of string the oscillations are influenced not only by the resonant properties of the instrument, but also by the intensity of the magnetic field. The result is due to the way the string disturbs the magnetic field in which it moves and the movement in the magnetic field induces the coil to translate it into electric current.

On the another hand the string tends to be attracted by the magnetic field which, if too strong, may cause the vibrations to be inhibited. The wider oscillations relating to the fundamental frequency of the note and the harmonics closer to it are less easily inhibited by the attraction of the magnetic field, but the shorter ones, relating to the higher harmonics, are greatly influenced, at times to the point of being completely cancelled. For this reason the magnet must be neither too strong nor too weak.

If the magnetic field is too strong there is an excessive dampening of the vibration, resulting in a harsh sound with little sustain, if, vice versa, the magnet is too weak, the signal will have a low output and a lacklustre tone. The flux density has to be strong enough to give a loud signal, but not to the point of dampening the vibrations. Between those extremes a stronger flux, for the same coil, favours the presence of high frequencies.

During this process, depending on the relationship between magnetic flux density and number of turns in the coil, some harmonics are cancelled, others are strengthened, producing a further variation of timbre, this time purely electric.

The signal sent to the amplifier is the result of the player's style, the string's properties, the acoustical qualities of the instrument and the colour added by the pickup. The Bigger the strings are, the more the magnetic flux is disturbed, and the result is a louder sound and a fuller timbre.

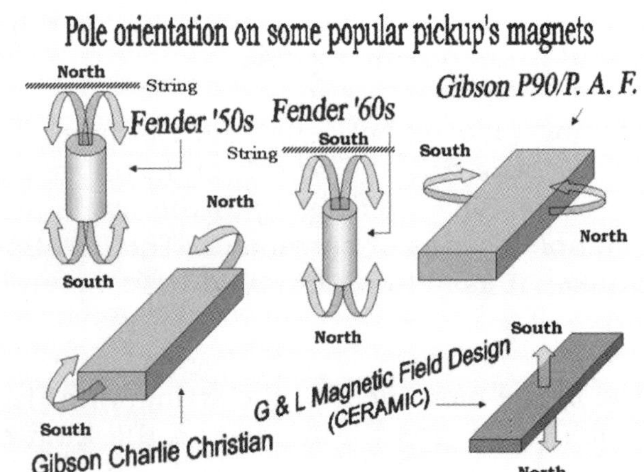

In a magnet the atoms can be aligned in the desired direction.

On Fender style pickups the flux runs parallel to the axis of the cylindrical magnets with the poles at the extremes of the cylinder.

On bar magnets as used on Gibson style humbuckers, the flux runs across the bar with the poles on the longer sides, resulting one north, the other south.

The magnets used to make pickups are mainly of two types: Alnico or ceramic.

Alnico magnets are made from an alloy of aluminium, nickel and cobalt plus steel or iron, common on almost all the models produced up to the sixties. These magnets are necessary whenever certain sounds are required.

Ceramic magnets are made from a mixture of barium or strontium ferrite particles, used at the end of the fifties on some models of loudspeakers and then in pickup production after the early seventies. At this time the search for a more powerful sound and the increasing price of Alnico prompted several manufacturers to experiment with them.

Ceramic magnets typically favour high frequencies, that's why they are preferable on high power pickups. They are efficient in balancing loss of trebles when using several turns of wire in the bobbins, which is necessary to increase the output. One of the first makers to effectively use ceramic magnets was DiMarzio on the Super Distortion, and since then most brands now offer similar pickups.

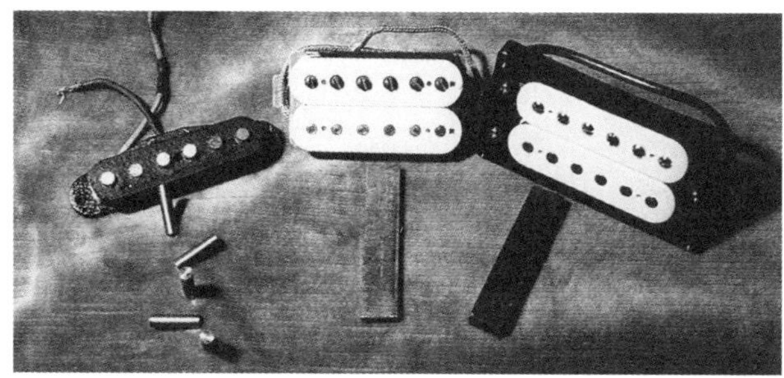

From the left: the cylindrical Alnico magnets of a Fender-style pickup, the Alnico bar magnet of a Gibson-style humbucker and the ceramic bar magnet of a high output model (C. Prosperini).

Alnico magnets used in pickups are found in two shapes, cylindrical or bar-shaped. Ceramic magnets, which are fragile and more difficult to work with, are mainly bar-shaped.

These are obtained by the agglomeration of materials at high temperature, without reaching the melting point. Alnico magnets can be made using the same method, but those used in pickup making are melted.

Today, any time the priority is sound quality Alnico magnets are desirable. They are available in several grades, the most common being 5, 2 and 3, and less often grades 4, 7 and 8. Ceramic magnets can also be found in similar grades and are used when either power or cost reduction is the priority.

The most powerful magnets are those in samarium-cobalt, but their use in pickup manufacturing is limited by their high cost.

All types of magnet are made up of various percentages of elements, as in a recipe, therefore Alnico magnets are composed of aluminium, nickel, cobalt, copper or cuprite, plus steel or iron to complete. Each grade has a different balance of elements in the formula, for example: in Alnico 5 the percentage of cobalt is double than that of Alnico 2, which has a higher percentage of nickel, while in Alnico 3 and 4 there is only a quarter of the cobalt present in Alnico 5.

Occasionally a formula can be altered when some component, such as cobalt, important for the military industry, is temporarily unavailable in sufficient quantity. In this case the percentage is lowered accordingly.

Each recipe gives a different flavour to the sound of the pickup, so the choice of grade is not only a matter of available power, but also of timbre nuances. Therefore Alnico 2 will be chosen for a sweeter sound rather than Alnico 5, Alnico 8 is preferable when looking for a bright sound and so on.

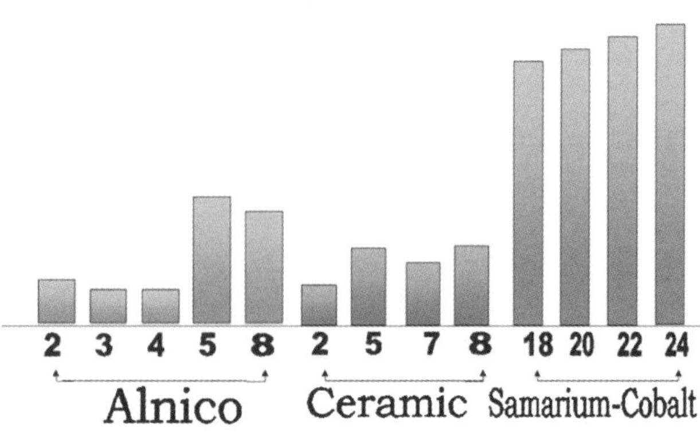

Alnico 5 has the highest flux density of this type of magnets, Alnico 8 is close, the 2, 3 and 4 grades have around one third of the density of Alnico 5. Ceramic magnets can have, according to the grade, from values similar to those of Alnico 2 up to two thirds of the energy of Alnico 5, but their sound is even brighter than the Alnico 8; another interesting characteristic is their low price. A samarium-cobalt magnet can have four or five times the energy of an Alnico 5 magnet.

Alnico 5 has become the industry standard and is the most used by almost all pickup builders, but the increasing interest for exact replicas of the old pickups has prompted accurate research on the characteristics of these units. According to several experts, such as Seymour Duncan, Bill Lawrence and others, most pickups from the fifties were made with magnets less powerful than Alnico 5. Probably Alnico 2, 3 or 4 magnets were used, and even when Alnico 5 magnets were used, they were weaker than those in use today, which are more powerful due to progress in the industry (some experts contend that there are no noticeable differences between old and new magnets of the same grade).
In fact, the magnets in many original pickups are varied, some more powerful, some weaker. It seems that makers, usually, would simply order Alnico magnets, without specifying the grade.

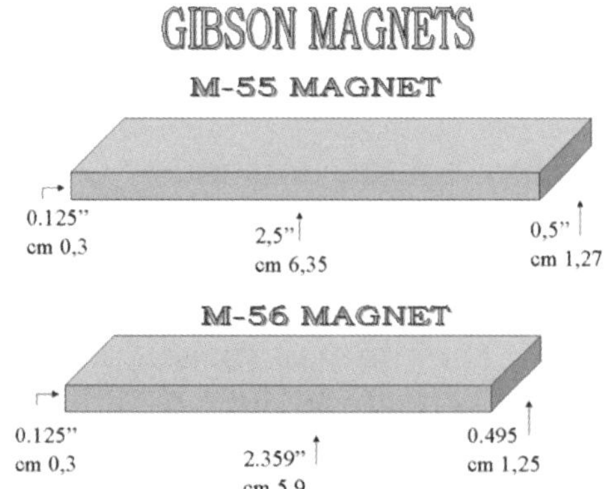

The bar magnet used on P 90 and humbucking pickups from the fifties, was named M 55 by Gibson and probably refers to the size of the bar.

In 1960 Gibson started to use a smaller alnico bar, called M 56, but those in pickups after the seventies, though sharing the same dimensions, were slightly more powerful.

Duncan, who buys the magnets and magnetizes them in his laboratory, to reproduce the characteristics of old pickups uses two different methods: on some models he magnetizes the magnet at a lower rate than it's full potential, so to get from a modern Alnico 5 the same power as the originals, on others he uses weaker magnets, such as Alnico 2. Other makers, such as Fender or Fralin, use Alnico 3 on models intended to sound the same as units of the Fifties.

DiMarzio uses normal Alnico 5, but on some models, like those in the "Air" series, such as the Air Classic, Air Norton etc., the magnet is mounted in a way, patented, which reduces the flux directed toward the strings, imitating the softer magnetic field of Alnico 2 magnets.

DiMarzio Air Norton. The patented mounting system uses plastic rings to keep the Alnico 5 magnet slightly far from the polepieces, in order to reduce the intensity of the magnetic field for a sweeter tone and more sustain.

The actual flux density of the whole pickup depends on the power of the magnet and the structure of the unit. For instance, if the magnets are inserted in the wiring, as on Fender pickups, or on the base of the unit with ferrous polepieces directing the flux toward the strings, as on Gibson's P 90 or humbucking pickups, the result is different.

The unit of measure for the flux density is the Gauss and the values found on an original humbucking pickup, according to Duncan, are 20/25 Gauss without a cover, 16/20 with the nickel cover, while on a Fender pickup it is about 40 Gauss. A minihumbucking can be about 15 Gauss in the Epiphone/Deluxe model and 20 Gauss in the Firebird model. On some modern pickups those values can double those on the vintage models. The magnet can be magnetized before or after inserting it into the pickups and the resulting sound is slightly different.

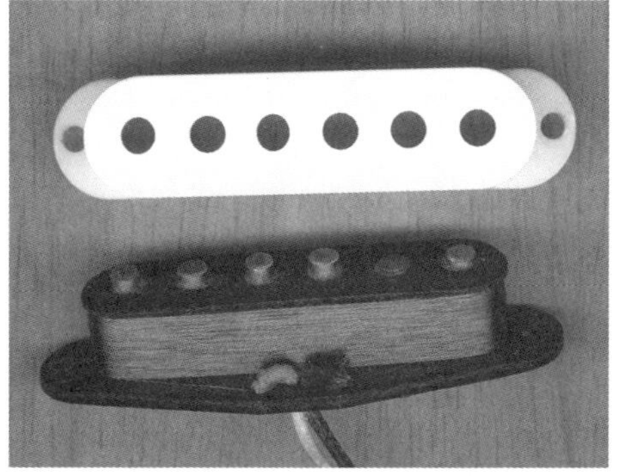
Duncan APS-1 “Alnico Pro”, with Alnico 2 magnets.

In order to obtain a sound similar to vintage units, Duncan uses Alnico 2 on the Seth Lover, Alnico Pro and Pearly Gates models, Fender uses Alnico 3 on the Telecaster models, as does Lindy Fralin on the Real 54 and on the Vintage Broadcaster model and Ibanez uses an Alnico 3 bar on the Super 58.

Duncan Antiquity “Texas Hot” with calibrated Alnico 2 magnets (C. P.).

Fralin prefers the sound of old PAF pickups using Alnico 4 magnets and that's what he probably uses for his PAF-style humbuckers.

Duncan uses "calibrated" Alnico 5 magnets. This means that they are not magnetised to their full potential, but to obtain the desired value in Gauss, used on most Vintage models.

"Calibrated" Alnico 2 is used on the Antiquity models (“calibrated” Alnico 5 on the Antiquity 2 series).

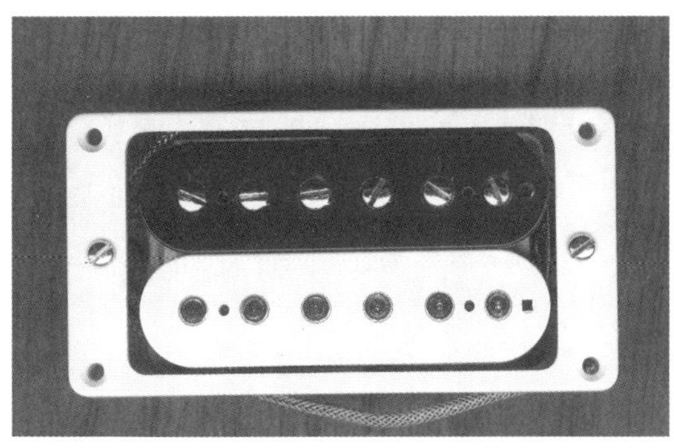

’59 humbucker from Voodoo Pickups. It’s a faithful copy of the old PAF model with an Alnico 3 magnet and AWG 42 Plain Enamel wire, hand made by luthier Peter Florance. Other models are the ’57, with Heavy Formvar wire, the ’60, similar to the ’59 but slightly louder, all with Alnico 3 magnet with the option of Alnico 5. Then there is the ’62, copy of the early “Patent Number” with Alnico 5 magnet. Also ‘50s, ‘60s and ‘70s models for Telecaster and Stratocaster are offered.

TV Jones, on his Classic model uses Alnico magnets especially formulated to match specifications of the fifties, for sweeter high tones, but used to offer the option of the slightly stronger 1960s style magnets.
Previously Stratocaster, Telecaster and P 90 replacements were also available, with a choice of Alnico 3, 4 or 5 magnets, while PAF-style models were obtainable with Alnico 2 or 5 magnets.

On models of medium-high power intended to sound similar to classic pickups with increased output or more trebles, full power Alnico 5 is used, as on the Gibson 498, the DiMarzio Humbucker From Hell, Breed, Norton, PAF Pro, FRED, Tone Zone, Class Of ’55, Twang King, SF-1, Blue Velvet, Red Velvet, the Duncan J. B. Model, Jazz Model, Screamin' Demon, Original Trembucker, Blues Trembucker, SF-1 Minihumbucking, Seymourized Mini, Pearly Gates Plus (specially designed for Fender), most "hot" models for Telecaster, Stratocaster, Jaguar and Jazzmaster.
Alnico 5 is also used in all those pickups made by Rio Grande, most Wolfetone models (some of which are available in a brighter version using Alnico 8), and most other modern makers. Both Duncan and Wolfetone offer high output humbucking models using Alnico 2 magnets, similar to the overwound PAF pickups self made by Eddie Van Halen. Duncan with the model "Custom Custom", Wolfetone with the Fenris.

Alnico 2 is used on another Duncan model, the “Stag Mag”, a humbucking with staggered magnets directly in the coils, Fender style.

Ceramic magnets are cheaper and for this reason are often used on low priced pickups. However due to their tendency to produce tight basses and cutting trebles their sound may be harsher. This is due to poor quality windings, but when used in well balanced solutions can deliver good timbre and a loud signal, as on the Distortion style pickups.
Models of this kind are the DiMarzio Super Distortion, Super 2, Evolution, the Duncan Custom, Distortion, the Gibson 500 T.

The concentrated flux of ceramic magnets permits the use of small bar magnets and these are preferred on Stratocaster and Telecaster sized humbuckers, such as the DiMarzio Chopper, Duncan Hot Rails and Little '59 and similar units. Some makers use ceramic magnets for their brightness, to get a more open sound, almost high fidelity. One of these is Joe Barden.

Other models with ceramic magnets are the Gibson Super humbucking, introduced on the seventies' SGs, the True Blues, which had three ceramic bars and a resistance of only 6 kOhms to create a really bright sound. The Dirty Fingers and the Velvet Brick, which were the first real "Hot" models from this brand.

Ceramic magnets are also used on models from Peavey, on the EMG-H, EMG-S, EMG-T, EMG 81, EMG 60, the Burns Reissues made by Kent Armstrong and the Rickenbacker High Gain.

Some makers offer pickups with different magnets on the same unit, such as Duncan, with the Nashville series for Telecaster and Stratocaster, with Alnico 5 magnets under the E, A and D strings and Alnico 2 under the G, B and high E strings, producing snapping basses and sweet trebles. Fralin made some models with Alnico 3 under the E, A and G strings, Alnico 5 under the D, B and high E strings (Alnico 3 has less low mids than Alnico 5, resulting relatively brighter).

A Fender Stratocaster made in 1958. It still sounds clear and biting (A. Angelucci).

Rickenbacker used samarium-cobalt magnets in the humbucking model to get a clear timbre similar to that of their famous single coils, but with more output.

It is possible to measure the magnetic flux of a pickup only with special and costly equipment, but to get an idea it is possible to touch the magnet or the polepieces with an iron object, such as a screwdriver, then try to detach it, the stronger the effort required, the more powerful the magnet.

Really strong magnets give the pickups more output or a brighter sound, but they can cause loss of sustain and intonation problems, specially Fender-style single coils. That makes necessary to adjust them farther from the strings, thereby reducing the theoretical benefits.

A powerful pickup is not difficult to make, but to make one with a balanced sound requires experience. If you exceed the limit the extra power may send too strong a signal to the amplifier thus overloading it.

A common opinion is that magnets lose their power with time, this must explain the difference in sound between old and new instruments, from our experience we tend to disagree, as many instruments from the fifties sound very clear and some twenty year old guitars have no appreciable difference in timbre still today.

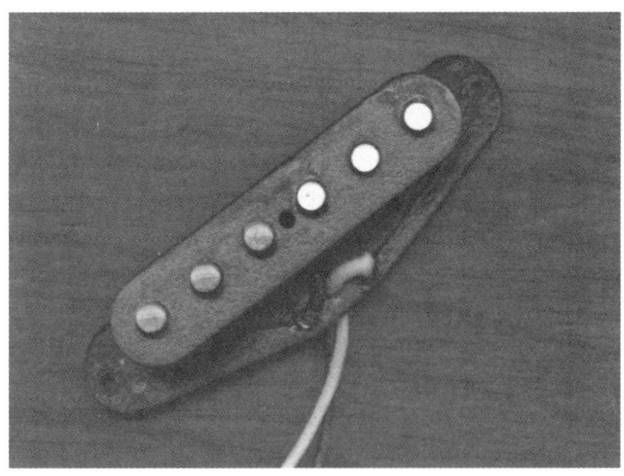

Duncan SSL-52-1 “Nashville Studio”, with Alnico 5 magnets for the bottom strings and Alnico 2 for the top strings for a full and sweet sound.

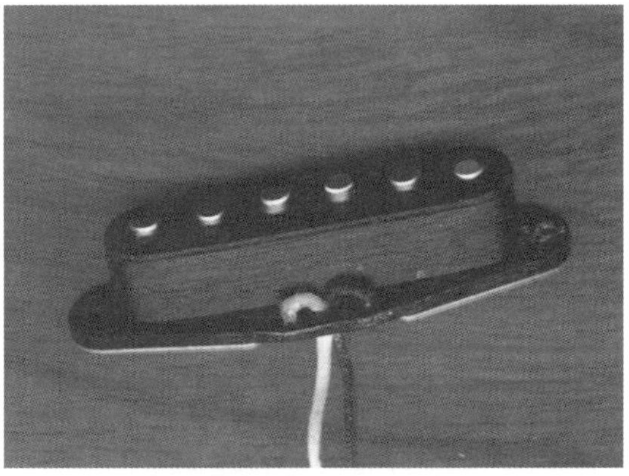

Duncan APST-1 “Twang Banger”, made with plain enamel wire, Alnico 2 magnets and copper plated steel bottom plate, to add Broadcaster/Telecaster-style lead unit’s punch to the bridge position of the Stratocaster.

Permanent magnets are supposed to lose 1,2% of their power after two years, then about 0,2% in the next thousand years, unless shocks, exposition to high temperature or much stronger magnetic fields affect the alignment.

Our opinion is that the magnets used in the past were weaker than today's magnets of the same grade, even when new.

Anyway almost all makers in order to avoid damage, advise: not to expose the pickups to strong magnetic fields, to avoid shocks or very high temperature, not to leave the guitar leaning on an amplifier, close to the loudspeaker for a long time, or close to big transformers whose intense magnetic field could weaken the magnets.

Seymour Duncan advises, when storing pickups for long time, not to put them one on top of the other, but to leave some distance between them (which is contrary to what happens in most shops).

Generally speaking we are sure that by taking reasonable care of the pickups, they will last without problems, and so be passed on from father to son, in perfect working order. Notwithstanding age, the truth is that in order to use magnets and wire similar to those used thirty or more years ago is not easy, as those materials are difficult to find and expensive. That's why the best quality reissues have such high prices, and sound similar to the classics they imitate.

Most new pickups sound different simply because they are made with different materials, different techniques and are mounted on different guitars and before they change, the chances are that the wood used for the guitar and our tastes will change much more.

The windings

Great attention has always been given to the wire used for the windings. The coil, solicited by the magnetic field running through it, when this is disturbed by the string's movement, generates the electric signal going to the amplifier. The gauge of the wire and the number of turns are of great importance in determining the quality of the signal: too many turns and the sound will lack high frequencies, too little and the output level will be not high enough.

The thinner the wire, the higher the resistance / length ratio.
The further the windings are from the magnets or polepieces, the less they will be solicited by the magnetic field.
The more turns of wire there are in the coil, the less extended is the range of the high frequencies.

The way the wire is wound is important too: if the windings are very regular the sound is cleaner and brighter, if they are irregular, with some turns running on top of each other at random, the sound will be more rich harmonically. However, if this is exaggerated there will be undesired distortions and eddy currents will limit the sound's clarity.
The gauge of the wire is given in AWG, which stands for American Wire Gauge, and indicates a diameter which decreases as it's number increases so, for instance, an AWG 43 wire is thinner than an AWG 42 wire and so on. The wire is made from pure copper with different kinds of insulation, to avoid short circuits, and the specifications might refer to the diameter of the wire only or to the wire including the insulation. This is an important difference because it means that the insulation can vary in thickness (other magnetic materials could be used, for the wire, but copper is the one with the best cost/sound quality ratio).
Below is the nominal diameter of some gauges of wire and the resistance in Ohms for the same length.

American Wire Gauge	Inches	mm	Ohms at 20°C
AWG 38	0,0040	0,1107	648 Ohms/1000ft
AWG 40	0,0031	0,0799	1080 Ohms/1000ft
AWG 42	0,0025	0,0633	1660 Ohms/1000ft
AWG 43	0,0022	0,0564	2140 Ohms/1000ft
AWG 44	0,0020	0,0508	2590 Ohms/1000ft

If we suppose to wind a Stratocaster pickup with ft. 3700 of AWG 42 wire, the resistance would be of 6,142 kOhms, using the same length of AWG 43 the value would raise to 7,918 kOhms. Using AWG 44 an even higher resistance of 9,583 kOhms could be obtained.

The diameter of the wire used to make pickups is very small, the most common being of mm. 0, 056 or 0, 063 (AWG 43 and 42 respectively) and the insulation consists in a very thin coat of lacquer, which is made from different chemical formulas, and applied in one or more layers. The difference in insulation thickness, between two brands, may seem irrelevant but becomes important if we think that in a P 90 winding there are about 10000 turns and in a Stratocaster pickup 8700 or 7600 turns, depending on the era. With such a high number of turns, even a minimal variation in thickness can make the outer windings a little closer or further to the magnets or polepieces, sometimes enough to affect the timbre.

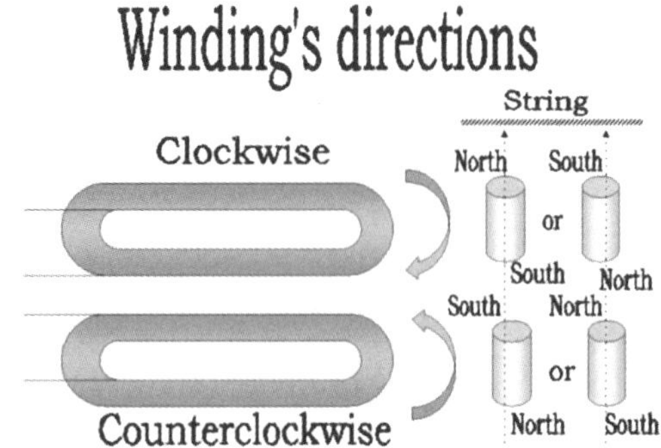

Single coil pickups can be wound both ways and the magnets can be inserted with the north or south poles toward the strings.

Often when a pickup is rewound, it's difficult to get exactly the same sound as when it was new. When it is necessary to rewind a pickup it is important to take note of the gauge of the wire, the direction of the winding and the number of turns. Even using the same number of turns and the same gauge of wire, the insulation on the new one can be made using more layers of lacquer or from a different material and that can change the specifications.

The direction of the winding is important to make sure that the pickups are in phase with the others, on guitars with more than one unit. To ensure that two pickups are in phase with each other, they must have the same magnetic polarity and the windings in the same direction or opposite polarity and opposite windings. Most models are standardized, for instance humbucking models have, almost always, south polarity on the adjustable poles, north on the fixed poles with anticlockwise windings. Fender style pickups have south polarity toward the strings, north toward the bottom. Occasionally on humbucking pickups, the direction of the windings doesn't follow the Gibson standard. Also on many models with three or four conductor cables, each maker uses a different code colour, therefore things can become confusing when mixing models from different brands.

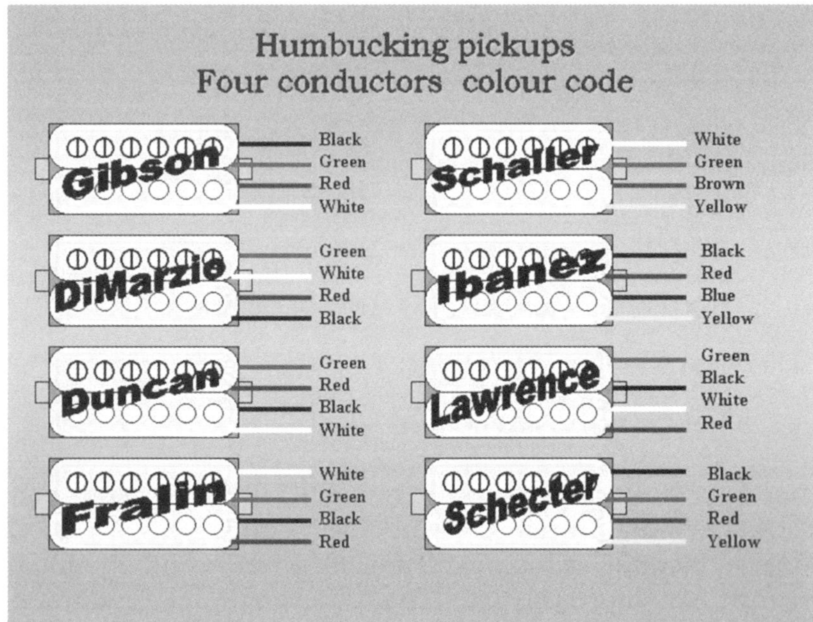

Code colour used to identify the wires from each bobbin on pickups from the most popular brands. Although the scheme can be helpful to confront the different codes, it's necessary to keep in mind that not always the coils are wound in the same direction. Usually, following the Gibson model, the windings are made counter-clockwise. In case a pickup results out of phase with another, will be necessary to reverse the hot output and the ground, corresponding respectively to the red and the green wire on a DiMarzio model.

Fender, over the years, changed the direction of the windings and in the beginning the magnets were inserted with the north facing the strings. In order to reproduce the vintage models of those years, some makers changed the specifications accordingly.

The winding can be done clockwise or anticlockwise, to find out whether two single coil pickups are compatible follow the scheme:

1) Same direction of winding and same polarity - in phase without humbucking effect.

2) Opposed direction winding and opposed polarity - in phase with humbucking effect

3) Same direction of winding but opposed polarity - out of phase

4) Opposed direction of winding and same polarity - out of phase

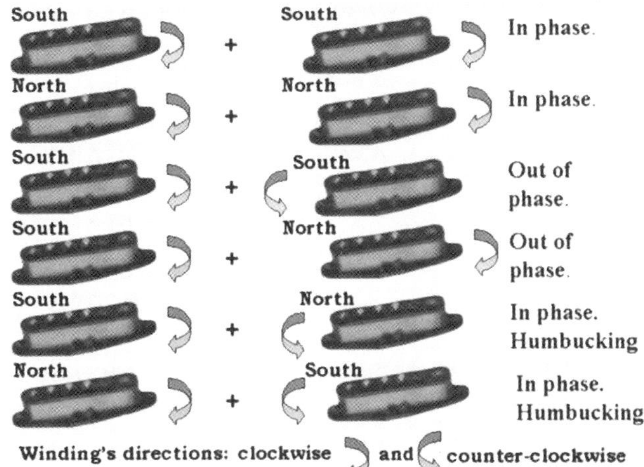

Modern Fender pickups for the American Standard Stratocaster, for instance, are wound anticlockwise and have south polarity toward the strings, the middle unit has clockwise winding and north polarity, to obtain hum rejection when used with any of the other two.

The first pickups using this system were those of the Fender Duosonic, with a reverse wound and north polarity neck unit, also the two units, when selected together, were in series, for a fuller sound with humbucking effect; the first maker to use a reversed wound/reverse polarity pickup in the centre slot of a Stratocaster was Seymour Duncan.

Supposing we need to substitute another brand of pickup for the bridge unit, for instance with a Duncan, we have no problems if we chose a SSL-1, SSL-2, SSL-3, APS-1 or APS-2 as well as any of the same production line, because they are all made with the same winding direction and magnetic polarity as the Fender. A Duncan Antiquity Texas Hot, wound clockwise and with north polarity, would be in phase with the middle pickup, but without humbucking effect; A Duncan Antiquity 2 Surfer, wound clockwise and with south polarity, would be out of phase.

Fender Mustang. Introduced in 1964 it was an improved Duo-Sonic with contoured body, vibrato and more versatile circuitry (A. A.).

This means also that we must pay attention even when using models from the same maker but from different series because, in our example, the Surfer would be out of phase with other Duncans in the standard line, such as the SSL-1. Once we know this, there is always the possibility of ordering the desired model with reverse winding and reverse polarity (RW/RP), to get humbucking effect if mounted in the middle or to put it in phase with other models.

The wire gauges used to make pickups are many, going from AWG 38 to AWG 44 and for special designs Duncan even used the rare intermediate gauges, like AWG 42,5. Fender and Gibson, used two kinds of magnet wire, on their old models, which were distinguished by the insulation, made of Heavy Formvar or the thinner Plain Enamel. In the seventies the even thinner Polysol was used and is still the standard wire for the American Standard Stratocaster and the Made in Mexico pickups.

The difference is slight but gives different results, as on the Fender Stratocaster pickups, on which AWG 42 Heavy Formvar was used until about 1964, then the introduction of automatic winding machines and the use of AWG 42 Plain Enamel resulted in the same electric specifications with a noticeably different sound. AWG 42 Heavy Formvar was used on most Lap Steel, Duo-sonic, Jaguar and Mustang pickups, AWG 42 plain enamel on Telecaster lead and Jazzmaster pickups, AWG 43 Plain Enamel on Telecaster neck pickup and AWG 42 Polysol on the Fender humbucking and X-1 models.

Seymour Duncan measured the wire used on many Fender pickups from the fifties up to the CBS years and found that the average diameter of the Heavy Formvar type, used in the fifties and part of the sixties, ranges from 0,0027 to 0,0030" (the most common), the plain enamel kind used by CBS ranges from 0,0025" to 0,0027". The thinner insulation permits the outer turns to be slightly closer to the magnets and the use of automatic winding machines gives more regularity to the winding and improves the alignment of the layers. During the sixties Fender also decided to decrease the tension of the winding because with the automatic winding machines of the time the thin wire could be easily broken.

These factors together contributed to a thinner, brighter, cleaner sound on the new models, compared to the older ones.

On Gibson pickups, such as the P 90 and the humbucking model, the wire is, traditionally, AWG 42 Plain Enamel, with a brownish colour. Around 1963 Gibson switched to Polyurethane coated wire, with a clearer, reddish colour. By the end of the sixties the wire used had a dark colour, but was sometimes dark red on some pickups. The sound, all else being equal, was slightly thinner on the treble and darker on the mids, although the change in tone was also due to the use of smaller Alnico 5 magnets, which began in the sixties.

Most replacement pickups have to retain the same dimensions as the originals they are supposed to replace. To make a replacement model for Stratocaster, for instance, the AWG 42 Heavy Formvar wire is used on the best replicas. To get more output on some models, a wire with a thinner insulation, but the same nominal gauge, such as Plain Enamel, can be used to obtain more turns. For even more turns the even thinner Polynylon can be used instead, as on some Fralin models. This means that if with Heavy Formvar we may have a coil measuring as much as 7 kOhms, by using Polynylon we can get up to more than 7,5 kOhms, thus producing a slightly louder, thicker and darker sound.

For hotter models AWG 43 Plain Enamel wire is generally used so as to be able to put many more turns in the same space. For a given number of turns, a thinner wire has a higher resistance, a lower output and more sensitivity to dynamics. Since the output level is made higher by increasing the number of turns in the winding, it is possible to make a pickup louder by substituting a thinner wire for the original. In this way one is able to wind more turns on the same bobbin, but this method also increases the resistance, thereby reducing the treble content: the pickup will sound louder, with more mids and less highs. D. C. Resistance can be higher than 13 kOhms.

On the very first Broadcaster bridge pickups, Fender used 10000 turns of AWG 43 Enamel wire, with a resistance which could exceed 9 kOhms, Gibson, on the P 90, used the same number of turns of AWG 42 enamel wire on a larger bobbin with a resistance of about 8 kOhms; even though the Broadcaster pickup is louder than later Telecaster pickups using less turns of AWG 42 enamel wire, it's output is lower than that of the Gibson P 90. This example shows how the resistance alone, if the wire gauge is unknown, is not enough to guess the power of a pickup.

Only by comparing two pickups made with the same wire, can the resistance be useful in determining which one is more powerful.

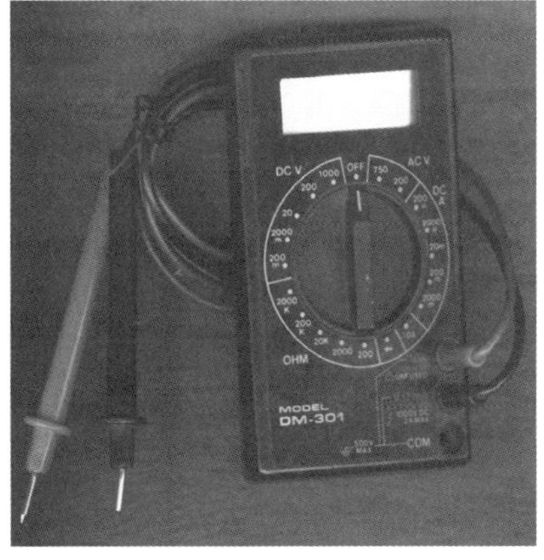

The D. C. resistance can be checked with a simple Ohm-meter, better if digital, and is usually given on catalogues, generally taken at a 68° F temperature. The resistance for any model is usually the value resulting from the average of several units measured, therefore it is quite normal to find slight differences between what's stated on the catalogue and what's found on the pickup just bought from the shop. The resistance increases with high temperatures, so if we measure our pickup in a room with a 96° F temperature we should expect to see some hundred Ohms more than the value given by the maker.

The tension of the winding affects the results. With high tension the wire tends to stretch and become slightly thinner, especially around the corners, with a proportional increase in resistance. The turns may be more or less tight, regular or tangling casually. This depends on whether the wire is hand wound or an automatic winding machine is used and then also on how the machine is adjusted.

In the past a worker used to keep the wire running between his fingers and adjust its inclination toward the bobbin, making, according to his ability, the winds more or less regular and determining how many turns would pile up on each coil. A mechanical counter would show when the number of turns for that model was reached and the worker would stop the machine.

The precision of the counters was not accurate and pickups were not wound to exactly the same number of turns, but to obtain a certain resistance, measured with testers which had a precision of 20% tolerance. The worker could stop the

Marsili winding machine from the sixties (Claudio Prosperini).

machine when required for any reason; add to this the difference of inclination impressed on the wire, the precision of the layers which differed according to each worker's ability and the way each machine was adjusted and it's easy to understand that any single unit would have its own character. (Lets raise a glass in honour to the women and men who while winding every day kilometres of wire, infused their personality to create sounds which made history).

During the sixties automatic winding machines became available, with precise counters and better adjustment possibilities, thus permitting more regular layers, greater consistency in the specifications of the pickups, and gradually reducing tolerances.

By the end of the decade the resistance values of pickups of the same model were fairly similar and the tension was constant without tangles in the coil.

Today most pickups are wound with precise machines (DiMarzio used digitally controlled winding machine from the end of the seventies), on which it is possible to adjust the winding speed and the tension for very tight and regular windings. For the reproduction of vintage models, however, different methods are possible, one adjusting the machine to tangle the coils after each number of turns, a sort of "programmed" irregularity, another is to use original machines and hand guiding the wire (the so called "hand wound" models).

On fifties' pickups the windings were very tight but irregular, when the first automatic machines came into use, to avoid breaking the delicate wire, the windings were made with lower tension, but with more regular layers.

This is why two pickups made in different years, for instance in 1959 and in 1968, can have the same resistance values, but different sounds, warmer the first, cleaner the second.

This happens because irregular windings cause differences in tension between layers, resulting in eddy currents which, if limited, make the sound richer and more harmonic.

Since these differences in tension are unpredictable, even though the number of turns is the same for two pickups, they might have a slightly different timbre.

Although these small details may seem of little importance, all together they can create audible differences between one unit and the other, even if made the same day by the same person.

The most important variables occurring in a coil are the following:

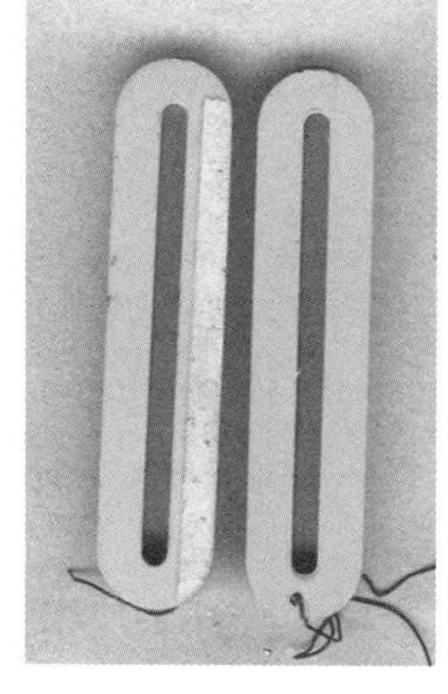

Nylon bobbins from an Höfner humbucking pickup. Thin and less expensive than the plastic ones used by Gibson, nylon bobbins were used by most pickup makers in USA, Europe and Japan. Gibson too, used them in the Melody Maker single coil and in the small sized Epiphone/Deluxe Minihumbucking.

1) Each kind of wire is delivered with some allowance on it's specifications, therefore slight variations in diameter from the nominal value may occasionally occur.

2) When the wire is wound around a bobbin or the magnets, variations in the tension can cause occasional stretch reducing the diameter of small segments of the coil which, when repeated turn after turn, noticeably increase the total resistance of the winding.

3) The coil has its own capacity, and acts as a small capacitor by cutting the highest frequencies. Thus the more turns there are in the coil, the more trebles are limited.

4) Inside each coil there are eddy currents affecting the timbre positively when the phenomenon is limited.

5) The more the turns are regular and have even tension, the lower the content of eddy currents. The sound is cleaner or, depending on taste, less rich; looser windings would give a brighter sound, but if too loose, feedback can become a problem.

6) As with any material, the coil has a resonance and the relationship between the intensity of the magnetic field, the number of turns and other factors determine the frequency of peak level sensitivity (resonant peak). The higher the number of turns, the lower the frequency at which the resonant peak occurs.

Although the type of magnet used is undeniably important, the winding method is much more important in obtaining the final sound.
The use of hand guided machines is a true art, and to understand even the smallest details is fundamental.

Imagine that the amplifier, reproducing the signal a lot louder than the original level, acts as a very powerful magnifying glass.

Lets say that we have two pickups of the same model and there are slight differences in the kind of wire, the number of turns, the tension in the windings and the intensity of the magnetic field. Any of these small differences is then amplified many times by the amp and the total percentage of variations could easily result in concluding that these units are two different models.

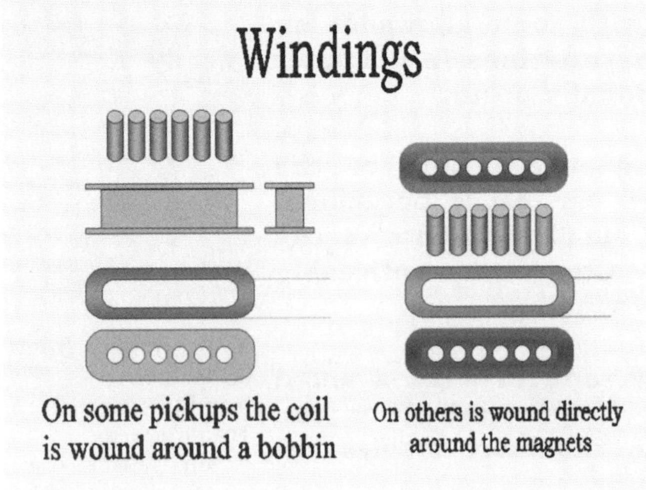

Some pickups have the winding directly around the magnets, others have the magnets inserted into a plastic bobbin around which the coil is wound. With the first method the magnetic field is more effective and the tone has more attack and is more open, with the second the material from which the bobbin is made, even though very thin, puts some distance between the coil and the magnetic field, resulting in a softer tone.

Both methods are correct according to the design of the pickup, but if one of them is used to make a model originally designed using the other, obtaining the right tone could prove difficult.

The Stratocaster pickups, for instance, had the coil wound directly around the magnets, today some copies are made using a plastic bobbin and rely on the stronger magnetic field of modern magnets, but the sound, compared to models using the original method, is less authentic.

The designer's solutions

The physical structure of the pickup plays a big part in the way the unit sounds. Different solutions in assembling components gives a different shape to the magnetic field and can have a relevant effect on the timbre.

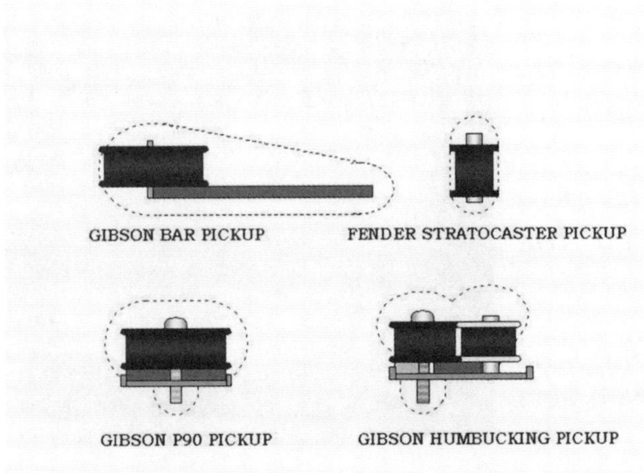

The Gibson bar pickup (Charlie Christian) has two big magnets running parallel to the strings under the guitar top and this is a factor which contributes to the sweet sound characterizing this model, especially if compared to the P 90, which uses the same coil, but has two more powerful magnets parallel to the winding and perpendicular to the strings. The Stratocaster model, with magnets directly under the strings has a very focused field.

The humbucker has a wide magnetic field similar to that of the P 90, but with a slight different shape.

The most popular models produced by Leo Fender are all very simple and with only small structural differences distinguishing one from the other, yet they all have a strong sonic personality.

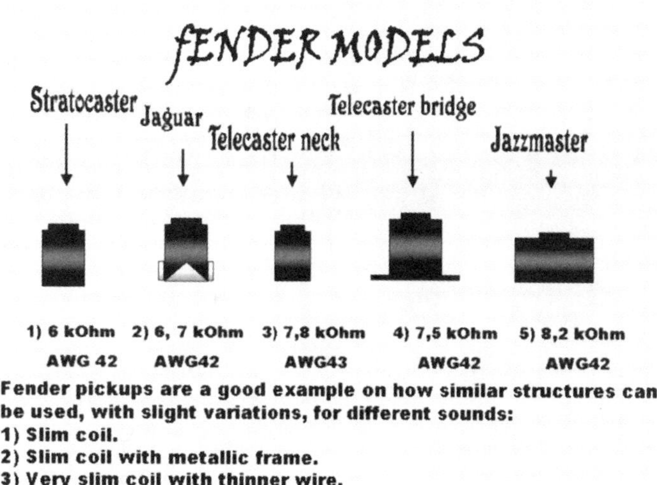

The models for Telecaster, Stratocaster, Jaguar and Jazzmaster, are all made by winding a single coil around six cylindrical magnets, but Fender's clever use of variants on this basic concept gives each of them their own signature sound.

The first noticeable difference is in the way the coils look. The Stratocaster and Jaguar coils are tall and slim, the Jazzmaster's is short and fat, the Telecaster's bridge unit is middle way and very thin on the neck unit.

A closer look shows that the Telecaster bridge pickup has a metallic plate in the base, the neck unit has a nickel cover, the Jaguar model has a notched metallic ring surrounding the coil.

There is more: the number of turns in the Telecaster bridge model is higher than in the Stratocaster pickup and even higher in the Jazzmaster unit, while on the Telecaster neck model a thinner wire is used (AWG 43 instead of AWG 42 as in the others) with a slightly higher number of turns than in the bridge unit. The coating protecting the wire is different too, as the Stratocaster and Jaguar units have Heavy Formvar wire coating, the Jazzmaster and Telecaster models are wound with a wire coated with slightly thinner Plain Enamel lacquer.

How do they sound? The Stratocaster model sounds bright but warm, the Telecaster bridge model, more punchy and with a fuller bottom end (thanks to the bottom plate extending the magnetic field and more turns in the windings). The neck model sounds softer and sweeter (the thinner wire has higher resistance and the cover softens the highest frequencies).

The Jaguar model is brighter than the Stratocaster unit because the metallic ring directs a more focused magnetic field toward the strings, the Jazzmaster model has a bigger sound because it has more turns in the winding and a wider magnetic window.

Leo Fender, using a simple basic idea, with clever expedients achieved five different sounds.

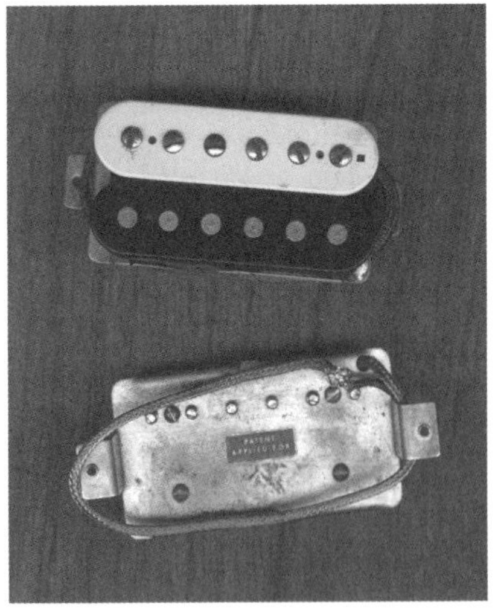

The concept behind the humbucking pickup is that two identical signals, with their phase opposed, cancel each other, while two signals with the same phase strengthen each other. The hum runs across the bobbins, which are out of phase, and gets cancelled, the musical frequencies produced by the strings disturb the magnetic field, of opposed polarities, thus resulting in phase with the bobbins. In this way they are not cancelled but strengthened.

The total number of turns in the two bobbins is the same as in the single coil of the P 90 (2x5000), the magnet is only one instead of two, but the actual sound level is equal or even greater, due to the efficiency of the system.

It has a similar timbre and a wide magnetic window due to the distance between the polepieces.

The hum is not cancelled totally because the signal picked up by the two rows of polepieces is not identical and some frequencies get cancelled. The relationship between the width of oscillation of the strings and the distance between each row of polepieces, strengthens some harmonics and cancels those falling in the centre of these two points. Since the highest frequencies have the shorter oscillation, these are the ones most influenced by this phenomenon and this is one of the reasons why a humbucking pickup sounds sweeter than a single coil. Even if the hum reduction is not 100% achieved, it's enough to quieten the pickup and the use of a nickel cover as a shield makes it even quieter.

While the best noise rejection is achieved using two identical coils, in the fifties it was difficult to find precise solutions, so some humbuckings have better matched coils than others. Those with more variations between the coils have a slightly brighter and rawer sound and some players love it, which is why Gibson now offers the Burstbuckers, and produces these units with not-so-well matched coils.

The original structure of the model designed by Seth Lover used two identical bobbins side by side, but in 1969 the low impedance models used on some Les Paul guitars had the bobbins on top of each other, with a magnet in the centre and polepieces running through the coils. Today there are many designs using thin bobbins on top of each other, made to look like single coil pickups, with windings made by utilizing very thin wire. This is necessary to obtain sufficient turns in such a small space. The purpose is to cancel hum while keeping the narrow magnetic window of Fender-style single coil units, but advertising hype notwithstanding, the result is a timbre which is, at it's best, very similar, though never identical to real single coils.

The humbucking pickup, with a magnet under two rows of polepieces, generates a wide magnetic field and a relatively great length of the strings becomes magnetized. The adjustable polepieces, extending over the base of the pickup, through six holes, direct some of the energy in that direction, while the non adjustable polepieces, leaning on the bottom, are less dispersed, and direct toward the strings a stronger magnetic field, thus producing a slightly more powerful and brighter sound. With the cover on, the magnetic field becomes weaker, so reducing variations. The screw poles can then be adjusted closer to the strings for an even more focused magnetic field and a little more brightness.

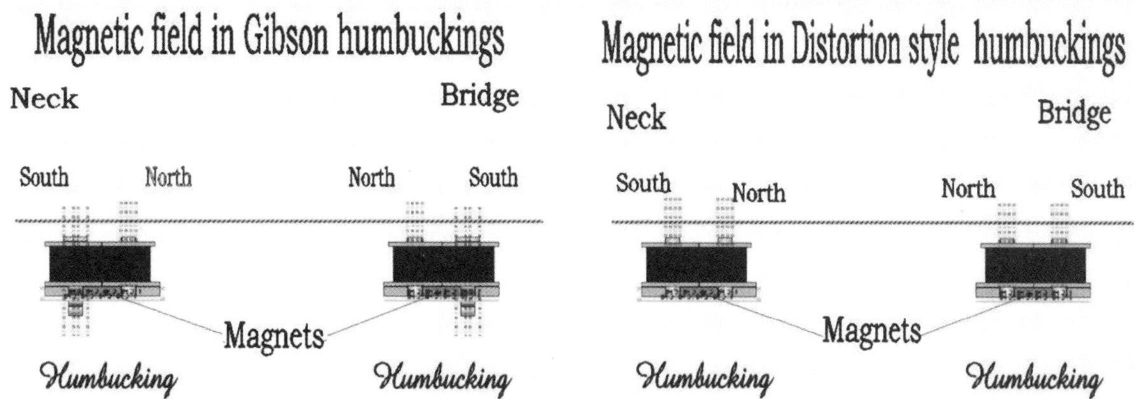

On humbucking models with identical polepieces for the two bobbins, as in those with Allen screws, the magnetic field is the same for both bobbins. These are usually sold without a cover.

There are several characteristics which give a pickup it's distinctive voice and these are all interdependent.

The magnet's flux density, the number of turns on the windings, the wire gauge, the shape of the magnetic field, the level of concentration toward the strings, are all factors which affect the output level and timbre.

The resonant peak

The wood and other materials from which the instrument is made, each has its resonance. This is also true of the pickup which creates a sudden increase in level on it's frequency range, almost flat up to that point, which is called resonant peak. After this peak the frequency level decreases rapidly. The frequency at which the peak is reached depends on the power of the magnet, the number of turns in the winding and the structure of the pickup.

The resonant peak is the frequency at which the pickup is most sensitive and the highest limit of acceptable range, therefore a model with a peak at 8000 Hz has a more transparent sound than one that has a peak of 4000 Hz. These details must be thoroughly considered.

A magnetic pickup is not meant to be a high fidelity device, but a component made to enhance the timbre of the instrument with it's musical tone.

The tonal balance of the frequencies reproduced is of utmost importance and a further extension in range is not necessarily more desirable.

The P 90, for instance, has a resonant peak of 4700 Hz, a resistance of 8 kOhms and an inductance of 7,5 Henries and is much loved for its hot and warm sound, the Fender Stratocaster pickup, which has a resonant peak one octave above, is appreciated for its open and clear sound.

DiMarzio has patented some humbucking models with different windings in each bobbin, so that each has a different resonant peak, which is like having an amplifier with a 12" and a 10" loudspeaker thereby producing the sonic characteristics of both formats. This technique is used on models such as the FRED, Tone Zone, Norton, Evolution, Cruiser and others. Some musicians love these results, while others prefer the traditional models.

Fralin makes the Unbucker, a pickup similar to a Gibson style model, the difference being that one of the bobbins is under wound. Uneven coils makes the humbucking effect less effective, but the sound is more open with some of the character of a single coil and a higher resonant peak.
The use of bobbins with wire of different kinds is also common on some humbucking models with stacked coils, such as the Kinman and other models of the last generation of single coil sized humbuckers. Due to the small space available and the thin wire required, which must be wound with great precision, the production of these pickups is very difficult and only possible using high technology winding machines.

In order to comprehend the resonant peak, imagine emphasizing a narrow portion of the audio range using a parametric equalizer. This instrument permits us to choose the frequency, the width of the band and the amount of level increase. On a pickup this is the result of the structural characteristics and the length (number of turns) of the wire in the coil.

A pickup such as the P 90, with the magnet under the coil, transfers the energy through polepieces and a high resistance. The peak has a narrow band but is very high and occurs at 4300/4700 Hz.

On a Stratocaster model, with its lower resistance and stronger magnetic field of the magnets directly in the coil, close to the strings, the peak is at a frequency well above 7000 Hz, is less pronounced and a larger band is affected. An humbucking pickup has a resonant peak around 5000 / 6000 Hz.

The width of the band emphasized is determined by the Q factor: the higher the value, the narrower the band, in our example they are 5,6 for the P 90, 2,7 for the Stratocaster.

The open and clear sound of the Stratocaster pickup is due to a higher resonant peak with a large emphasized band.
The warm but nasty sound of the P 90 is the result of a narrower band, which has more emphasis, at a lower frequency.

In the graphic the peaks of two imaginary pickups are shown as occurring at the same frequency for ease of comparison.

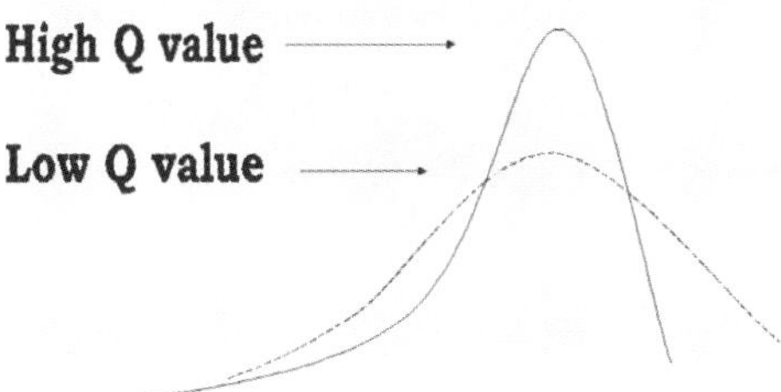

When the pickup is connected to the guitar's circuitry, the height and width of the peak is modified by the potentiometers. As the resistance of the potentiometers decreases, the peak height gets diminished and it's width increased, the frequency too is lowered.

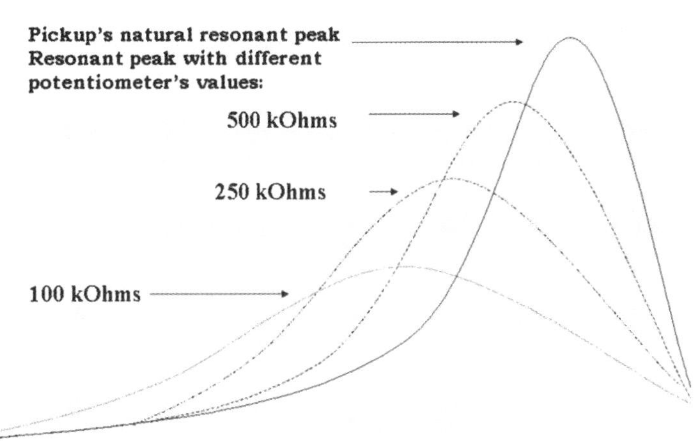

On a guitar with 1 MOhm potentiometers the natural resonant peak is almost completely preserved, with 500 kOhms potentiometers the frequency and the height of the peak is lowered and the band gets larger, with 250 kOhms potentiometers the amount of peak reduction is higher with an even larger band and so on.

The result is that the higher the potentiometer value, the brighter the instrument will sound, for this reason with trebly pickups, as in most single coils, lower value potentiometers are used, to avoid the tone becoming shrill, conversely with warmer sounding units, such as high output single coils and humbuckers, high value potentiometers are preferred to reduce the loss of high frequencies.

The relationship between the coil and the metallic parts of the pickup gives the inductance, measured in Henry, a higher value means a louder signal and less trebles.

Considering the pickups used as an example, the P 90 inductance is between 7/8 Henries and the Stratocaster has about 2/3 Henries. A humbucking pickup, PAF style, has an inductance of 4,5/6 Henries. This value is seldom stated in catalogues, but when available, if the resonant peak of a model is unknown, it is easy to presume that one with an inductance of 6 henries will sound louder and warmer, and will have a lower resonant peak, than a model with 4 Henries.

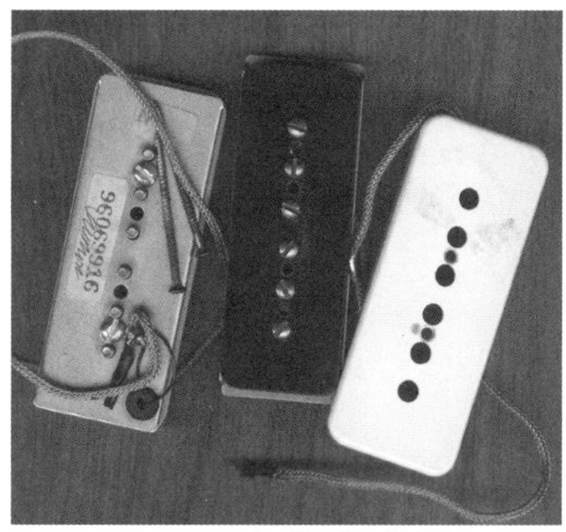
Duncan Antiquity P 90

By the end of the seventies, probably in order to give an image of professionalism and high technology, most makers used to publish catalogues with plenty of technical information, but later, gave more emphasis to "vintage" models, with more descriptive prose, often colourful and imaginative and less detailed specifications. Several DiMarzio catalogues from the early eighties and recent Duncan Antiquity and Fender catalogues report the inductance values of their pickups. This makes for an interesting comparison, if we presume that the measurements were made using similar methods.

Remember that a higher value means more power and a warmer sound, while lower values indicate less output and a clearer tone.

DiMarzio	Super Distortion	Resistance: 13,68k	Inductance: 8,2h
	PAF	Resistance: 7,65k	Inductance: 4,5h
	FS-1	Resistance 13,35k	Inductance: 6,7h
	SDS-1	Resistance: 8,68k	Inductance: 8,8h
Duncan	Antiquity Humbucking	Resistance: 8,52k	Inductance: 5,12h
	Antiquity Humb. Neck	Resistance: 7,8k	Inductance: 4,22h
	Antiquity P 90 style	Resistance: 8,52k	Inductance: 7,41h
	Texas Hot (Strat Style)	Resistance: 6,3k	Inductance: 2,87h
Fender	Custom 1954 Strat	Resistance: 6,5k	Inductance: 2,75h
	Original Vintage 57/62	Resistance: 5,6k	Inductance: 3h

As a point of reference lets compare these values with those measured on pickups we had the opportunity to test.

Gibson	Patent Applied For c.1959	Resistance: 7,6k	Inductance: 4,26h
	Patent Number c. 1964	Resistance: 7,76k	Inductance: 4,35h
	Patent Number c. 1970	Resistance: 7,81k	Inductance: 4,5h
DiMarzio	PAF	Resistance: 7,87k	Inductance: 4,32h
Duncan	Seth Lover bridge	Resistance: 8,09k	Inductance: 4,8h
	Antiquity Humbucking	Resistance: 8,56k	Inductance: 5,15h
	Antiquity Humbucking n.	Resistance: 7,72k	Inductance: 4,4h
	Pearly Gates	Resistance: 8,13k	Inductance: 5,32h
Fender	Stratocaster 1960	Resistance: 5,65k	Inductance: 2,3h
	Stratocaster 1960	Resistance: 6,02k	Inductance: 2,54h
	Stratocaster 1960	Resistance: 6,12k	Inductance: 2,6h

Even slight differences in measurement conditions and equipment used can cause variations in values, but, on pickups of the same style, the "vintage" models have more or less comparable values to those on original samples.
Others are completely different, for instance the DiMarzio SDS-1, even though its resistance is lower than that of the FS-1 from the same maker, it has a higher inductance and sounds, indeed, closer to a P 90 than to a Stratocaster model, (even a "Hot" one).
The Duncan Texas Hot and the Fender 54 are very similar to original models and their inductance gradually increases when the resistance is higher.

The Fender 57/62, despite a lower resistance, has a higher inductance, and so presumably should produce a cleaner sound, a bit less open, or warmer, depending on taste.

The polepieces

There are different ways for the magnetic field to be concentrated on the strings. There are two methods mainly used on pickups, one is to insert the magnets directly in the windings, under the strings, the other is to put an alnico or ceramic bar on the bottom of the coils, with ferrous polepieces directing the magnetic field toward the strings.

A rudimentary but effective system is the one preferred by Leo Fender, with cylindrical magnets in the coil, a polarity toward the strings and the other toward the base, but this method makes it impossible to adjust the level for each string.

DeArmond tried to solve the problem by mounting each magnet in a cylindrical holder which, by means of a screw and its respective spring, could be adjusted in height to balance variations in output of the strings. A similar system, was used on the Gibson Alnico pickup designed by Seth Lover but instead used square magnets.

The bottom of a DeArmond pickup, with the magnet holding cylinders and the adjusting screws (Claudio Caldana).

On the Gibson P 90 two bar magnets on the base of the unit, with the south polarity toward the centre, touch six adjustable screws which transfer the magnetic field across the winding to the strings. An interesting peculiarity of this system is that the opposite polarity (north), facing the external sides of the coil, tend to be attracted by the south polarity in the centre, so the magnetic field completely surrounds the pickup and widens the magnetic window. This is one of the reasons for the potent sound of this model.

On his humbucking Gibson used a similar technique, with a magnet under the coils and polepieces in the plastic bobbins around which the wire was wound.
On the prototype Seth Lover used non adjustable cylindrical polepieces, but on the production model one of the bobbins, the one with south polarity, received adjustable screw poles, as on the P 90.
Since the distance between the two pole rows is smaller than that between the external sides of

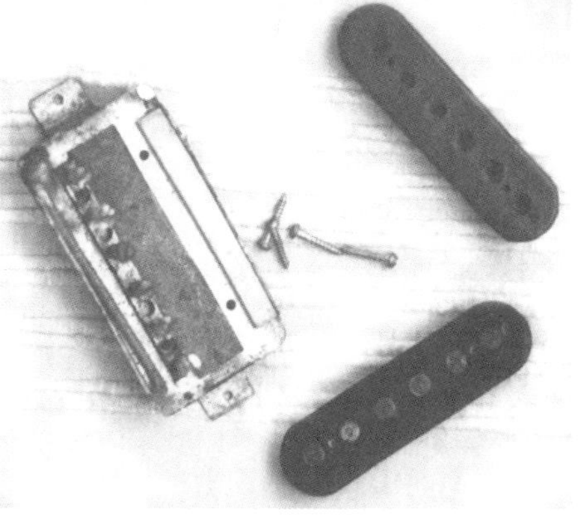

Duncan SH-AH-1B, designed for Allan Holdsworth. Made with two rows of adjustable polepieces and an Alnico 5 magnet, with windings for about 16 kOhms of D. C. resistance, it has a warm and smooth sound.

the pickup, the magnetic field is more concentrated and is more efficient than the single coil model.

Therefore even though the total number of turns used in the windings (2 x 5000) is the same as the single coil model (10000 turns) and only one magnet is used instead of two, the result is a comparable output level, a lower inductance and a higher resonant peak.

Gretsch, on the Filter'Tron, used a structure similar to the Gibson, but with adjustable screws in both bobbins. This should allow a smoother sound, but since Gretsch used less turns of wire, of a bigger gauge, the low resistance resulting gives a brighter tone.

DiMarzio, on the Super Distortion, introduced two rows of adjustable Allen screws as polepieces, not extending under the base of the pickup as on the Gibson and the Gretsch, in order to avoid dispersion and create a more focused magnetic field, thus obtaining a greater sensitivity to high frequencies and reducing the loss of highs due to the numerous turns in the coils. In other models, such as the Humbucker From Hell, DiMarzio used the same kind of polepieces with different windings to get a timbre closer to that of Fender-style single coils, but in a humbucker format.
Bill Lawrence seemed to favour a single blade polepiece, thought to transfer a more uniform magnetic flux and to give a cleaner sound.
Barney Kessel and other musicians used to prefer the Charlie Christian pickup over the P 90 because they thought that the blade pole gave a cleaner tone than the screw type.

Gretsch, on the Super'Tron 1, chose several thin blades as poles, which was similar to that used on a transformer core, thus creating the most efficient and perfect method in obtaining the clear tone sought after by country musicians.

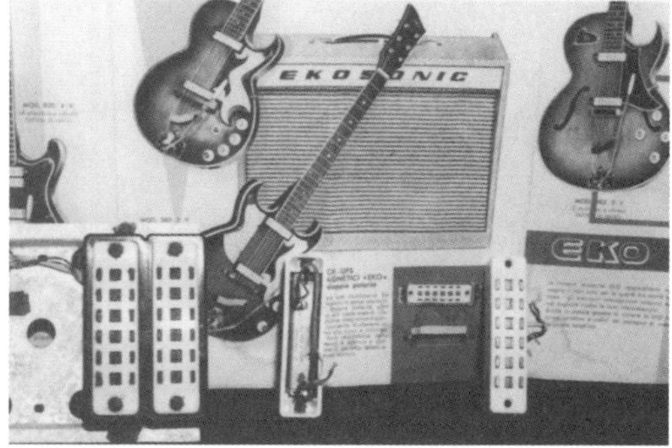

The Italian EKO used a similar method, but chose to use small blades under each string, in a single coil model, creating a pickup with good output level and a bright sound. Unfortunately this was not appreciated due to the poor quality of the guitars on which it was used.
Carvin used eleven polepieces in each bobbin for evenness of flux.

The Italian Red Push put twelve alnico cylindrical magnets in each bobbin, a diagonal pair under each string in single coil and humbucking models, to produce a wider magnetic field than on traditional Fender style pickups (in the humbucking a quicker attack is obtained).

As far as string spacing is concerned, guitars are all different. The main difference is apparent between the Gibson and the Fender standards. On Gibson-style guitars the spacing is narrower than on Fender-style guitars, for this reason pickup makers, whose humbucking models follow the Gibson standard for pole spacing, also offer versions with a Fender-style spacing for a better fit when mounted on that particular style of guitar.

Seymour Duncan designed the Trembucker series specifically for vibrato equipped guitars, following the Fender standard, with two rectangular polepieces under each string. The magnet can be Alnico or ceramic according to the model. The series includes also a model with stacked coils and dimensions similar to a Fender-style single coil.

Duncan offers several of the standard models in Fender-style spacing, described in the catalogue as “Trembucker spacing” versions. DiMarzio makes most models in the optional "F" version, which stands for Fender-style.

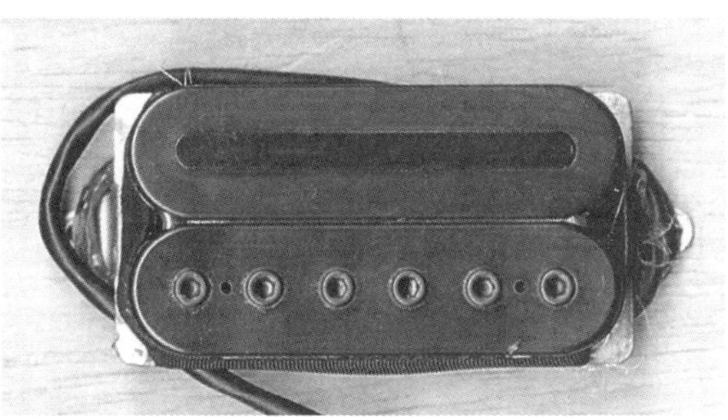

DiMarzio Megadrive

On some humbuckings different polepieces were used in each bobbin, so as to obtain the best characteristics of both, such as on the Duncan Screamin' Demon, with screw poles in one, Allen screws in the other.

DiMarzio used to make the Megadrive, with six Allen screws and a large blade, that model is no more produced, but the system is used again in the recently issued Dropsonic. The shape and the dimensions of the polepieces or magnets used could affect not only the magnetic field, but also the inductance.

No system is better than the other, it depends on the design and the sound sought after.

The important thing is that the polepieces must be made from ferrous materials, otherwise the magnetic flux is not transferred properly.

Other materials, such as brass, cannot transfer the magnetic field toward the strings.

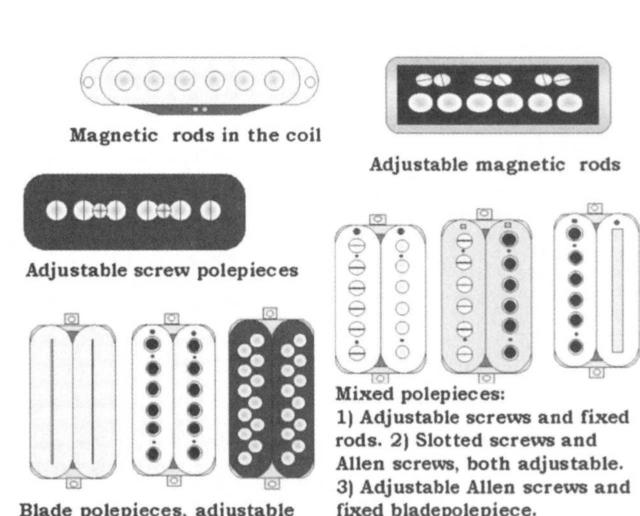

Models with active electronics

There are two kinds of instruments with active electronics: those with transistorized preamplifiers or equalizers coupled with traditional pickups and those using specially designed low impedance models made to work only with those circuits.

The first type differs from traditional guitars only for the presence of a miniaturized circuit, but the pickups are the same as those on passive instruments and can usually work normally in passive mode, by inserting the active circuit when desired at the flick of a switch. The latter has low impedance pickups and its' output level is too low for passive use and needs a battery powered circuit to raise the signal to the level necessary to feed the input of a high impedance guitar amplifier.

Amplifiers have been developed with the magnetic passive pickups and their input impedance is high, usually 1MOhm, suitable for the strong signal of these models.

Active pickups, structurally, are similar to passive models, but are wound for a lower resistance to produce a better frequency response, low noise and a cleaner sound. The output level is low, compared to passive pickups, but this is not an important factor since they are meant to be used with a preamplifier. In both cases the real problem is the quality of the circuit, because if the components are cheap or the project not well designed, excessive noise and poor tone can result.

Les Paul was the first to believe in low impedance pickups and designed such models for the Gibson Les Paul Recording and Les Paul Professional, offered in 1969. They were less prone to catch noise and when using long cables more high frequencies were retained, but were designed to be use directly in a mixer's input and to be connected to a normal amplifier required the use of an impedance transformer. With active circuitry a preamplifier, miniaturized and mounted on the guitar, increases the signal to the level necessary for a perfect match to an amplifier's input and the problem is solved.
The first to use transistorized preamplifiers on a guitar is thought to be Alembic in 1968, for Jerry Garcia of the Grateful Dead.

The progress in miniaturized electric circuits in the seventies, permitted the production of complex systems often including active equalization. These were small enough to be mounted on the guitar, powered by a simple 9 volt battery, and were able to increase the output to levels much higher than those possible even with the hottest passive units.

The availability of integrated circuits of better quality, made active systems more popular and by the end of the seventies it was not uncommon to see guitars factory-fitted with active electronics on sale. Several makers, in the USA as well as in Japan, by that time, had active models in their catalogues.

The leader, in the eighties, was EMG, whose models were appreciated by professional players because of their low noise, flat sound and ability to retain a clear sound. This was possible even when the signal was heavily processed through massive rack sized effect devices, which were very popular in those days. The success of EMG was the result of research carried out by Rob Turner, who in the early seventies designed pickups specifically conceived to be used with a preamplifier. His idea was that in this way it was possible to make the pickup without compromising a clean and faithful tone, leaving the preamplifier to do the job of increasing the output as needed, while active equalization would modify the timbre at will for more versatility.

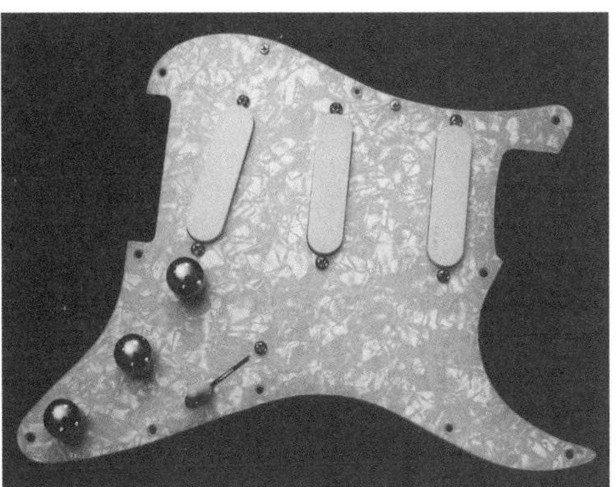

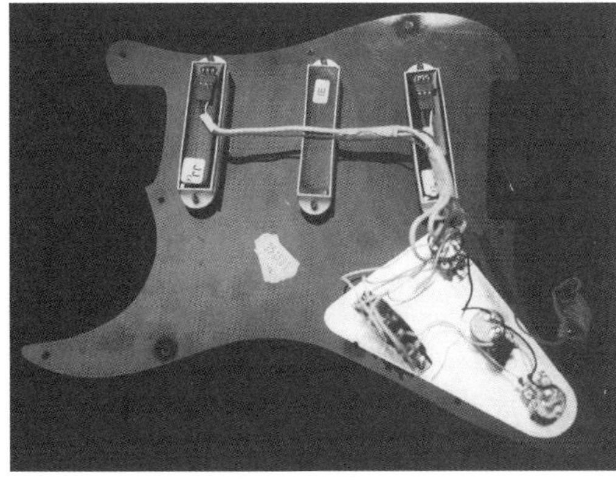

EMG-SA Set

Miniaturized components enabled the circuit to be small enough to mount on most popular guitar models without alteration, the increased quality made the system quieter and more efficient. It also consumed less power and had longer battery life.

The first models were the EMG-SA for Stratocaster, in 1974, with low impedance preamplifier for reduced hum, and the EMG-H, a single coil with a humbucking-like cover. After 1979 the range was broadened with improved versions of the first models added to by the humbuckers EMG-59 and EMG-81.

To confirm the success of the brand, well known players such as Peter Frampton, Steve Lukater and David Gilmour used EMG pickups and Ned Steinberger chose them as standard equipment for his innovative guitar.

Today EMG produces models in standard humbucking format or in single coil size for Telecaster and Stratocaster, with Alnico or ceramic magnets. Regardless of the size, all recent models are humbucking. Any pickup can be coupled to different circuits for a broad range of tones and characteristics. The popularity continues and new EMG users are James Hatfield and Zakk Wylde.

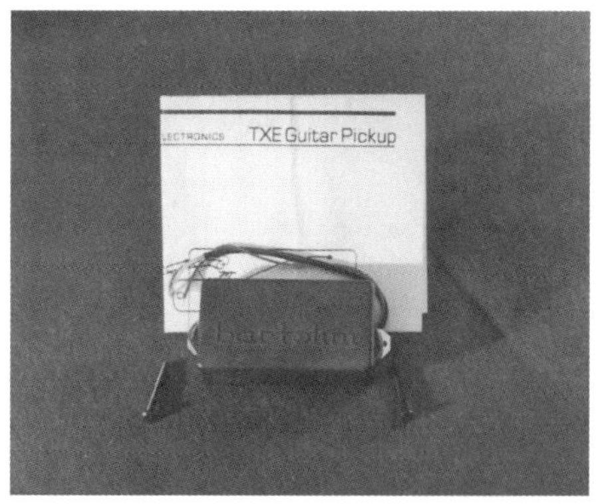

Bartolini TXE, a hi-fi active model designed to amplify the tone of an archtop guitar as pure as possible (Claudio Prosperini).

In the seventies many looked at active electronics as the way toward the future and used it with regular passive pickups or with specially designed low impedance models. Amongst those following this path we must remember Alembic, Bartolini, with active and passive models, some with multiple windings for increased possibilities of connection (the Beast II has two windings per bobbin with eight output cables), and models with variable Q.

Other brands offering active circuitry were Ibanez, Gibson, Aria, Fender, Steinberger, but commercial results didn't pay for the investments in this field, at least not for all of them.

The Fender Stratocaster and Telecaster Elite, the Gibson Artist and RD series, were all commercial failures.

In Italy the best known active pickup maker is Magnetics, with the models designed and built by Piero Terracina.

Today the interest for active models seems to be low, at least concerning the electric guitar, for which the warmer tone of the best passive models is reputed more suitable than the colder and more clinical timbre of active pickups; bass players seem to be more receptive to this kind of product.

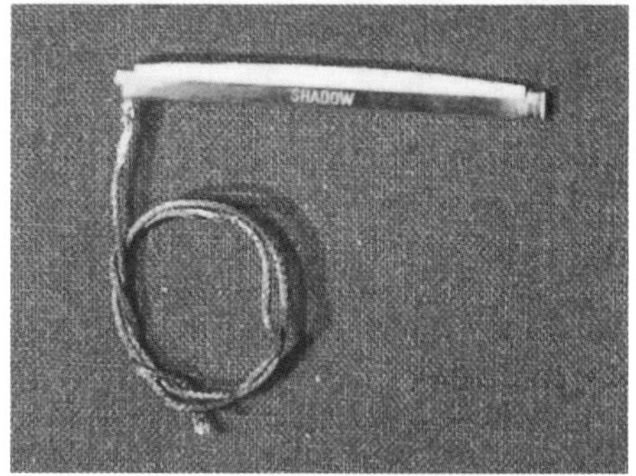

A piezo-electric pickup (C. P.).

The increasing availability of high quality passive models and the vitality of blues based music styles, particularly after Stevie Ray Vaughan's success, seemed to bring a general lack of interest in heavy processed sounds and a search for purer sounds. Even EMG, without betraying its commitment to active pickups, offered models designed to give "vintage" tones.

In the past cheap instruments with poorly designed electronics and low level components gave active guitars a bad reputation because of their shrill tones and high noise, but today the quality is very high and the decision whether to use active pickups or not, is a matter of tone preference. This is more of a philosophical rather than technical nature.

With active models it is certainly possible to obtain more fidelity and more possibilities of tone shaping, but these qualities, appreciated by acoustic players, seeking even more purity of tone, and bass players, are not the most sought after by most electric players.

Despite this, a certain number of players favouring active models are found in every music style, from jazz to rock, and from ethnic to experimental.

Barcus-Berry contact pickup on a Bouzouki (Claudio Prosperini).

The acoustic guitar seems to benefit more from the better quality of active electronics, the piezo pickups, pioneered by Gibson in 1960 for the classic CE-1, then perfected by Ovation who added stereo models, are now the common solution for acoustic guitar amplification. High quality systems are produced by Fishman, L. R. Baggs, Martin, Gibson and are also available in versions suitable for electric guitars therefore giving a solid body some acoustic-like qualities.

Some systems use a piezo pickup coupled to a magnetic pickup to mix the sonic characteristics of both types, for a sound with clarity and warmth. Others use a piezo pickup and a microphone. All relate to the preamplifier for output level and tone equalization.
Most contact mikes, are not really active pickups because they often have an output powerful enough to work without a preamplifier, although using one gives better performance and more control.

With today's electronics is possible to solve many problems, especially for live performance.

The acoustic guitar can be amplified reducing the risk of feedback, with great fidelity to the original sound,

In the recording studio, however, for the best results, a good choice of microphones and their careful positioning remain the preferred solutions for most artists.

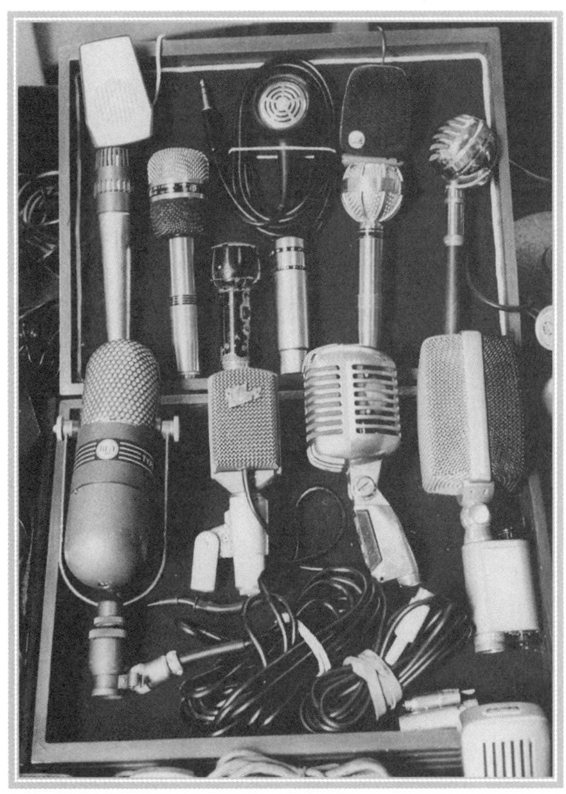

Part 3 – Utilization

1) How to read technical specifications

To choose a pickup on paper is not an easy task, the best thing, although seldom possible, would be to try it on the guitar on which it's supposed to be mounted. Pickups can be faithful copies of old models, modern versions of classic designs or new high output monsters.

Often the models are described with plenty of enthusiastic words which tend to be very optimistic regarding the sonic results, therefore, we must read them with care.

The most prestigious names have a reputation to defend, so in this case caution is advisable not only owing to the possible exaggeration of the product quality, which we can take for granted, but because, assuming that the text is reliable, the description of the sound of a pickup is a very subjective criteria.

To correctly interpret the advertising message, we must understand the sound policy that the maker had in mind (the same model can be "bright, with wonderful treble" for one person and "harsh, with biting highs" for another).

Even though some makers produce an impressive number of models, each maker has his own tone preference, so that a DiMarzio, whatever the model, has a different sound than a comparable model from Duncan.

This is because the techniques used to make them, the materials used and the decisions regarding the required tone, are different and, in most cases, applied consistently by each brand to the whole production line.

Technical specifications, in most cases, are included in catalogues without exact information on how the parameters were obtained, making it impossible to compare results documented by different makers.

The main measurements to be carried out on a pickup are the D. C. resistance, the inductance, the resonant peak, and the magnetic flux.

D. C. resistance: this is the resistance of the coil to the Direct Current flow and is measured in Ohm. As the diameter of the wire decreases, the resistance increases. In a wire of a given gauge, the resistance increases proportionally to the length of the wire (number of turns).

Inductance: this is a product of the relationship between the coil and the magnet and other metallic parts in the pickup and is measured in Henry; again a higher value, on two otherwise similar pickups, means more power and less highs.

Impedance: this is the resistance of the coil to the flow of Alternating Current and is measured in Ohm. The value increases proportionally with the frequency.

Resonant peak: this is the frequency at which the impedance reaches the highest value and the pickup sensitivity is greater. The frequency at which it is centred is the limit of the frequency range of the pickup, after that point the level decreases rapidly. On pickups of the same kind a higher resonant peak indicates a brighter sound.

Magnetic flux: this indicates the strength of the magnetic field in a pickup and is measured in Gauss. It is seldom documented in catalogues.

Some catalogues report only the D. C. resistance, others the resonant peak and inductance too (one of the most complete is the catalogue issued by DiMarzio in 1978). The resistance is the only characteristic a customer can check using a simple Ohm-meter (better if digital). All the others require specialized and costly equipment. In order to utilize this information correctly, it would at least be necessary to know the wire gauge used in the pickup.

In two pickups with different resistance values, the one with the higher value can have more turns of the same gauge wire or can be wound using a smaller gauge wire; if two models are wound using the same wire, the one with the higher resistance will sound louder and darker.

The resistance value is useful to ascertain whether a pickup can be included in the supposed category. If a model, for instance, is advertised as a reissue of a "vintage" model, in the style of the Gibson "Patent Applied For", which was made with about 5000 turns of AWG 42 wire, with a 20% tolerance, it should have a D. C. resistance ranging from a minimum of 7 kOhms to a maximum barely exceeding 9 kOhms.

If we measure on our unit a 16 kOhms resistance, we can deduct that it is not a faithful copy because such a high resistance can only be the result of a higher number of turns using a smaller gauge wire, AWG 43 or 44, which permits more windings to fit into the bobbins (if such a measurement were found on a pickup presumed original, it would be without any doubt, rewound). The tension of the winding, whether carried out with regular turns or with a tendency to get entangled, has a definite effect on the timbre, especially with single coil models.

Since any single unit of the same model shows slight differences and, all other elements being equal, a higher resistance means more output level and a warmer sound, we can put the unit with the higher value near the bridge for a calibrated set and several makers offer factory-calibrated sets.

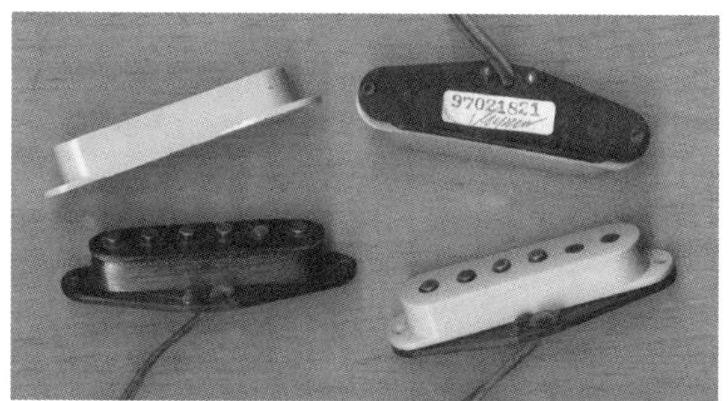

Duncan Antiquity "Texas Hot" calibrated set.

It is important to note that details such as the kind and quality of the wire used, the use of hand guided winding machines, well trained workers, the selection of first choice materials, will all definitely have an effect on the resulting timbre, and also on the price of the model. Even if it is possible to find relatively inexpensive good sounding models, it is not reasonable to expect the same rich timbre of a model worth double its price only because the brochure shows similar technical specifications.

Due to the difficulties in interpreting the specifications, several catalogues are complete with "Tone Charts", expressed in numbers, reproducing a scale similar to the tone controls for bass, middle and treble of a typical guitar amplifier.

These occasionally contain a graphic representation, in order to give some hints regarding the perceived tonal balance of the model in question.

Of course with values such as, 5/4/8 for bass, middle and treble, for instance, there is no indication of the width of each band nor of the frequency on which they are centred, but these may prove useful in comparing other models: if another has a value of 9 for the treble we can presume it sounds brighter than the first one.

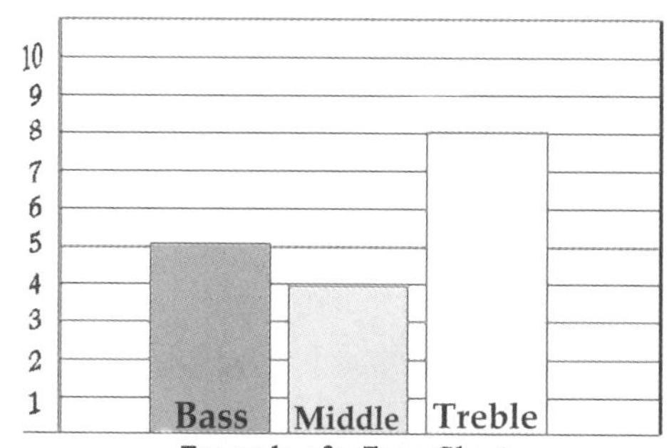

Example of a Tone Chart, referred to an imaginary model, showing values of 5/4/8 for bass, middle and treble

RESONANT PEAK

100 200 400 800 1,6k 3,2k 6,4k 12,8k

100 200 400 800 1,6k 3,2k 6,4k 12,8k

The graphic shows how the frequency response of two pickups with different resonance peaks would look according to our imaginary "Tone chart". Even if the balance between bass, middle and treble bands is similar, the harmonic content is different enough to give two distinct sonic characters.

Duncan in his catalogues gives the resonant peak and by using the tone chart and this information we have a better idea of the sound of the pickup. If a model has a similar tone balance, but a lower resonant peak, we can presume that the inductance is also higher and the peak is narrower and more emphasized than the one with a higher frequency, which produces a thicker, darker sound. Duncan wisely advises to use the "tone chart" only to compare models in the same class and never, for instance, those of a different type such as a single coil and a humbucking model.

The values reported in recent catalogues from DiMarzio show slight differences, if compared to previous ones, not because the sound of the pickups has changed, but because the scale used has been changed in order to give a broader range, with more nuances. Supposing we want to compare an old model, already out of production, from a previous catalogue, with a new model recently introduced in a new brochure, we might have problems comparing the two pickups because the parameters have been changed, although they refer to the same brand.

Based on the same concept, the kind of wire and inspiration (the old P. A. F.), we can compare the Duncan models '59, Seth Lover, Pearly Gates and APH-1. In the "Hot" class, with most models based on a ceramic magnet and several turns of smaller gauge wire (often AWG 43), we can compare DiMarzio models following variations of this classic Super Distortion recipe, such as the Distortion 2, Evolution, Super 3. Consequently we can compare different models from the same maker, the comparison with values given by a competitor are of little use because of the lack of a standardized method in obtaining them. It is like comparing the tone settings on the amplifiers of two players without knowing the brand and models used.

The most we can do with the information given in the catalogues, if we have the opportunity to listen carefully to one model from a given brand, is to use them to try to understand how another model can compare with the one we already know.

If, for example a known model does not appear bright enough on a certain guitar, by looking at the tone chart it is possible to choose another model to try, taking note of those with a higher value for the treble and avoiding those with a lower value, using the known one as a reference point. It is however advisable to bear in mind that the indications given are merely generic and should not be taken literally. In some cases more technical specifications, such as the D. C. Resistance, are different than those stated in previous catalogues, because a maker will sometimes decide to change certain characteristics.

Simply because a 1999 pickup has the same model name as a 1986 one, doesn't means they will sound exactly the same, some of the materials used or the technique used in making them is subject to change over the years.

When choosing a pickup it is better to remember that it must balance well with other units already present on the guitar. Putting a "hot" style pickup on a Stratocaster style instrument, for instance on the treble position, will also change the tone of the second position when the centre pickup is also selected. The emphasis on different harmonics, of course, will affect the timbre when using both units.

These days DiMarzio no longer gives specifications concerning resonant peak and inductance as in the past, but taking into consideration the fact that a higher resistance means more windings or a thinner wire, we can presume a lower resonant peak when encountering a very high value. The X2N, for instance, seems to have pronounced treble and flat middle and bass, with values respectively of 7/5/5, with a resistance of 14,5 kOhms, but a PAF PRO, which has a less emphasised treble, with values of 6/5/5, and a resistance of 8,40 kOhm, presumably has its resonant peak at a higher frequency, but with a lower Q factor, thus less pronounced but broader. Not surprisingly, the sound of the PAF PRO, compared to the X2N, is clearer and more transparent with a lower output.

Elements such as the polepieces, can have an effect on tone. Two Distortion models, DiMarzio and Duncan, have similar characteristics, but simply the use of Allen screws polepieces on the first and studs and screw polepieces, (Gibson-style) on the second, produces different timbres.
The structure of a pickup has a lot to do with the resulting timbre, therefore when a maker states that he has produced a model with the same sound as a certain single coil pickup from the fifties, but humbucking and with an original magnetic field, we must translate all that as "somewhat similar", imagining the difference occurring between a book and a movie "freely based on..." (having ascertained this, it is possible that some will prefer the movie to the book).

The original technical specifications for the Gibson humbucking pickup, are two bobbins wound with the same number of turns in each, nominally 5000 turns for 4k with AWG 42 plain enamel wire. This gives the best effect of hum rejection, but due to the winding methods of the time, some old pickups have slightly uneven windings, and one bobbin with more turns than the other. When this happens the sound is a little brighter and rawer but the decrease in humbucking efficiency is unnoticeable, especially if the pickup is shielded by the nickel cover (this kind of PAFs are reproduced by Gibson with the Burstbucker models, available in vintage versions with Alnico 2 magnets and the brighter Alnico 5 version fitted on the new Les Paul Standard 50 and 60).

Today some humbucking models are made with different windings in the bobbins to achieve a sound otherwise unobtainable; by using a different wire gauge or different turns, each bobbin has its own resonant peak. DiMarzio calls this system dual resonance pickups, where one bobbin has a higher frequency peak and when in series with the other, according to the maker, acts as two speakers of different sizes in a cabinet. Lindy Fralin makes the "Unbucker", a model wound with traditional AWG 42 enamel wire, but using less turns in one of the bobbins (i.e. 5k and 3k), thus obtaining more treble, a little lower output and one third less humbucking effect, while retaining single coil-like sound quality. Most single coil sized humbucking models of the last generation, such as the Kinman, Fender Noiseless and DiMarzio Virtual Vintage models have stacked bobbins with different gauge windings. All these models have a sound different from traditionally wound pickups.

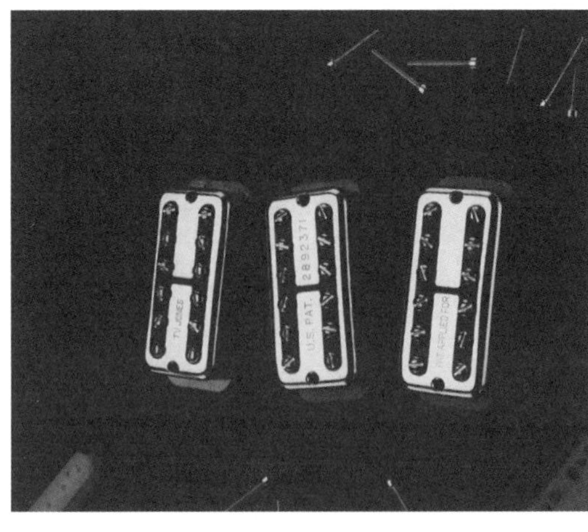

TV Jones Classic (left) and original Gretsch pickups (courtesy of TV Jones).

The first choice must be made according to the kind of sound we are looking for, whether that of a "vintage" style pickup or a "hot" one, whether to choose alnico magnets or ceramic ones. Another factor, albeit relative, is sometimes due to the desire to imitate a musician who uses a certain brand and whose sound we admire, although we must bear in mind that an artist can use one kind of pickup in a phase of his career and a completely different one in another and in the same way uses different instruments live or in the studio. Once we have defined the field, we can further analyse the available specifications.

There is a wide choice in Fender and Gibson copies of models from the fifties and the sixties while the choice is more limited for other brands. For those interested in the Gretsch models, a reissue of the DeArmond Dynasonic is available as stock item on some guitars. Fender used to make the 2k a reproduction sounding a bit louder and brighter than the originals. A faithful reproduction can be obtained by the Duncan Custom shop. Most Gretsch guitars are equipped with Filter'Tron reissues with vintage specs (previous copies had ceramic magnets and more output). High quality reproductions of the Filter'Trons are made by Tom Holmes and TV Jones, whose models are used by Brian Setzer on some of his guitars, also available in a format which can be mounted on guitars with the Gibson-style humbucking rings. Guild recently uses some Duncan models and his own copy of the original HB-1.

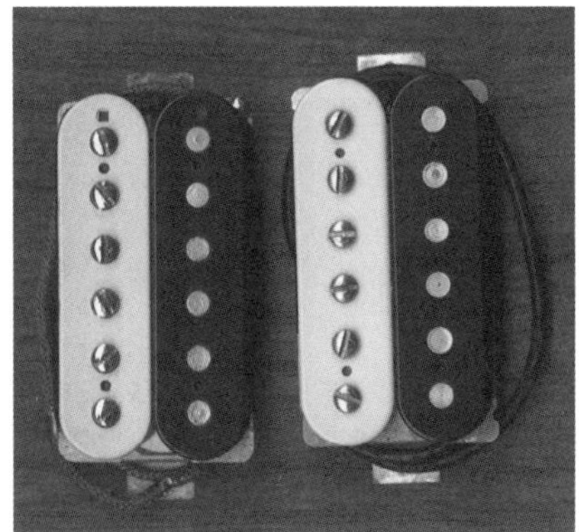

PAF copies: Duncan Antiquity (left) and Fralin (right).

Rickenbacker offers in his catalogues modern versions and "vintage" versions of his pickups, but without the old "Horseshoe", which is available, in a slightly different version, for bass only. Rick Aiello and Jason Lollar cooperate to make reproductions of the “Horseshoe” and Duncan makes his own version available, on special order, in his Custom Shop.

The reborn Danelectro makes two different versions of the old "Lipstick", normal and the "Original", which has slightly less powerful magnets for a warmer sound.

A copy is also offered by both Kent Armstrong and Seymour Duncan.

Fender and Gibson, whose copies are without doubt the most widely diffused, have only recently seen the potential and have introduced really accurate versions of their old models, particularly regarding the magnets. Whilst some models have been available for a long time, such as those offered by Seymour Duncan, specialist Jack Jones, with his models for Stratocaster, and Tom Holmes for the humbuckers whose PAF-style models are much respected.

DiMarzio offers very good models based on the vintage designs although not exact reproductions of any specific model. Of the Gibson P 90 very good copies are available from Fralin, Duncan in the Antiquity series and Jason Lollar.
The Gibson Reissue and Duncan Vintage are louder and brighter than the originals, and DiMarzio offers several P 90 inspired models with ceramic magnets.

Each maker has their own recipe and, because of the inconsistencies in specifications of the old units, has to make a choice when deciding which one to copy. The most respected makers all make excellent copies, the differences between these products usually reflects the personal preferences of the manufacturer.

For Fender pickups everybody seems to have different ideas about how strong should be the magnets or the exact number of turns in the windings and so everybody makes copies sharing the same average specs but sounding all different. Fender periodically claims to have made more accurate Reissues using old formula Alnico magnets and Duncan offers Alnico 2 and Alnico 5 versions as well as the Antiquity models with “calibrated Alnico” magnets, several manufacturers offer models based on original sets from different decades, so to have ‘50s, ‘60s and ‘70s replicas.

Gibson used almost any magnet available at the time, in the Patent Applied For pickups, Alnico 2, 3, 4 and 5, therefore in order to make a modern replica the manufacturer has to choose which one to use as a model. Some makers let the customer choose between Alnico 2 and 5, Duncan likes the sound of relatively weak magnets such as Alnico 2, which he uses for most PAF copies.

Fralin favours PAFs with Alnico 4 magnets and a slightly tighter sound, so he makes his models accordingly while Tom Holmes seems to use Alnico 2 for a warmer tone and so on. On the old PAF pickups, although AWG 42 Plain Enamel wire was used for about 5000 turns on each bobbin, the actual D. C. resistance can vary from as little as just over 7 kOhm, to values slightly exceeding 9 kOhms. With this in mind Fralin makes his models with varied windings, giving the customer the possibility to choose between 7, 5 kOhm and more than 9 kOhm, on a gradual scale of 15% increase (for Fender style pickups the increments are of 10% which range, for vintage models, from 5,7k to 7k).

Duncan produces several models, each representing a possible variation, Gibson offers the medium power '57 Classic and the '57 Classic Plus, which is a copy of the units with more windings than normal and three versions of the Burstbucker (under wound, normal and over wound).

Those quoted, schematically, are the specifications of some very popular "vintage" models, which, according to most musicians and collectors represent a sonic excellence and remain a reference point despite technical progress. The dates for the changes are approximate, we would also like to point out that after the second half of 1955, the Telecaster bridge unit has slightly taller magnets under the D and G strings.

Brand	Style	Model	Magnets	Wire type and gauge in AWG	Resistance	Polarity toward the strings	Production
Fender	Telecaster	Neck	Alnico	Enamel 43	7,3-8k		1950-1968
	Broadcaster *	Bridge	Alnico	Enamel 43	7,5-10k		1950-1951
	Telecaster	Bridge	Alnico	Enamel 42	5,9-7,6k		1952-1954
	Telecaster	Bridge	Alnico	Enamel 42	5,9-7,4k	South after 1957	1954-1968
	Stratocaster	Same for all positions	Alnico	Formvar 42	5,5-6,5k	North up to 1956, then South	1954-1964
	Stratocaster	Same for all positions	Alnico	Enamel 42	5,7-6k		1964-1968
Gibson	PU-498	Humbucking	Alnico	Enamel 42	7,1-9k	South adj. Poles	1957-1960
	PU-498	Humbucking	Alnico	Enamel 42	7,4-8,5k		1960-1963
	PU-498	Humbucking	Alnico	Polyurethane 42	7,6-7,8k		1964-1968
	P 90	P 90	Alnico	Enamel 42	7,3-9k	South	1946-1968

* The term Broadcaster also includes the instruments called Esquire and "No-caster"; for the neck model, on which the specs remained unchanged, we kept the more general name Telecaster. Polarity on earlier units used to vary since it was not possible to select both models simultaneously, and was probably not considered important.

Now we can analyse the most popular reissues and the small details which distinguish them. As we can see on the table above, the resistance values, on the originals, show a certain amount of variations. The average values are most common while the extreme ones are relatively infrequent, therefore each maker decides which values to choose in this range, as the basis for his production. After examining several original units, one person might have a preference for a certain PAF with a resistance of 8,2 k and decide to copy that one, another person may choose a different one, showing a resistance of 7,8 k. Either copy would be correct, but they would sound a bit different.

It is curious to notice that on Fender Stratocaster pickups and Gibson humbuckers, the units with the higher resistance values are found more often amongst those manufactured in 1959, so it comes as no surprise that many use this year as a reference point when discussing these kind of pickups.

The most accurate "Reissue" models available on our market:

Brand	Model	Magnets	Resistance
For Telecaster			
Fender	No-Caster Lead	Alnico 3	7,3k
	Or. Vintage Lead	Alnico 3	7,2k
	Or. Vintage Neck	Alnico 3	7,7k

Duncan	Antiquity Bridge	Alnico 2 calibrated	6,4k
	Antiquity Neck	Alnico 2 calibrated	7,6k
	APTL-1	Alnico 2	6,2k
	APTR-1	Alnico2	8,1k
	STL-1B	Alnico 5 calibrated	7,6k
	STL-1 stile'54	Alnico 5 calibrated	7,2
	STR-1	Alnico 5 calibrated	7,3k
Fralin	Stock Telecaster	Alnico 5 or 3 on order	7k
	High Output Tele	Alnico 5 or 3 on order	9,5k
For Stratocaster			
Fender	Original 57/62	Alnico 5 Old Style	5,6k
	Custom 54 Bridge	Alnico 5 Old Style	6,5k
	Custom 54 M & N	Alnico 5 Old Style	5,9k
Duncan	Antiquity Texas Hot	Alnico 2 calibrated	6,3k
	APS-1	Alnico 2	6,4
	SSL-1 Vintage	Alnico 5 calibrated	6,5k
Fralin	Vintage Bridge	Alnico 5	6,3k
	Vintage Middle	Alnico 5	5,9k
	Vintage Neck	Alnico 5	5,7k
	Real 54 Bridge	Alnico 3	7k
	Real 54 Middle	Alnico 3	6,1k
	Real 54 Neck	Alnico 3	6k
Humbucking			
Gibson	Classic 57	Alnico 2	8,2k
	Classic 57 Plus	Alnico 2	9k
Duncan	Antiquity Bridge	Alnico 2 calibrated	8,56k
	Antiquity Neck	Alnico 2 calibrated	7,8k
	Seth Lover Bridge	Alnico 2 calibrated	8,1k
	Seth Lover neck	Alnico 2 calibrated	7,2k
	Pearly Gates Bridge	Alnico 2	8,35k
	Pearly Gates Neck	Alnico 2	7,3k
	SH-1 59 Bridge	Alnico 5	8,13k
	SH-1 59 Neck	Alnico 5	7,43k
	APH-1 Bridge	Alnico 2	7,8k
	APH-1 Neck	Alnico 2	7,6k
Fralin	Humbucker	Alnico (probably 4)	7,5k - 9,5k
Tom Holmes	H 450 Neck Humb.	Alnico 2	7,6 - 8k
	H 455 Bridge Humb.	Alnico 2	8,2 - 8,6k
Voodoo Pickups	59 Humbucker	Alnico 3	8 k

As we can see all the values are in the range of specifications found in the original models they aim to copy. The occasional exception concerns the bridge unit, especially on the Stratocaster model, which pushes the resistance value to more than 6,5 k or even 7 k, to comply with the preference of most contemporary guitar players for more fullness in that position.

The measurements taken on several examples show some slight inconsistencies, probably due to the fact that the most accurate copies, made using hand guided machines, reflect in this aspect a striking resemblance to the originals. Therefore, the Gibson '57 Classic can vary between 7,8 k and 8,3 k, the Duncan Antiquity models are supplied with a label stating the individual resistance of the unit. The "Seth Lover" models have a serial number stamped on their base plate through which the maker can find the technical specifications of that particular unit on a “data base”. Fralin offers the possibility of personalized windings in a range of minimum and maximum resistance values, which differ for each model.

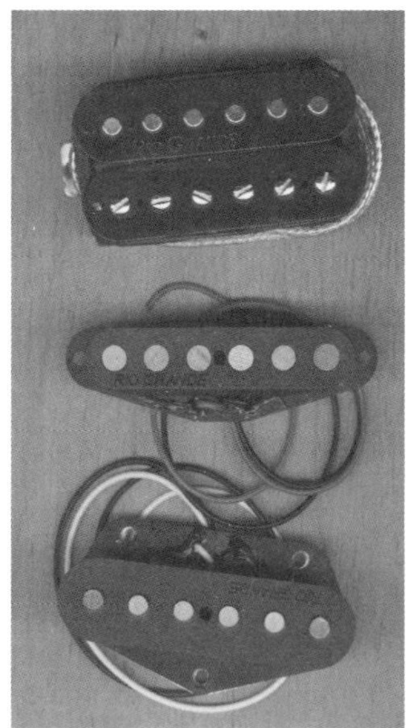

Rio Grande models: BBQ, Strat-style Muy Grande and Tele-style Tallboy.

The use of materials similar to those used on the originals and winding machines of that time, permits only a relatively limited production with a larger investment, which is duly reflected in the final price. The difference between models made using hand guided machines and calibrated magnets and those produced using more standardized techniques and materials is enough to justify the high cost for some musicians, but not for others. We must also remember that the better the quality of the guitar, the higher the possibility of appreciating the sonic benefits offered by the best pickups.

The high quality handcrafted products, characterised by hand guided windings and premium materials are not limited to copies of the classic models from the past. Joe Barden makes pickups with blade polepieces, windings in humbucking configuration, for an original, clean and crystal clear sound, with a medium high output level. The Red Push represent the maker's preference for sounds which are warm and rich in harmonics.

When the amplifiers were relatively simple and built to avoid distortion, rock players needed more powerful pickups to saturate their input and get a fat tone. Today, with amplifiers made with multiple gain stages, a high output pickup is not anymore a priority for most players, but a specialized tool for specific music styles. In recent years, the possibility to get an overdriven sound simply switching channels on the amp, turned many players to pay more attention to tone than pure power and the manufacturers answered offering almost any flavour desirable, from pure old style pie to hot peppered soup and everything in between.

We have a reference point for the copies of the old models, although uncertain due to inconsistencies. Beyond this field things become even more difficult.

To make comparisons easier, we can distinguish between different classes of pickups. For example, there are those inspired by vintage models for structure and general characteristics, with medium output, similar or a little louder than corresponding vintage models, those with increased output but with a sonic character not dissimilar to the first ones which usually have alnico magnets. Finally, there are those not aimed at reproducing the sound of the old ones, but created for an original timbre, often using ceramic magnets.

Some models are made using new technologies and original designs, but are aimed at producing timbre and output inspired to the vintage pickups. We call them medium output. Such models are the Fender Noiseless, the DiMarzio Virtual Vintage, Twang King (for Telecaster), the Blue Velvet, the Duncan Classic Stack and Nashville Studio, all made to replace single coil units. For the humbucker replacement there are the Gibson 490, the Rio Grande Genuine Texas, the DiMarzio PAF, Classic PAF, Air Classic, PAF Pro, the Duncan Jazz Model.

More powerful than vintage pickups, but still offering similar tone quality and which we will call medium-high output are the Fender Texas Special, the DiMarzio Pre B-1 and FS-1, the Duncan Custom for Telecaster and Stratocaster, the SSL-3 "Hot", the Red Push Single, the Rio Grande Vintage Tallboy. In the humbucker department we have the Gibson 498 the DiMarzio Norton and Air Norton, the Humbucker From Hell, the Duncan J. B. Model, the Custom Custom, the Screamin' Demon, the Fralin Overwound, the Rio Grande BBQ. All these models have more windings than vintage replicas but are made using Alnico 5 magnets for a traditional tone.

For the models with an output more than double than on vintage models, called high output, we can find Alnico pickups as the DiMarzio Tone Zone, the Red Push Humbucker, the Rio Grande Muy Grande Humbucker, the Duncan Quarter Pound single coils, but for very loud models the ceramic magnets are more common, as on the Gibson 500T, the DiMarzio Super Distortion, Evolution, X2-N, Duncan Distortion, Custom, most single coil-sized humbuckers.

Some manufacturers makes only a few models in each class, so it's not difficult to chose, Rio Grande, for instance, makes two Gibson-style models, the medium output Genuine Texas and the traditionally toned but very loud BBQ, but others, as DiMarzio or Duncan have so many models that things can become confusing.

Very important is to read very carefully the specs, but also the description and the output category (moderate, medium, high) or even better the output in millivolts, when available. The resistance alone can be misleading, as some models can have a very high value, like the DiMarzio Air Zone (17,49k), but to be actually less powerful than another showing a lower value, as, for instance, the Evolution Bridge (13,84k).

A higher resistance value does not always correspond to a louder output, as differences in wire gauges and magnetic flux as well as other structural details have to be considered.

When the difference in output is easily perceptible, as in the case of Rio Grande's Vintage Tallboy for Stratocaster compared to the much louder Muy Grande we can make decision according to our priorities about tone and power, but when the differences are more subtle, as between a DiMarzio PAF Pro or a FRED, choice would be more wisely made according to the desired timbre rather than their output level.

Other characteristics are far more important than the loudness, for example a Duncan Distortion and a DiMarzio Tone Zone both have screw polepieces, Gibson-style, the first with a ceramic magnet, the second with a alnico one. The Red Push humbucking has twelve cylindrical magnets in each bobbin, each couple inserted diagonally under each string. The Rio Grande Muy Grande humbucking and the Duncan Stag Mag have six magnets in each bobbin, the first

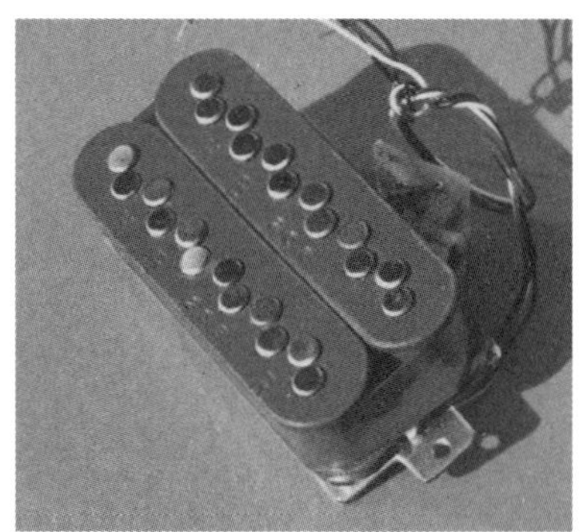

Red Push humbucker (Vincenzo Tabacco).

in alnico 5, the second alnico 2, the Wolfetone Fenris has alnico 2 magnets and blade polepieces and although these models share a similar output level, the timbre and distortion characteristics are very different.

The models for Telecaster or Stratocaster in humbucking configuration, such as the Duncan Stack, DiMarzio Chopper, "Virtual Vintage" and others of similar design, like the Fender Noiseless and the Kinman, are less bright than the original single coil models, so in order to approach their more open sound it is advisable to use potentiometers of a higher value than the stock 250 kOhm, such as 500 kOhm or even 1 MOhm.

The simple fact that a maker calls a model "neck" or "bridge" doesn't mean we cannot experiment with different positions. For example, we could install a Duncan "Jazz Bridge" near the fingerboard to obtain a little more punch than that available from the "Neck" model, and coupling it with a "J. B." model or a "Custom" near the bridge. To obtain a bright sound without harshness, we can place a DiMarzio "PAF" in the front position and a "Air Classic Neck" in the back. We don't have necessarily to couple an "Evolution Bridge" with the "Evolution Neck", to vary the timbre, we can put a "Humbucker From Hell" near the neck for single coil-like cleanness, or, for a warmer sound, a "PAF Classic" or a Duncan "'59 Model".

When both pickups are selected, some musicians prefer the sound of two units with similar outputs, others prefer a more powerful bridge position model to compensate for the decreased energy of the strings in that area. Above a certain point the more we increase the power, the more we sacrifice the timbre, with a premature cut of high frequencies. From this point of view the models with a medium-high output are more balanced. A relatively clean pickup, as proved by many old models, can have a big, open sound and a terrific tone in distortion, most high gain pickups are better when distorted, but lack lustre when used clean.

The characteristics of the amplifier are important too, as with high gain models it is not necessary to have very powerful pickups and a choice can be made based more on the quality of timbre. The pickup of the electric guitar is not, and does not pretend to be, a high fidelity device, therefore the relative balance between the reproduced frequencies is not everything (it can be efficiently modified using the amplifier's tone controls). Characteristics such as sustain, attack, and dynamics, are far more important than frequency response and are not disclosed by the aseptic technical specifications.

It is always best to consider that the pickups, the guitar lutherie, the characteristics of the amp and the loudspeakers are used as separate components of a single instrument, with the end result being the tone produced

by the sum of their qualities. The more evenly the chain is balanced, the better will be the resulting tone quality.
Speakers come in two general types, the low wattage ones, like most vintage speakers, which have a tendency to add their own distortion to the sound when played at high sound levels.

Jensen speaker on a '50s Fender Deluxe (Claudio Caldana).

The other type are the heavy duty. The first type is mostly preferred by blues and rock players. Generally these speakers have a power rating between 15 and 30 watt, but some 50 watt speakers are included in this category and some Celestion models can handle 70 watts. The most sought after speakers of this kind are the old Jensen used in vintage Fender, Gibson, Supro and Gretsch amps, just to name a few, and not forgetting the first 15 watt Celestion speakers used in vintage Vox amps, known as Bulldog and the Celestion G 12 "Greenback" used on several Marshall amps.

Jensen speaker on a '60s Supro (C. C).

The Heavy Duty speakers, able to handle 100 watts, such as the J. B. Lansing D 120 and similar models from Electro-Voice and others, are built to deliver a clean tone even at high sound levels, without adding any distortion of their own. They will reproduce the tone and the attack of the pickups with more fidelity, without break-up.
With these speakers a warmer sounding pickup may be preferable.

The technique of the musician has to be considered as well, as the same set-up will sound dramatically different if used by Jeff Beck, for instance, or Steve Vai. If a musician relies on long, sustained notes, Santana-style, a humbucking pickup would be preferable; for short, quick bursts of note, a bright single coil would be just the right pickup. The context is also important, as high output pickups are often better suited in small combos to obtain a bigger sound even with few instruments. When playing in an orchestra or a band with keyboards and horns, a relatively clean pickup, with a more extended range, can cut through better.

Jazz players, usually, are less inclined to modify their instruments, but eventually they decide that timbre is much more important than loudness, so it has to be expected that their preference would go toward models with a clean and warm sound, such as most PAF copies. Some musicians such as Tuck Andress, like the Bartolini models, others might find the "SH-2 Jazz" and the "APH-1 Alnico Pro" by Duncan sufficiently clear. Duncan also produces models designed by Bob Benedetto, a luthier specialized in the production of archtop guitars. The

Gibson ES 175 D, a model very popular among jazz musicians (Claudio Prosperini).

Duncan made Benedetto line consists of models designed to be mounted near the fingerboard of a guitar without having to put a hole on the table, such as the minihumbucking S-6. Other models produced as replacements for standard humbucking, like the A-6, the B-6 and the P. A. F., all have alnico magnets, and their specifications are: **S-6** - D. C. resistance 9,55 kOhm, inductance 3, 85 Henries. **B-6** - 12,10 kOhm and 7,10 H. **A-6** -11,84 kOhm and 5,76 H. **P. A. F.** - 8 kOhm and 4,56 H (higher inductance values suggests more power and a darker sound).
Some models designed for archtop guitar are also offered by Lindy Fralin.

No matter what kind of music is played, hard reality brings us to one conclusion. Direct experience, not always easy to achieve, is the only way to choose without making mistakes.
Catalogues can help our choice by restricting the field of those models which have technical specifications in line with our needs, but we first need to decide, whether we require a vintage or a hot model and then try to fine tune our choice through a careful scrutiny of the other characteristics.

As far as high class products are concerned the quality is guaranteed by the reputation of the brand, which is a hard gained position that nobody would like to jeopardize by introducing low level products. To choose a Fralin or a Duncan Antiquity is a matter of personal preference and the only way is to try them on the guitar after coming to an agreement with the retailer, where possible, to exchange it, if not satisfied after a short trial period.

The kind of music played and the style of the player create further elements which are important in the choice of a pickup. Gibson models from the fifties and some early Fender pickups were not waxed and some makers reproduce these characteristics, therefore if tone is priority, these models come much closer to the originals. However, if a musician plays at very high levels, with high gain amps, a waxed model might be preferable, especially if their command of the instrument is less than perfect, although this model causes some loss of nuances.

On some Duncan models the same plastic used on the originals is used for the copies, like the Antiquity humbucking and the Seth Lover, therefore waxing them is unadvisable because the bobbins would be damaged by the high temperature necessary for the process.

For small handcraft factories or single craftsmen the contact with the client is direct, based upon personal relationship and trust with the added advantage of obtaining a custom-made product. When looking for a product in a catalogue, on the internet or other kinds of communication, it would be wise to have assurance regarding the right to obtain a refund if not completely satisfied before ordering.

The replacement of one or more pickups is still the easiest way to customize a guitar and is always reversible if done wisely. These kind of components are influenced by many small and often unsuspected details such as the quality of the output cable, therefore the desired timbre improvement may contrast with the amount one is willing to spend. Before deciding to invest on a "boutique" model, it is important to estimate whether the instrument on which we would like to make the substitution has enough sonic qualities to fully exploit the subtleties offered by an excellent pickup. There are cheap Korean models on the market, and others with a good quality / price ratio. Many specialized products and high class items made using hand guided winding machines and with mainly handcrafted parts; in general the more we spend, the more we get. The competition is hard and prices are, after all, reasonably contained, even though they may sometimes seem excessive.

Of course those who are lucky enough to own instruments made before 1965, with mainly handmade pickups, will hardly feel the necessity for replacements, which is not advisable anyway because it would decrease the value of the instrument. However, for anybody owning a good quality guitar, fitted with mass produced but good quality pickups, and who decides to upgrade to a hand-wound model there is the opportunity to discover nuances never before thought possible.

2) Pickup adjustments

On the first pickups there was no possibility for adjustments and their relationship to the strings was decided by the maker of the instrument, but after the forties each model allowed for adjustments of a more or less subtle degree. According to the type and gauge of the strings, the playing style and the way the guitar was set up, it was sometimes necessary to change the factory adjustments and in case of replacement of the original units, of course, it was necessary to start from scratch.

On the Gretsch Filter'Tron is not possible to adjust the height of the unit, only the polepieces can be adjusted (Attilio Giacomini).

Models with magnets which are inserted directly in the winding, such as the Fender style units or humbucking models with a similar structure, and the Duncan Stag Mag or several Rio Grande models, can only have the overall distance from the strings and the inclination of the whole pickup adjusted.

It is important to find a good balance in order to have a strong enough signal, without reaching the point at which the attractive force of the magnetic field interferes with the vibration of the strings. Let's imagine that we have to amplify a singer's voice: if the microphone is too close to his mouth we'll get distortion, excessive sensitivity to sibilants and explosive "p". If however, we move it away a little the sound will improve and a further distance may produce a more natural and richer sound. If the microphone is too distant, the signal will be too weak.
If we substitute the guitar strings for the vocal cords and reason in millimetres instead of centimetres, substituting the instrument's resonant characteristics with the ambience of the room, the idea, we hope, will be clear.

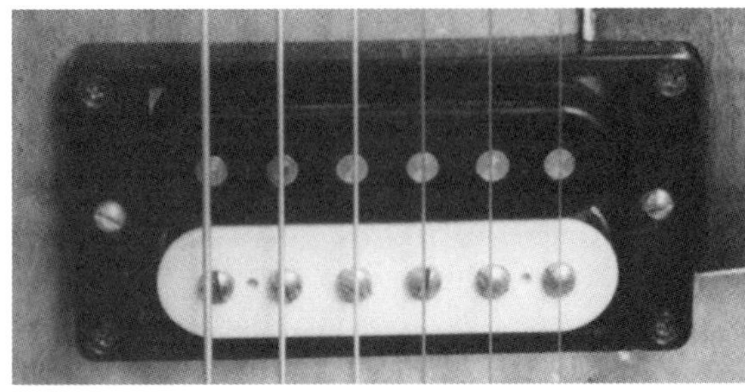

If the pickup has adjustable poles we can balance the output of the single strings and / or the general harmonic spectrum.

On Gibson style models one bobbin has adjustable screws, the other has fixed cylindrical polepieces.

On the first one, since the screws extend through the base, part of the magnetic field is directed toward the under side of the pickup and so the sensitivity is a bit lower than the other one. Adjusting the poles to protrude a little from the surface of the unit can help to balance the output, concentrating the magnetic field; if we adjust them closer to the strings we have an even more concentrated magnetic field, which is like focusing a camera. This gives a sound which is brighter but not as full; on most guitars the best tone is achieved by adjusting the polepieces following the curvature of the fingerboard, with the centre screws a little higher than the external ones.

The distance from the strings must be, in general, around mm. 2 for the treble strings and a little more for the bass strings, and more still for most humbuckers and other models with polepieces, such as the P 90.

For those that have magnets directly under the strings, it would be better to start with at least mm. 3 while maintaining a further distance for the bass strings. Then we can start to try with slight increments or decrements until we find the best balance between timbre, dynamics and output. If the magnets are powerful, such as ceramic magnets or full power Alnico 5, a slightly greater distance is required, weaker magnets, like Alnico 2, can be adjusted closer to the strings.

Some "Hot" models have really powerful magnets, to compensate for the decrease in treble due to the increased number of turns in the windings and they must be kept more distant from the strings. This method partially decreases the theoretically available power, sometimes we can get a louder sound with medium output models adjusted closer to the strings than with some overwound pickups that we have to keep lower because of their characteristics.

Adjusting unpotted models too close to the strings will give a louder sound but there are more possibilities of feedback. Feedback is a problem which already exists for semi-hollow guitars, therefore when using these models for loudness and distortion, it would be advisable to use potted pickups, although this would entail loss of nuances when playing clean.

One common mistake is to judge pickups by trying to adjust various models in the same way. Each one has it's own sweet spot and sometimes a pickup which may not sound as good as another, if adjusted in the same way, if set closer or further to the strings will have a much better tone.

On some pickups, such as the Telecaster bridge unit or some Guild and Ibanez humbuckers, the inclination to the strings can be adjusted, allowing more subtle nuances.

On the Telecaster lead pickup, three screws allow to adjust height and inclination of the unit (C. Caldana).

Most humbucker replacements are sold without a nickel cover, in order to reduce cost. Most players like their appearance, especially when they have cream bobbins, although the cover, which is intended to shield and protect them from moisture, has a slight effect on the sound, slightly reducing the magnetic flux and giving a softer, slightly rounder tone.
A wonderful sound is created by a balance of the maximum gauge of strings used, and individual playing style and technical abilities.

The bigger the strings, the more efficiently the magnetic field is stimulated to give a fuller tone.

The strings for an electric guitar have to be made from magnetic metals, in order to be affected by the magnetic field from the pickups. The alloy used to make them can have a great effect on tone. The unwound strings are made from stainless steel, the wound ones may have the outer windings made from pure nickel, nickel plated stainless steel or stainless steel, and each will produce a different sound. Pure nickel seems to give the fullest sound, stainless steel is brighter, while other materials are somewhere between these two.

Each brand has its own formula and even the actual diameter of the string can vary from a common nominal value. This means that two 010s from different brands can have a slight difference in actual thickness. The process used to make them and the alloy used to make some strings more elastic than others will probably produce a variation in sensitivity to the magnetic field. Therefore it's worth experimenting with different gauges and brands to find the best match for the pickups used.

Light gauge strings are more easily dampened by a strong magnetic field, so the finer the strings, the less the pickups need to be adjusted closer.

If light gauge strings are used when choosing a pickup, for a big sound, it is possible to select a higher resistance model. With heavy gauge strings a 7,8 kOhms PAF-style humbucker can sound good, but it is possible to have an equally fat sound with light gauge strings, using a model of the same kind with a resistance of 8,3/8,5 kOhms.

3) Pickups and lutherie

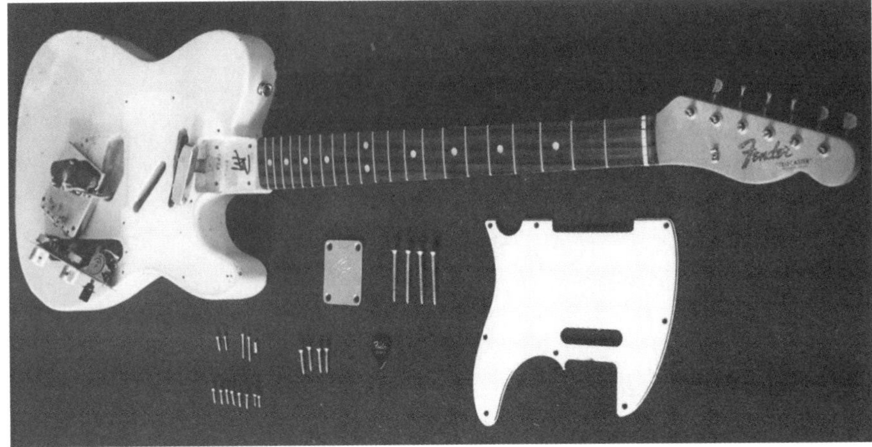

Even an excellent pickup with a strong sonic character, is not the sole determining factor for the final timbre of the instrument, which is due mainly to the materials from which the body and the neck are made, in a complex balance of each component.

The Gibson Les Paul: body and neck made from Honduras Mahogany and top carved from Michigan Maple (A. Angelucci).

The basic rule is that the more rigid the material, the higher is the frequency at which it resonates. This is as true for the parts made of wood as for those made from metal. For example, the harder the alloy used for the bridge and tailpiece, the brighter the sound, while with more weight the vibrations are transferred to the wood less quickly. Heavy tuning machines, with the added mass, can decrease the neck resonance.

Wood is a complex subject. Plants with very different characteristics are often called by the same name, such as mahogany, used for 200 types of plants (the Philippine mahogany, used on many oriental productions is not of the same family), some of which is suitable for making musical instruments, and others not; the same can be said about rosewood or ebony.

The weight is indicative, generally, of the rigidity and density of the material, higher values give more treble and sustain, while lower values give a warmer sound.

To list good quality wood, according to density, and starting with the softer ones, would give, in generic terms, these results: balsa, spruce, cedar, basswood, poplar, alder, mahogany, Philippine mahogany, maple, ash, rosewood, ebony.

Some examples of the weight of wood

Balsa (chromite in Gibson literature): can vary between 60 to 250 kg/m3.
Spruce: can weigh an average of 430-470 kg/m3. Sitka Spruce is lighter than European spruce and has a higher weight /strength ratio.
Poplar: is around 450 kg/m3.
Basswood and Alder: 430-450 kg/m3 with medium density.
Mahogany is not very rigid and weighs around 540 kg/m3.
Maple varies between 620-720 kg/m3, soft maple being the lighter and softer, rock maple the heavier and more rigid.
Rosewood is very rigid and weighs about 850 kg/m3.
Ebony is the stiffest and the heaviest of them all, reaching an average of 1030 kg/m3 and even 1190 kg/m3 with some species, depending on the region it comes from.

A greater rigidity gives a brighter sound, that's why the same pickup will have more treble and sustain on a guitar with an ash body, maple neck and ebony fingerboard and a warmer tone if fitted on a guitar with mahogany body and neck and rosewood fingerboard. All else being equal, the neck can shift the balance towards itself, therefore between two guitars with a mahogany body, one with a maple neck, the other with a mahogany neck, the first one will have a clearer sound. The same applies to fingerboards: one made from ebony gives more highs and sustain than one made from rosewood. The kind of fibre is important too, as an example, maple is less porous than rosewood and for that reason, although less rigid, generally, has a clearer timbre. On the same type of instrument less weight indicates more resonance, so if we have two instruments made from ash, the lighter one will sound warmer and fuller, the heavier one will have more sustain.

Shape and dimensions of the body, according to the amount and distribution of mass, have an effect on timbre (C. Prosperini).

Generally speaking very little importance, is given to the shape of the body of an electric guitar, although a wider body, will have a deeper low end than one made from the same wood but smaller or thinner.

The scale used for the fingerboard too has an effect on the sound, a long 25½" scale, as used on most Fender models and some Gibson Archtop such as the L-5 CES or Super 400, with its higher tension, makes the tone brighter and with a more pronounced attack. The shorter 24¾" scale, as used on Gibson Les Paul, ES 175, Fender Jaguar, has a smoother sound. Some makers, such as Danelectro

Components such as a Bigsby vibrato contribute to the tone of the instrument (C. C.).

and Paul Reed Smith, use an intermediate 25" scale, thus looking for a compromise between the two.

A neck made from different pieces of wood (generally three) is more rigid than a one piece neck and has a higher resonant frequency. To take advantage of the increased clarity, three piece maple necks are often used on high class electric archtop guitars, although not always desirable. Gibson used three piece maple necks on Les Paul guitars in the seventies, switching to three piece mahogany necks after a while and reintroducing, in the eighties, one piece mahogany necks, because too much high end in a solid body may produce a cold sound.

The way wood is cut is important too, and the most efficient method is flat cut, although in instrument making quarter sawn tables are preferable for increased resistance and more even figures. This applies especially for necks, where strength is a priority, however, for other applications, such as Les Paul tops, flat sawn and quarter sawn pieces are used according to availability and beauty of the figures (some customer like the more straight figures of quarter sawn tables, others the more wavy figures of flat sawn tables). Apart from aesthetic considerations, all else being equal, flat sawn timbers are supposed to sound warmer, quarter sawn ones slightly brighter.

Finish is another contributing factor to the timbre of the instrument, and depends on chemical composition and thickness. Nitrocellulose lacquer is the finish used on vintage instruments and still the favourite because, although difficult and expensive to apply, it allows the wood to breathe and age and is preferable for the best tone. Polyester finishes are easier and faster to apply, for mass production, but it is a bit like enclosing the wood in a plastic glove giving it less freedom to vibrate and especially reducing the higher frequencies. This gives the sound a somewhat dull and plastic-like character. Urethane and acrylic finishes are a little less rigid, and thus preferable for obtaining a more open sound. The nitrocellulose finishes of today have chemical additives to make them dry faster and remain more elastic thus avoiding the cracking seen on many vintage instruments. On some high end instruments the old formulas are still used, or so some makers state, but sometimes it appears to be too thick on otherwise well built instruments.

A resonant instrument is always desirable, but a good acoustic guitar, when amplified, can be used only at relatively moderate loudness otherwise the sensitivity makes feedback impossible to control. This is why most archtop electrics, such as the Gibson ES 175 and even some acoustic guitars fitted with piezo pickups have a laminated top, to reduce resonance and thus sensitivity to feedback. Solid top archtops, such as the L-5 or the Super 400 are intended for the purist musician who is looking for the best timbre and, presumably, playing at moderate volumes without distortion, but some use their tendency to feedback as an intentionally provoked sound effect. On some guitars the pickup is mounted near the fingerboard with a bracket to avoid cutting the top, this way preserving the acoustic tone of the instrument, usually a quality model with solid spruce top.

Gibson ES 120 and ES 125 T. The hollow body of these instruments can make the tone richer, but feedback can become a problem (C. Caldana).

With solid body guitars parameters are different and an instrument made from very rigid wood may sound harsh and be too heavy, which is the reason why Gibson chose to make the Les Paul by mixing the warmth and resonance of mahogany and the brightness and sustain of maple.
The reasoning was that using the stiffer timber only for the top would be enough to add high end without exceeding in overall weight.

Different systems of mounting pickups are used on solid body guitars, the most common being to mount the pickups suspended through screws and springs, so as to allow adjustment of the eight screws in relation to the strings, in a plastic ring as on Gibson style instruments or in a large pickguard as on Fender guitars.
Some pickups are screwed directly on the top, such as DeArmond pickups on some Gretsches, or at the bottom of the hole, such as the Telecaster neck model or the P 90s on original Gold Top Les Pauls.
Some musicians believe that fixing the pickup directly on wood, instead of suspending on a ring or pickguard, improves transmission of resonance and the resulting tone. This is why Eddie Van Halen even mounted humbucking pickups this way.

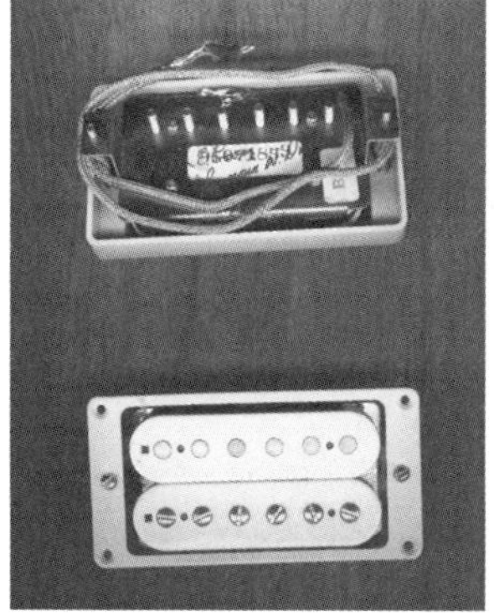

Mounting ring with elevating screws. Below an early sixties Gibson bridge-tailpiece (C. C.).

The bridge and tailpiece are also important. The more movable parts are involved, the less the sustain, so much so that the old one piece bridge-tailpiece introduced by Gibson in the fifties, although is missing the tuning adjustments available with more advanced bridges, is still popular and other makers, such as Paul Reed Smith, have introduced new versions of the same design.
Another element affecting tone is the material the nut is made from. Here too, stiffer materials favour high frequencies.

All these elements contribute to the tone of the instrument and the pickup simply amplifies it, which is why it doesn't matter how good a model is, it cannot improve a poor sounding guitar, if made from cheap wood and immersed in a thick polyester finish; even if it may sound like a paradox, an expensive pickup on a cheap guitar can bring into evidence deficiencies that the old less efficient units used to hide. A good pickup should add its own colour to the basic sound, exalting some harmonics and adding its personality, by changing the balance between middle and bass, cutting some of the high end and so on. It cannot however, add to the limitation of the guitar, and so the richer the basic tone, the greater scope for the pickup to work on.

The legendary tone of most vintage instruments is a happy balance between a good lutherie, a good pickup, plus the nuances added with time, use and general settling.

4) Electrical circuits

On some pots the value is on the top, on others on the side. Some are made with a switch and a push-pull mechanism to activate it.

Whether simple or complex, the electrical circuit will always somewhat change, the sound of pickups. The moment we insert a pickup into an electrical circuit, depending on the value of the potentiometers, the frequency at which the resonant peak is reached will be lowered and the brightness reduced proportionally as the value of the potentiometer is lower, so we should have a brighter and more open tone with 500 k potentiometers than with others with a value of 250 k.

A better quality potentiometer will give more sound preservation to a pickup, so we must remember this when comparing pickups on different guitars. The choice of value must be based on the power of the pickup.

With humbucking models and high output single coils, such as the P 90 or "Hot" Strat-style pickups it is generally preferable to use 500 kOhm potentiometers. However, with lower output pickups, such as most Fender models, which are already very bright, 250 k seems to be more suitable.
Other values used are 100 k (Danelectro) and 1 MOhm (Fender Telecaster from the seventies and DiMarzio Virtual Vintage). After 1974, Gibson used values of 300 k and 100 k.
Fender and Gibson have changed the values several times, while others, like Gretsch, Guild and Rickenbacker have maintained more stability.

Since the resonant peak is lowered, by inserting a hot pickup in the circuit, it would be preferable to use 500 k potentiometers instead of the 250 k usually fitted to Fender style guitars. This is true also for models similar to Fender style single coils, although humbucking, such as the DiMarzio HS, Duncan Stack and

Rails series, Kinman and others of the same kind, which in most cases have a resonant peak already lower than that of the originals they are supposed to imitate.

On some Yamaha Pacifica and G&L Legacy guitars the potentiometers are 500k for a brighter sound. Some models, such as DiMarzio's Virtual 2.1 for Strat style guitars and the Virtual T for Tele style guitars are designed to work with traditional 250k pots.

The sensitivity of the human ear to changes in sound level differs with each band of frequencies. Therefore potentiometers have been invented to reflect this same sensitivity, and are called Audio taper potentiometers (logarithmic pots). On a linear taper potentiometer, the value of the centre position is exactly half the nominal value, thus if it's 500 k, on a usual 0 / 10 scale, we will get 250 k at 5, but electrically speaking this is half of the original level. With logarithmic, or audio, potentiometers, we will get 250 k around the position corresponding to 7, whereas at 5 we have a lower value which is not the electrical 50%, but what we register as half as loud. Each brand uses a slightly different logarithmic curve, so the effect is slightly varied between potentiometers from different manufacturers. With linear potentiometers any change in volume or tone, seems to happen abruptly, that's why we think they don't belong to electric guitars, even though some makers use them. (There is always a technician, who usually doesn't play the guitar, ready to explain that linear pots are "better" than those which, as it happens, are called "audio").

A 1964 Gibson ES 335 TD, with humbucking pickups and 500k “audio” pots (Claudio Caldana).

Each of us has different ears, so one person may find the results more balanced in one brand than another. However, some very cheap pots are not well calibrated and most of the time the effect seems to occur only for a limited range. Some guitar makers use pots of a lower value than usual to obtain a softer and smoother sound, such as 300k or even 100k with humbucking pickups. It is preferable to have the best value fitted for each pickup's model and then if necessary adjust the tone controls. The only alternative solution is to change the settings of the amplifier.

Sometimes the value is not stamped, or not visible on the case of the potentiometer. However it is easy to measure and replace, if necessary, with one of the correct value.

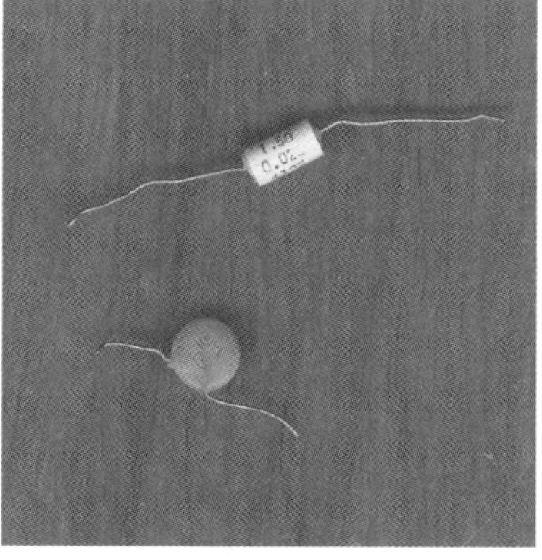

A simple experiment, which is easy and cheap to carry out, is to try different capacitors in the tone control circuit, buying different values for a few cents and replacing the stock ones with a slightly higher value for a darker sound, or a lower value for a brighter tone. Some people, on guitars with separate tone controls such as Gibson Les Pauls, use different values for the neck and bridge pickups (like a 0.033 MFD on the bridge tone control instead of the original 0.022).

It is important to make a clean job when soldering parts and to keep all the original parts in order to restore the original conditions if desired or if planning to sell the instrument.

Usually when lowering the guitar's volume control, the sound becomes darker and, in some cases, even dull. This is not a problem for some people, but for those desiring to keep a more open sound, a good trick is to connect, between the input and the output of the potentiometer a small capacitor of 0.001MFD, such as on post 1967 Telecasters. In this way the highest frequencies don't pass through the potentiometer and are unaffected, which is conceptually similar to the effect of using the bright switch on most vintage amplifiers. The effect is almost unnoticeable when at full volume, and increases gradually when it's turned down. With humbucking pickups the effect is less noticeable than with most single coils, so it may be necessary to experiment with different values to find the correct balance.

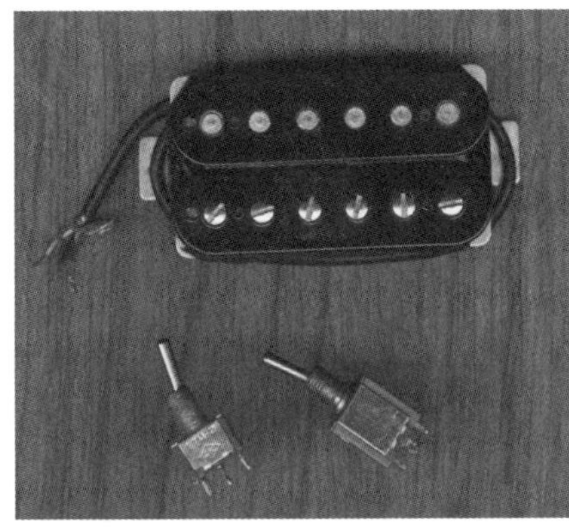

After the seventies the arrival of miniature switches and pickups fitted with four conductor output cables made it possible to obtain connections previously unavailable, widening the scope of available sounds.

On most single coil equipped guitars the units were connected in parallel, which is why when used together, such as in the middle position of a Telecaster or in positions two and four of a Stratocaster switch, the output became lower.

A miniature switch gives the option of a series connection producing a louder, fuller sound. This happens because two pickups of a resistance of 6 kOhm, connected in parallel, give 3 kOhm, while in a series connection the value becomes 12 kOhm.

Some "hot" models have three cables corresponding one to the full winding, another to a fraction of the winding, the last is earthed. Therefore if we have a resistance of 13 kOhm for the full power, we will have, lets say, 7 kOhm for the tapped output, with a brighter and thinner sound. Since the portion of the wire not selected is nonetheless present, and influences the inductance and resonant peak, the result is not exactly the same as using a pickup wound for only 7 kOhm. Taking into account also that in order to fit so many turns in the bobbin, a thinner wire is probably used, such as AWG 43 instead of the usual AWG 42, but for most applications the result is similar enough. In the full power position we have the same sound as a model with the same specifications but untapped.

In a humbucking pickup, for a resistance of 8 kOhm, two bobbins wound for 4 kOhm each are connected in series and out of phase. If we connect them in parallel, keeping them out of phase, we get 2 kOhm and a much clearer sound with reduced output while maintaining humbucking (the resonant peak increases too). By connecting one of the bobbins to earth we get 4 kOhm without humbucking effect.

Ibanez AR 300. A three position switch for each pickup allows to have single coil-like sounds or to put the two humbuckers out of phase when both are selected (C. Prosperini).

These solutions, which are very popular in achieving timbres similar to those of single coil models, have the limitation of low resistance compared to true single coils and their sound is thinner and shallower. A model with more turns in the winding, such as one reading 14 kOhm, would have an output with a resistance similar to that of a Fender single coil or even bigger (i.e. a 16 k humbucking split gives 8k). In this case a thinner wire is used, thus changing the parameters. In most humbucking pickups the magnet is a bar at the bottom of the unit with polepieces transferring the magnetic field toward the strings, while in most single coils the magnets are inserted directly into the winding, which also affects the tone.

Some humbucking models, such as the Rio Grande Muy Grande, the Red Push and Duncan's Stag Mag have cylindrical magnets in the bobbins and the same wire gauge as on Fender style single coils and when split have a similar sound. Used with both bobbins in series their timbre is different from normal Gibson style humbucking models, (a certain amount of compromise has to be accepted in single coil or in humbucking mode).
Another possibility is to connect two pickups out of phase with each other. In this way, when used together, some frequencies are cancelled, giving a more nasal sound, with less bass and a slightly lower output (resistance reading is the same as in phase connection).

To effectively use four conductor pickups is necessary to remember that every maker has a different code to identify output cables.

Since a humbucking pickup is made with two bobbins in series, with opposite magnetic and electric polarity, the same principle is used on some three pickup guitars, to avoid excessive noise when the switch is in the combined position(such as two and four in a Stratocaster).

By mounting a unit with inverted magnetic and electric polarity in the centre position, and playing with the centre pickup coupled with any of the other two, we will get the humbucking effect. Since the connection remains in parallel, the original sound is almost totally preserved.

To obtain rejection of hum with only two positions out of five may seem a small improvement, unless the player uses only those positions. This system however, is now very popular and several guitar models arrive straight from the factory with a reverse wound centre pickup and with reverse polarity.

1967 Gibson ES 345 TD Stereo with Varitone (C. Prosperini).

The more complex the circuit, the more important it is that all the included parts are of very good quality, from switches to potentiometers, from capacitors to cables.

With active circuitry, since the pickups are low impedance, the potentiometers are of a lower resistance, most often 50 k, and of the linear type; in this case too it is important to use high quality components to maintain the noise level as low as possible, especially hiss.

While it is still possible to fit active circuitry on a guitar with high impedance pickups, using specifically designed circuits, it is impossible to use these pickups with active circuits designed to work with low impedance units.

After the seventies, switches have become available for out of phase connections, to cut one of the bobbins in humbuckers and to produce single coil type sounds.

Even before that, filters were used which comprised of several resistors and capacitors connected to a rotary switch gradually changing the tone of the pickups, as on the Gibson Varitone.

The purpose is always to increase the versatility of the instrument, but it would be wise to decide on priority (purity of tone or versatility), considering that the most simple circuit looses less sonic quality.

Each component, such as a switch, a potentiometer, even a short wire, has its own capacity, however small, which acts like a small capacitor, filtering the signal, and each time we add something it is like increasing its value by filtering a larger portion of the signal.

It is important to remember that when installing components a clean and well executed soldering, avoiding any excess, is essential in obtaining not only a more stable and durable connection, but also a better sound.

When working on a guitar circuit, it is better to use low power and a small pencil-type soldering iron, as a soldering gun can damage the pickups.

5) How to modify and build a pickup *by Giovanni Gaglio*

A pickup may look fairly complex, but as it's assembled in various forms with a number of factory made components, it is not that difficult to replace, modify or repair and even to make your own. Other simpler looking parts, such as volume and tone knobs, which are just plastic pieces, on the contrary have to be made by a specialized factory.

Let's start with some simple operations.

One of the most common modifications made to humbucking pickups, which became fashionable due to some rock musicians in the sixties, such as Clapton and Beck, is to remove the cover in order to improve the sound or the appearance.

Here is some useful advice for avoiding most common mistakes.

1) Pickup covers, like those made by Gibson, Ibanez and others, are usually soldered in two points. Rather than try to unsolder them, it is better to cut the solder using a very sharp blade, such as a Stanley knife. If the unit is waxed it is possible, using a hair drier at maximum power, to heat it thus making the operation easier. Difficulty, from 1 to 10: 3/5

2) Some of the Gibson pickups which can pose a different problem, are those that look like a black circuit board on the base: the wire from the bobbins is soldered directly to little tips on that base and any slight movement can break the fine wire. To add to this problem, there is a very strong bi-adhesive tape which holds the cover firmly on the bobbins. Even an expert will have difficulty avoiding damage to the unit. Difficulty: 10

3) Plastic covers, which are only inserted to protect the wiring, as on the Stratocaster style units, are very simple to remove and refit the pickup on the guitar after protecting the delicate wire with masking tape. Difficulty: 1 or 2.
If the covers are filled with resin, and more or less rigid, as on EMG, Gotoh, Gibson Super Humbucking, Bill Lawrence and others, the operation is impossible, it doesn't matter how experienced the person is.

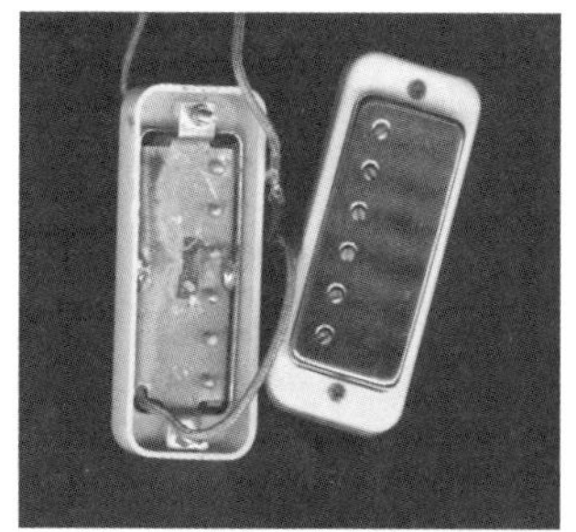

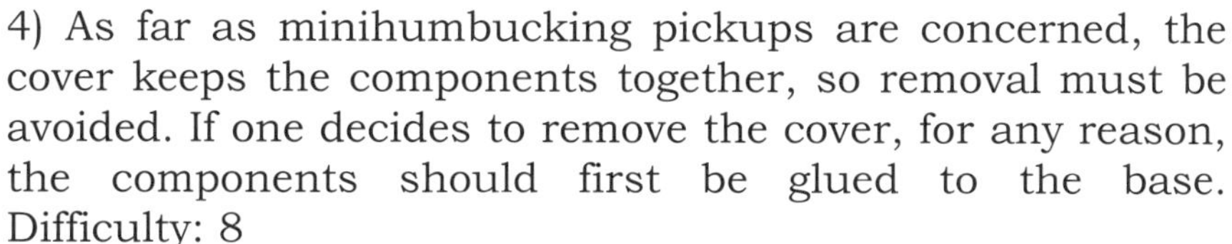

4) As far as minihumbucking pickups are concerned, the cover keeps the components together, so removal must be avoided. If one decides to remove the cover, for any reason, the components should first be glued to the base. Difficulty: 8

5) The neck pickup on a Telecaster has a small cover with three little tongues on the bottom bent around the base. One of them is soldered to the earth wire, and if removed

would probably result in one of the tongues touching the wire and cutting it. Difficulty: 7

Always remember that covers are put on pickups not only for aesthetic reasons, but to shield it and to protect the wiring, so it is possible, by removing it, to perceive an increase in noise. When playing, one must avoid hitting the bobbins with the pick, as the thin tape surrounding the wiring is not always a sufficient protection. On the other hand removing the cover can decrease the risk of feedback when playing very loudly.

Very important! When removing a pickup from the instrument NEVER unsolder the wire from the pickup, but only on the other side, where it's connected to a switch or a potentiometer. If it is difficult to reach that point, as on semi acoustic guitars, it is necessary to be very patient and remove the potentiometers from the F hole or the pickup cavity and then fit them back very carefully.
Some more impatient people, as an extreme solution, cut the cable half way and then solder the new one to the remaining part, insulating the junction with insulating tape. This is really not the best way to do it and in any case one should never try to unsolder the cable near the pickup.

With single coil units, such as the Fender models, the magnets should never be pushed down, as is often done to staggered units to make them flat, as the wire is wound around them and is very easy to break. Some have tried this experiment with no repercussions, but only because they've been lucky. It is really unadvisable to try it.

Even though it may sound strange, repairing a pickup is more difficult than making one from scratch; in this case, indeed, we cannot experiment, but we must know the kind of wire and, even more important, the number of turns in the wiring. On humbucking pickups things are even more difficult because there is no standard colour code or connection and some commercial units are very difficult to take apart. They are made in such a way, as if it was presumed they would never need a repair.

A last important piece of advice: any experiment, replacement, modification, must be avoided on old instruments, of historical interest or value.
Once the damage is done it is irreparable and another piece of our past is gone forever.

To make a homemade pickup is not impossible.

Obviously it is necessary to have some manual ability: do you know how to repair a motor scooter carburettor or a light switch? If the answer is yes you can build a pickup.

The first thing is to find the material for the structure, or the bobbin, any insulating material is suitable: plastic from a tomato box, cardboard and so on, which can be hardened by glue, such as Superglue.

Magnets of different shapes can be bought in a ironmonger's shop: magnetic locking, tool-holder, fridge magnets, and even a refrigerator magnetic gasket are suitable (I hope you won't take it apart from a new refrigerator!). For better magnets it is possible to refer to an antitheft company, as the cylindrical magnets they use are perfect.

Of course it is always possible to ask a repairman for a broken pickup, usually for little money or even for free, thus obtaining the raw material, wire excluded. In this way you will only reproduce something which already exists, but it would be much more exciting to make something completely on your own.

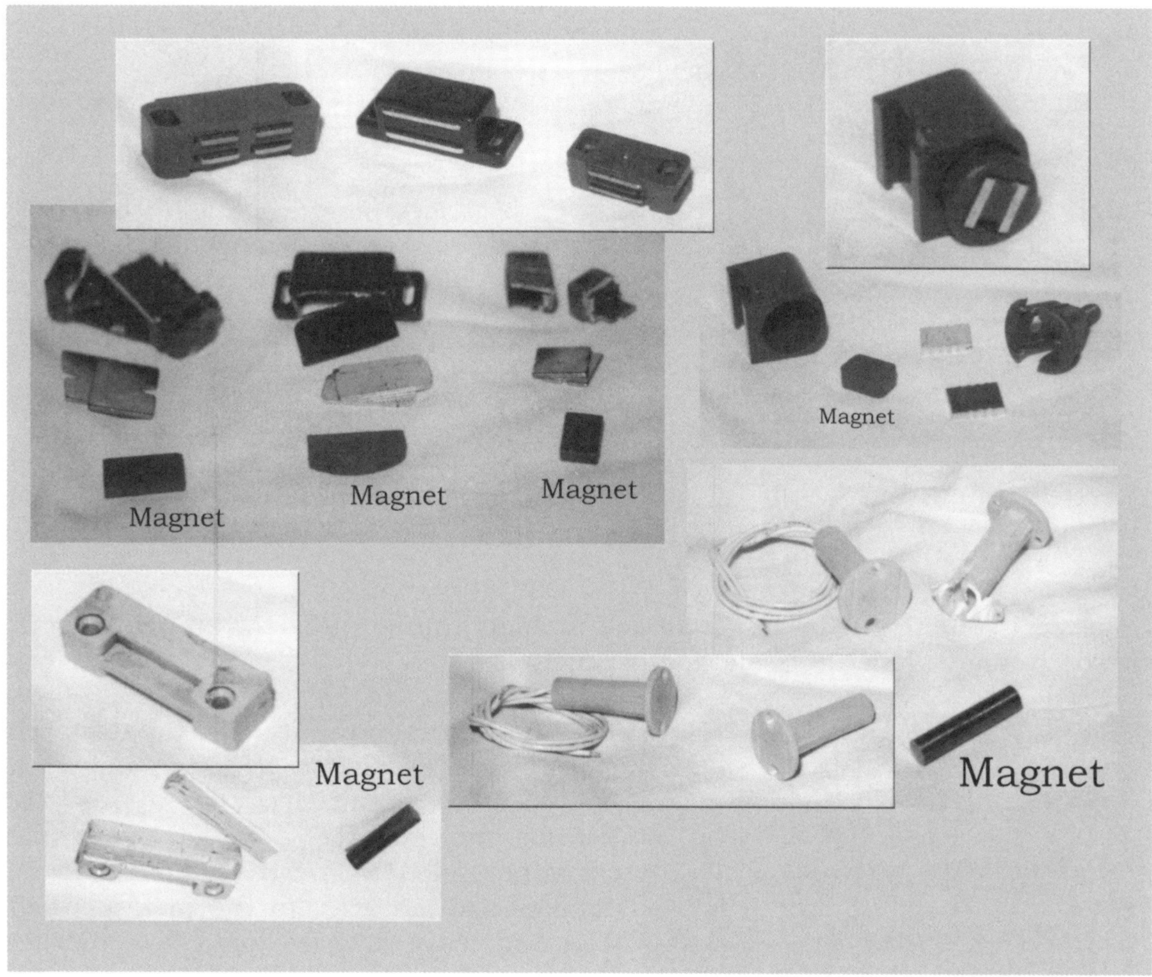

The wire, unfortunately, cannot be bought in small quantities, and it is better to look for transformer winding companies and ask the boss if he can sell you a small rocket of wire (it's sold by weight and two or three hectograms should be enough), with gauges AWG 43 or 42 (approximatley mm. of 0,05 or 0, 063).

On a pickup there are an average of grams 25 / 35 of wire, so with the quantity mentioned above many experiments can be carried out.

How to make the winding? To make a pickup work, it is necessary to wind at least 4000 turns (a Stratocaster pickup has twice as much). Therefore in order to avoid a nervous breakdown it is best not to do it by hand, but to fix the bobbin to a record player, a hand whisk, or a hand drill, provided they have a speed control. If the wire breaks don't worry (it will happen often the first few times), you can solder it and continue winding.

Luckily modern wire can be soldered without problems, and it is not necessary to scratch the insulation as on old style wire. The soldering iron is just hot enough to melt the lacquer and solder at the same time.

The first attempts will probably be frustrating, but don't give up, you could well be a new DiMarzio.

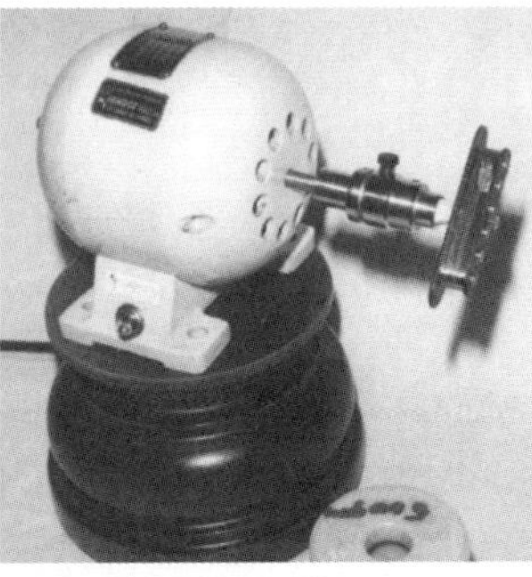

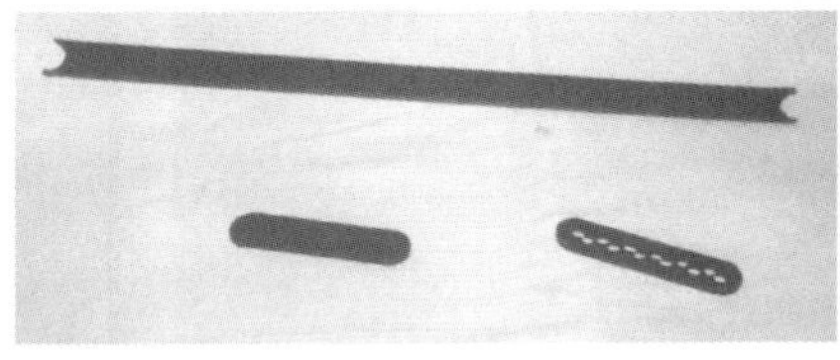

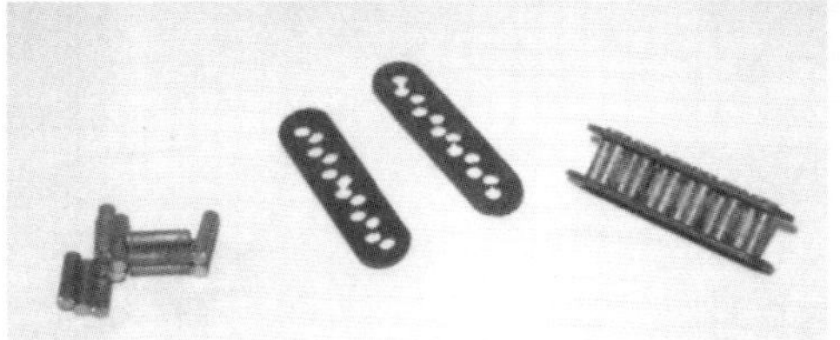

A pickup is often sensitive to feedback at high volume playing, and this occurs with both home made units and factory models.

A miniaturized PAF copy hand made by Giovanni Gaglio and perfectly working, compared to a standard size Gibson humbucker (C. Prosperini).

The solution is to dip it in wax (potting), by melting some candles in a pot using the hot air from a hair dryer or, if preferred, leaving the pot for a while in another container filled with hot water. When the candles are melted, dip the pickup in the wax and leave it there for a few minutes, just to allow the winding to absorb the paraffin. When dry it will solidify and stop the wire from vibrating thus reducing the insurgence of feedback.

A pickup becomes "microphonic" with an excessive vibration of the wire, especially if wound a bit loose. This makes the unit to "howl" when played loud and too close to the amplifier.

Before waxing a commercial model it has to be remembered that some old Gibson pickups were made with a kind of plastic (butyrate) which tends to shrink or bend if exposed to heat. The same applies to some reissues, on which the same material is used.

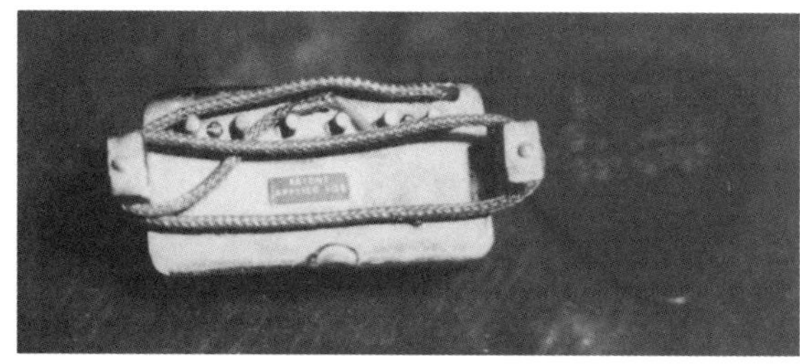

A scaled down PAF needs a scaled down label... (Claudio Prosperini).

Most modern models, however, are made to be waxed, and a more resistant plastic is used. In case of doubt consult a luthier.

On the right an example of how the magnetic flux can be extended through a nail used as a polepiece. The magnetism runs across the nail which so becomes able to attract the coin. The same way the polepieces in a pickup are used to transfer the magnetic field from the magnet on the bottom of the unit toward the strings.

Of course there is a lot more to say about pickup making and our description could continue further, but that would go beyond the purpose of this writing. If only a few readers are stimulated to experiment, it would give the writer sufficient satisfaction.

All the photographs on this chapter are from Giovanni Gaglio, unless otherwise credited.

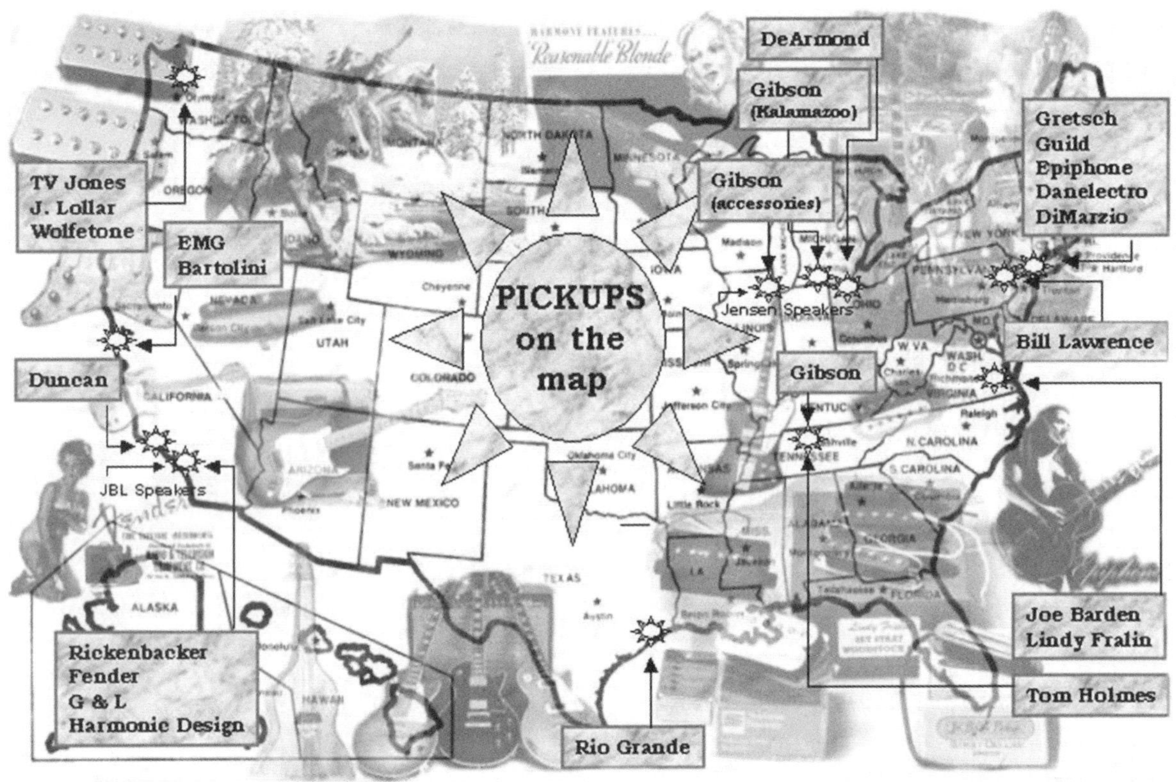

Pickup makers in USA

Actodyne
Lace-Music Products
5561 Engineer Dr.
Huntington Beach, CA 92649
Tel.: 714-898-2776
Fax: 714-893-1045
www.agi-lace.com
info@lacemusic.com

Bartolini Pickups & Electronics
Tel.: 925-449-7692
www.bartolini.net
Sales: T. J. Wagner
P. O. Box 129
Flagler Beach, FL 32136

Bill Lawrence Designs
Bethlehem, Pennsylvania.
Moved to 1785 Pomona Rd, Unit D
Corona, CA 92880 since august 2003.
Tel: 951-371-1494
Fax: 951-371-9191
www.billlawrence.com
Becky@billlawrence.com

Danelectro
P. O. Box 73010
San Clemente, CA 92673
Tel.: 949-498-9854
Fax: 949-369-8500
www.danelectro.com

Original Factory
Red Bank, New Jersey.
Moved to 207 W. Sylvania Avenue
Neptune City, New Jersey
(1959-1968)
The new Danelectro Company produces reissues of the original instruments and new models, inspired to the same philosophy but with updated features, made in the Far East.

DiMarzio
1388 Richmond Terrace
P. O. Box 100387
Staten Island, NY 10310
Tel.: 800-221-6468
718-981-9286
Fax: 718-720-5296
www.dimarzio.com

EMG
P. O. Box 4394
Santa Rosa, CA 95402
Tel.: 707-525-9941
www.emginc.com

Epiphone
Division of Gibson M. I.
645 Massman Drive
Nashville, TN 37210
Tel.: 615-871-4500
www.epiphone.com

Original Factory
68 West 39th Street (1923) New York, moved to Wilburn Avenue in 1925 and to 142 West 14th Street in 1935.
In 1957 Gibson acquired the brand and made instruments with the Epiphone brand in Kalamazoo until 1969.
Then the Epiphone name was used on instruments produced in Japan by the Matsumoku Company.
Production moved to Korea in 1983.
Selected models are again produced in USA since 1995.

Fender
Fender Musical Instruments Corporation
Attn: Consumer Relations Dept.
8860 E. Chaparral Road, Suite 100
Scottsdale, AZ 85250
Tel.: (480) 596-7195
Fax: (480) 367-5262
www.fender.com
consumerrelations@fender.com

Original Factory, 1946
South Pomona Avenue, Fullerton CA.
Distribution by R&TEC, 207 Oak Street, Santa Ana.
In 1953 was founded the Fender Sales Company, still in Santa Ana, manufacturing moved to a new factory in South Raymond Avenue, Fullerton.
Administration moved to Brea in 1985 and then to Scottsdale, Arizona, in 1991.
Production, since 1985, is carried out in a new factory in Corona, CA.

Fralin Pickups
2015 West Laburnum Avenue
Richmond, VA 23227
Tel.: 804-358-2699
Fax: 804-358-3431
www.fralinpickups.com

G & L
2548 Fender Avenue
Fullerton, CA 92831
Tel.: 714-897-6766
www.glguitars.com

Gibson Guitar Corp.
1818 Elm Hill Pike
Nashville, TN 37201
Tel.: 615-871-4500
Fax: 615-889-3216
www.gibson.com
Accessories (strings, pickups etc.)
1150 Bowes Road
Elgin, IL 60123
Tel.: 1-800-544-2766
Fax: 1-847-741-4644
strings@gibson.com
Custom, Art and Historic Division
657 Massman Drive Nashville, TN 37210
Tel.: 615-871-4500
Fax:615-871-9517

Original Factory
"Gibson Mandolin-Guitars Manufacturing Co." 1917-1984:
225 Parson Street
Kalamazoo, MI
(some guitars made in Nashville since 1975)

Gretsch
FMIC Specialty Sales
8860 East Chaparral Road, Suite 100
Scottsdale, AZ 85250
Phone: 480-596-9690
custserve@fender.com
www.gretschguitars.com

Original Factory
60 Broadway,
Brooklyn 11, New York, (1916-1972).
Baldwin bought Gretsch in 1967 and moved production to Booneville, Arkansas, in 1972. During the eighties other changes occurred and finally, in 1985, Fred Gretsch jr., nephew of the original founder, bought back the company and introduced, with help from Duke Kramer, in 1989, guitars made by Terada in Japan. A deal signed on January 2003 gives distribution duties to the Fender Corporation. The first electric guitars, introduced in 1939, used Gretsch-made pickups, but since 1949 had units built by **Rowe-DeArmond** of Toledo, Ohio, until the introduction of the Gretsch Filter'Tron model designed by Ray Butts.

Guild
Distributed by Fender

Original Factory
1952-1956
536 Pearl Street,
New York
1956-1966
300 Observer Highway
Hoboken, New Jersey
Pennsylvania
Then moved to Westerly, Rhode Island.
Now is part of the Fender family.

Harmonic Design Pickups
325 Jefferson
Bakersfield, CA 93305
Tel.: 661-322-2360

J. M. Rolph Pickups
Tel./Fax: 859-781-9334
www.cindernet.net/rewinder
rewinder@cinternet.net
rewinder@juno.com

Joe Barden Engineering
9161 Key Commons Court
Manassas, VA 20110
info@joebarden.com

Lollar Guitars
P. O. Box 2450
Vashon, WA 98070
Tel.: 206-463-9838
www.lollarguitars.com
info@lollarguitars.com

Rickenbacker
3895 S. Main Street
Santa Ana, CA 92707
Tel.: 716-545-5574
www.rickenbacker.com

Original Factory
6071 S. Western Avenue
Los Angeles, CA
Moved to Kilson Dr,
Santa Ana (1962 – 1989).

Rio Grande Pickups
3526 East T. C. Jester Blvd
Houston, TX 77018
Tel.: 713-957-0470
Fax: 713-957-3316
www.riograndepickups.com

Seymour Duncan
5427 Hollister Avenue
Santa Barbara, CA 93111-2345
Tel.: 805-964-9610
Fax: 805-964-9749
www.seymourduncan.com
tech@seymourduncan.com

Tom Holmes
P. O. Box 414
Joelton, TN 37080
Tel.: 615-876-3453

TV Jones Guitars
P. O. Box 2802
Paulsbo, WA 98370
www.tvjones.com
info@tvjones.com

Van Zandt Pickups
205 Robinson Rd
Combine, TX 75759
Tel.: 214-476-8844

Voodoo Pickups
Peter Florance
P. O. Box 328
Honesdale, PA 18431
Tel.: 570-253-1475
www.peterflorance.com
sales@peterflorance.com

Wolfetone Pickups
223 N 143rd Apt. A
Seattle, WA 98133
Tel.:206-417-3548
www.wolfetone.com
wolfetonepups@earthlink.net

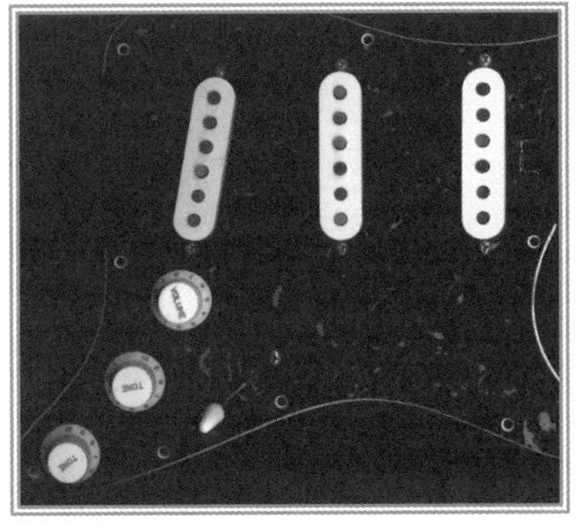

Part 4 - Famous models

Rickenbacker "Horseshoe" and "Toaster"

Designed by George Beauchamp, with help from Paul Barth, the "Horseshoe" pickup, so called for the distinctive horse-shoe shape of its magnets, was made with 5000 turns of AWG 38 wire around six polepieces and two big tungsten magnets surrounding the winding from the base and extending on top. The strings passed through the centre (between the polepieces and the superior extension of the magnets).

In this structure, the magnetic field completely surrounds the strings, but being of moderate density, as opposed to that of modern magnets. Having a lesser attraction, it does not interfere with the vibration of the strings, and therefore gives good sustaining properties. The polarity toward the strings is south. The resulting wide magnetic window guarantees a full sound, while the pickup position near the bridge naturally favours high frequencies, with a very balanced timbre, clear but fat.

Combo 800 c. 1955/56 Combo 800 c. 1957/58

Combo 400, 1957

Pictures courtesy of Rickenbacker

Conceived to amplify the lap steel which musicians soon lost interest in, the pickup was then used on several Rickenbacker guitars and basses. The first units were made in 1931. In 1932 Beauchamp applied for a patent, but it was such a novelty that it was difficult to determine whether it belonged to the electronic devices section or the musical instruments section (it was unexpected to combine the two things).

In 1934 the request was presented again with more details, but was accepted only after a Hawaiian band performance, which it is rumoured played with Sol Hoopii himself, convinced the officer that the system would work.

During the thirties and the forties several versions of the Horseshoe were offered, one of which, with smaller magnets, was sold as an aftermarket unit suited to amplify acoustic archtops. After Leo Fender's instruments appeared, the technical specifications were changed in order to obtain a brighter sound, even though most musicians didn't seem to like the results and the older units from the thirties were much more sought after.

A new version was installed on the guitar Combo 800 in 1954; hiding two selectable windings under the big magnets, one for a brighter sound, the other emphasising basses; with both selected on, the pickup was humbucking. Strangely Rickenbacker didn't apply for a patent on the system and the horseshoe disappeared from guitars in 1959. It was used on lap steels up to 1971 and on basses up to 1964 (1966 for exported models).

"Toaster" pickup on a 1967's Rickenbacker Model 1998, a version of the Capri 345 for the European market. (Claudio Prosperini).

In 1957 a new pickup model was introduced, with a more traditional look, at first with a black cover. After October of the same year it had a chrome cover showing two openings on top giving it the appearance of a toaster, hence the name by which it is still known. The new unit was made with six Alnico magnets around which was wound a very fine AWG 44 wire, which was a traditional gauge for Rickenbacker and is still used today. Old units had a resistance ranging from as low as 7 kOhm up to 16 kOhm.

The "Toaster" pickups have a clear sound which is distinctive in many famous recordings from the Beatles, the Who, the Byrds, Paul Weller with the Jam, Tom Petty, Johnny Marr with The Smiths, Peter Buck from R. E. M. and many contemporary bands.

In 1970 it was substituted with a new model, the High Gain, with ceramic magnets, and at the same time a short lived humbucking pickup was offered for some guitar models.

In 1988, a humbucking pickup was introduced, for a "Signature" John Kay guitar model, it had samarium-cobalt magnets, and was also used on the series 600 guitars. After 1984 the "Toaster" was reintroduced and is still produced, using the same specification as the originals and with a resistance of 11 kOhms (the value is based on the average measurements taken on several original pickups).

Some musicians contend that several sixties pickups had fewer turns and used to take out some of the winding on the new units in order to get the brighter sound of those under-wound samples. However we find today's Rickenbacker pickups to be very good reissues and with the right Vox AC30 it is easy to reproduce the classical sounds of the Beatles or the Byrds.

The Horseshoe too was reintroduced after 1984, but for bass only and with ceramic magnets.

The newer models, such as the "Toaster" and the "High Gain", have a distinctive clear sound, never too thin, and without harshness, but to most musicians the name Rickenbacker means Horseshoe and that model will always be related to the lap steel, for which many still think of it as the best. Recent faithful reissues of the Horseshoe are the Aiello/Lollar version and one available on special order from the Seymour Duncan Custom Shop.

The "Toaster" will always be connected with some of the most famous British bands, such as The Beatles, The Who and to California sixties rock, thus it's place in history is assured. The tone of the "Toaster" is still appreciated as one of the most distinctive sounds available. Totally different from those of Gibson and Fender pickups, although not as popular as in the sixties, it still provides subtle textures on many records, plus it is produced by a factory which makes the most eye-catching and original guitars on the market.

The Gibson Bar pickup, a. k. a. "Charlie Christian"

Rickenbacker's success pushed Gibson to research for his own solution to the problem of guitar amplification, which at this point could no longer be delayed. Gibson too started with the Hawaiian guitar, entrusting the job to John Kutalek, engineer at Lyon & Healy, a Chicago company well experienced in the field. Alvino Rey, a well known Hawaiian specialist was hired as consultant.

After months of experiments and at least one prototype, still owned by Rey, the realization of a commercially suitable unit seemed to still be out of reach, so the job was passed on to Walter Fuller, a Gibson employee, who had to find a solution original enough not to infringe Rickenbacker's patent.

The result of Fuller's work was a pickup with the wire wound around a blade polepiece with two big magnets on its base. At first the magnets were made from an alloy consisting of iron and nickel, while the winding was made from AWG 38 wire (mm. 0,1107) with low resistance. In 1937, when the Gibson model was finally "patent applied for", the alloy was iron and cobalt (36%) and the wiring was later changed to 10000 turns of the thinner AWG 42 wire (mm. 0,063) for an average resistance of 8 kOhms (20% +/- tolerance), values which became standard for Gibson pickups up until the sixties.

By the end of the thirties two models were offered, one for high level guitars, with magnets having a percentage of 36% cobalt, one for cheaper instruments with only 17% cobalt in the magnets, while the winding remained the same for both versions. One version had a single blade polepiece under the bass strings, notched to appear as three smaller blades under each of the high strings and was fitted to the EH 150 lap steel. The other had a single blade polepiece and was standard equipment on the ES 150 guitar.
A later version with six mini blades as polepieces was mounted on the fancier ES 250 guitar.

The two magnets, slightly smaller on the guitar version, were placed horizontally, with one of the smaller sides touching the polepiece, and extending on the other

Reissue of the Gibson Bar pickup made for the ES 175 CC (Claudio Prosperini).

side under the guitar top with three screws allowing small adjustments for slight changes in timbre.

The amplifiers, for lap steels and guitars, were built by Lyon & Healy. Together with the ES 150, the pickup became a classic fairly rapidly in the hands of jazz and blues musicians, such as Charlie Christian, T-Bone Walker, Barney Kessel, who used the pickup on a ES 350 P, and continued using it faithfully for many years.

It was also used by Tony Mottola, Mary Osborne and Alvino Rey, who had two units on his ES 250.

After the Second World War the powerful and gutsier P 90, became the standard fitting on all Gibson guitars up until 1955, when it was replaced on high level instruments by the Alnico pickup and later by the humbucker.

The success of the bar pickup brought Gibson to the top of the expanding electric guitar market. Due respect for this model is testified by the fact that, despite the introduction of new models, with which Walter Fuller tried to eliminate problems such as the sensitivity to hum, guitar players like Jimmy Raney, Oscar Moore and Barney Kessel continued to use it during the fifties. Gibson continued to produce it on special order for the next two decades and in 1977 a version of the model was reissued for the limited edition ES 175 CC guitar. Today Jason Lollar offers a replica made with Alnico 5 magnets and the Duncan Custom Shop makes copies of the original on special order.

Rowe-DeArmond 200 (Dynasonic)

Lovers of Gretsch guitars are equally divided between those who like the Dynasonic and those who prefer the Filter'Tron. The Rowe-DeArmond single coil became standard equipment on guitars made by the famous Brooklyn-based factory in 1950. Gretsch named it Fidelatone and later Dynasonic, which is the name by which it is known today. It became as important for those guitars, made famous by the likes of Duane Eddy and Chet Atkins, as the P 90 was for Gibson. The debate concerning these pickups and the Filter'Trons is very similar to that between fans of the Gibson P 90 or P. A. F. models.

The Dynasonic is made by winding about 9000 turns of AWG 44 wire around six cylindrical Alnico magnets, for a resistance of 10 / 12 kOhms, and has a clever system to adjust the height of each magnet. By slipping each magnet into a metallic cylinder fixed to the base of the pickup, under the coil, to which a screw is threaded, it is possible to move the cylinder up or down therefore adjusting the magnets closer or further from the strings.

The cylinders are actually open on one side and then tightened around the magnets, and this can cause them to become loose in time. The Dynasonic, fitted to the top of the guitar, cannot be adjusted as a whole, thus making the possibility to adjust the single magnets more important. Their dimensions make it impossible to fit them to guitars without pre-designed slots, unless the cavity is modified.

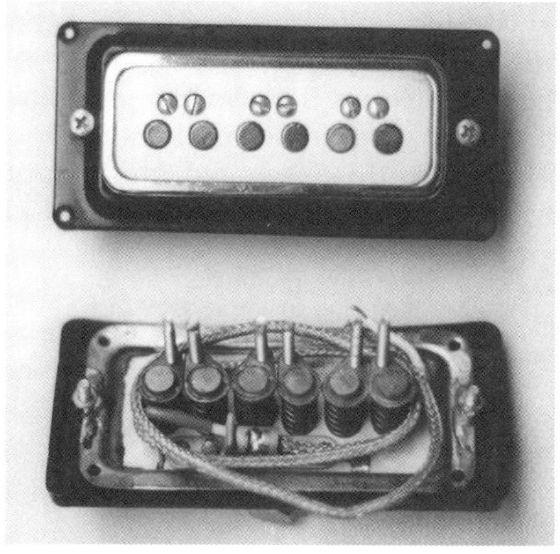

DeArmond M 200 with white top, as used by Guild (Claudio Caldana).

The voice varies from one unit to another. Some have a muffled sound, decidedly limited on higher frequencies, a bit boxy, while others have a sweet and clear high end. The better ones have a good balance between a strong attack on lower strings, the celebrated "twang", a clear middle range and round, sweet trebles.

By the end of the fifties other makers such as Guild used this pickup on their guitars, but gave it a white top instead of the black one as used by Gretsch. Encouraged by Chet Atkins, then consultant for a series of guitars, Gretsch adopted the new humbucking Filter'Tron models designed by Ray Butts. These were similar in concept to the Gibson humbucking, but had a larger magnet and a resistance of about 4 kOhms for a much clearer sound, and gradually substituted the Dynasonics. Fender then produced the 2k, a reproduction looking very similar to the original but with a bar Alnico magnet and cylindrical polepieces. Gretsch had his own reissues, built in Korea, while a good "boutique" version is available from the Duncan Custom Shop.

Fender Telecaster

The bridge model

The pickup conceived by Leo Fender for his first guitar was disarming in its simplicity, yet cleverly designed and very effective. Two black vulcanised fibre plates kept the six cylindrical Alnico magnets together and the wire was wound directly around the magnets, then simply a few turns of string protected the fine magnetic wire.

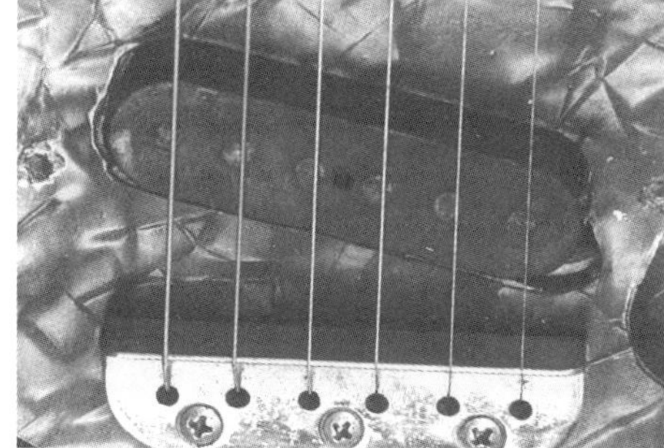

Fender 1949 lap steel's pickup (C. C.)

This pickup was very similar to the one used on the Lap Steels produced by Fender, but the base plate was pentagonal instead of rectangular and had a tin-plated sheet fixed underneath which acted as a shield anchorage. Three screws

permitted adjustment of the overall height and inclination of the unit. The metallic plate, in contact with the base of the magnets, widened the magnetic field, reflecting it toward the top, instead of being partially dispersed under the pickup as would normally happen.
Therefore this changed the relationship between the magnetic flux and the wiring, and increased sensitivity to high frequencies.

The copper plated steel sheet of the Telecaster lead pickup. In the background the nickel covered neck model (Claudio Caldana).

The winding used on the first units was AWG 43 plain enamel wire, for up to 10000 turns with a resistance in excess of 9 kOhms on some pickups. The numerous turns gave power and fatness to the sound, while the fine wire favoured dynamics and the metallic base plate a good presence of the high frequencies. The result was a pickup with a well balanced timbre, giving brightness and body, and a characteristic "singing" quality.

At first Fender didn't dip his pickups in wax, but during the fifties, to avoid feedback, he started to do so. At the end of the sixties CBS stopped waxing pickups for about a decade, and then tried to dip them in lacquer, which when dried, would crystallize, damaging the wire. It was not until the eighties, that proper waxing was resumed.

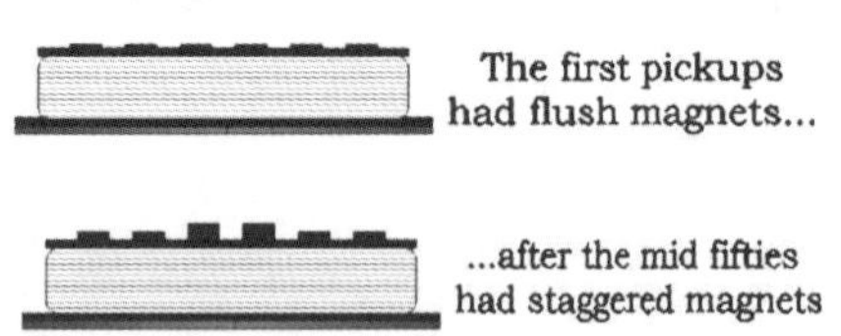

The sound pursued by Leo Fender was bright and full, without excess of middle frequencies, having the tone of the Lap Steel as a reference point. To his ears the pickup was still bottom heavy, so during 1951 he chose to change the wiring by using less turns of a slightly bigger gauge, 8000 turns of AWG 42 plain enamel wire, for an average resistance of 7, 5 kOhms. In 1951 the tin-plated sheet on the base of the pickup was substituted by a copper-plated one.
Not yet satisfied, in his search for more brightness, Fender gradually reduced the number of turns, although some units still showed occasionally high resistance values. By 1954 the magnets, which had been all of the same length up till then, were replaced with slightly smaller diameter cylinders and the middle ones were slightly longer, thus increasing the output of the D and G strings.

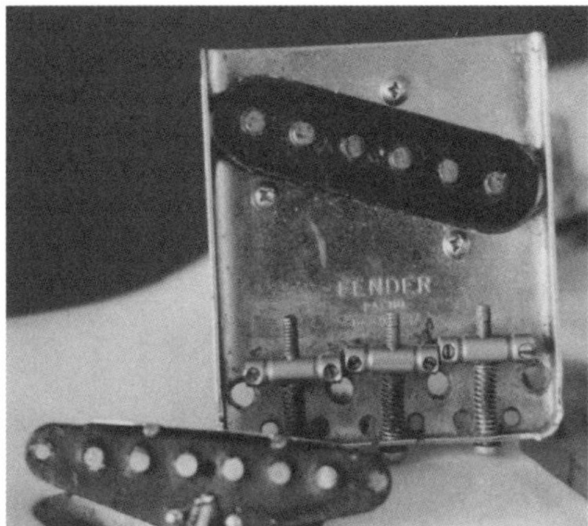

Late sixties Telecaster pickups (C. C.).

The result of these changes on the timbre of the guitar, made it brighter, with less bottom end, gradually evolving into the very clear sounding instruments of the late fifties. These characteristics were emphasized further by the brighter sounding amplifiers made by Fender in the sixties, and made the Telecaster the ideal instrument for funky rhythm.

Many players, however, still preferred the fatter, singing sound of the Broadcaster guitars. According to most experts the material for the magnets was Alnico 2 or 3 in the very first years of production, and changed to Alnico 5 during the fifties.

Originally the pickups were fed to two 250k audio potentiometers, one used as a volume control, the other as a mixer for the bridge and neck unit. The three position switch allowed to select the neck pickup filtered by a 0, 05 MFD capacitor for a very dark sound, the neck pickup alone with its natural sound and when both units were selected their output could be balanced through the mixer potentiometer.

In 1952 the circuit was changed, maintaining the master volume, but the capacitor's value was increased to 0, 1 MFD for an even darker sound. The middle position was for the neck pickup alone and the third position was the bridge pickup through the second potentiometer, which this time acted as a tone control with a 0, 05 MFD capacitor. It was not possible to select both pickups together. We don't know, if it happened by mistake or because it was considered irrelevant, but some pickups on these guitars, had one of the units with opposed polarity, so that when musicians rewired the circuit in order to use both pickups at once, sometimes they found them to be out of phase.

In 1967 the circuit was changed again, the 0, 1 MFD capacitor was discarded and now it was possible to select both pickups, or the neck or bridge alone, with master volume and master tone. A 0, 001 capacitor on the volume control retained high frequencies when the pot was turned down.

Esquire 2 Pickups / Broadcaster

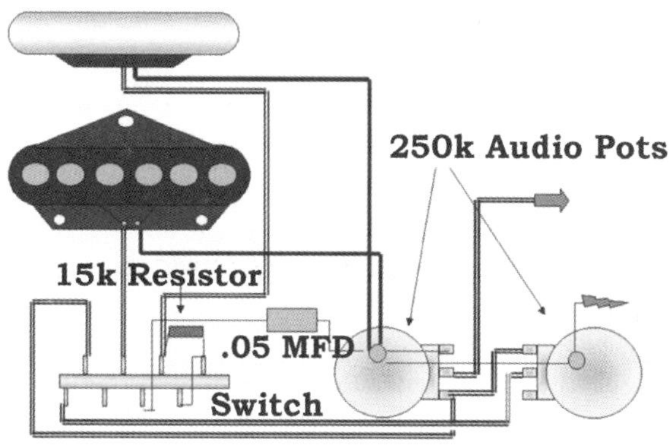

Telecaster '52

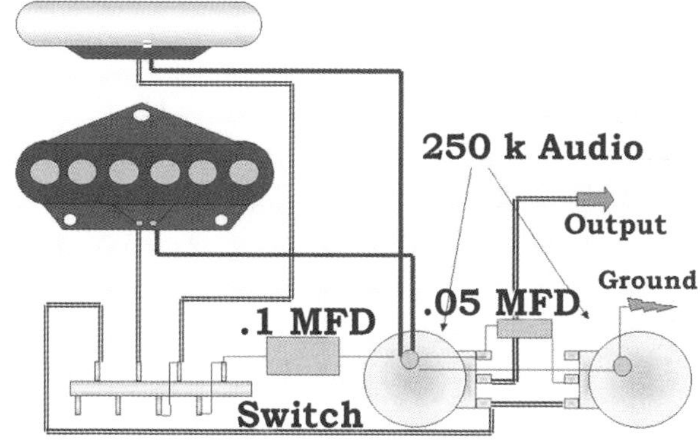

Telecaster '67

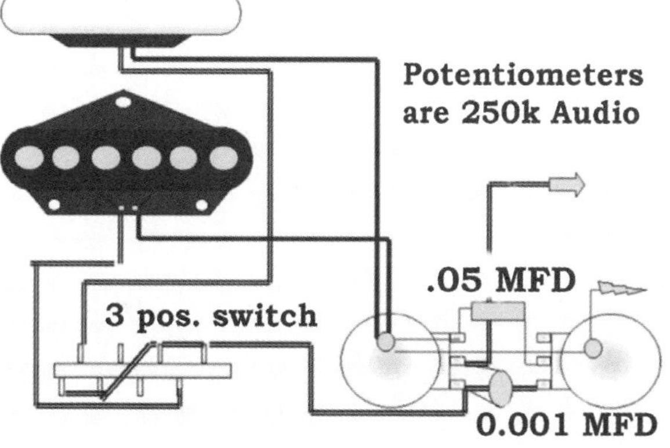

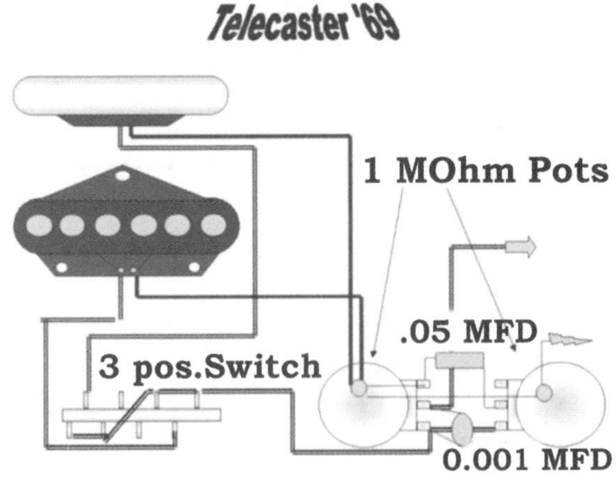

In 1969 the potentiometer value was gradually changed to 1 MOhm and on some instruments has been found a volume control of this value coupled with a 250k tone control. The change to higher value potentiometers made the guitars of that era even brighter (CBS also reduced the number of turns on both pickups to 7500), plus the units were not waxed, which increased the insurgence of feedback and prompted musicians to look for instruments made before 1968.

In 1981, encouraged by the excellent copies already manufactured by Duncan and others, Fender went back to 250k potentiometers and tried to make pickups which reproduced the technical specifications of older units. Today the Original Vintage model with Alnico 3 magnets and a resistance of 7, 2 kOhms, reproduces the 50s pickups, the No-Caster those made by Leo Fender before 1952. This model is available in two versions, "clean" and "relic", the first with the normal look of a brand new pickup, the second made to look like the old, used units; the magnets are Alnico 3. A hotter version is the Texas Special, with Alnico 5 magnets and a resistance exceeding 10 kOhms.

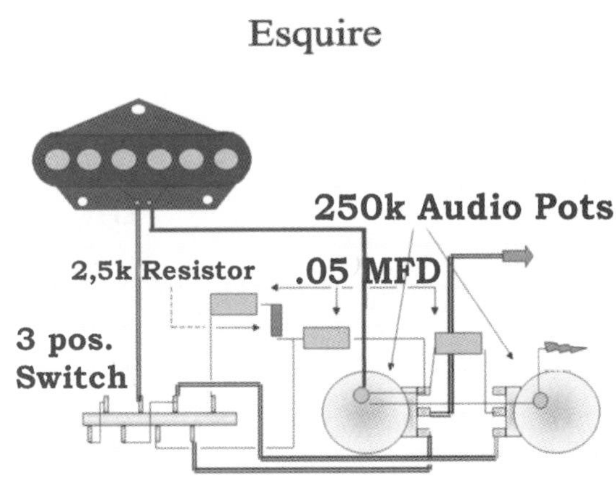

When the first guitar, Esquire, was introduced it was available with only the bridge pickup or with both units, then the second type was called Broadcaster and later Telecaster. Actually the two guitars were exactly the same, the only difference being that the Esquire had the neck pickup slot concealed under the pickguard. On this model the circuit had a control layout looking similar to the two pickups model, although the functions were different.

The two potentiometers were for volume and tone control, but the switch, on the neck position, fed the pickup through a resistance and capacitor filter cutting some of the high frequencies. On the centre position the pickup was controlled by the tone control, while on the bridge position the output was only controlled by the volume. The first position was meant to duplicate the tone of a neck pickup, the second was normal, the third, with the pickup free from any filter or tone attenuation, was to produce a slightly louder and brighter sound than normal. This last feature, not available on other Telecaster style guitars, was a reason for some musicians to prefer the Esquire because it had that extra punch they found appealing for lead playing. Late fifties and sixties models, with their already brighter pickups, were not so sought after, (some of them can sound very harsh) and were thought as more suitable for rhythm playing.

The neck model

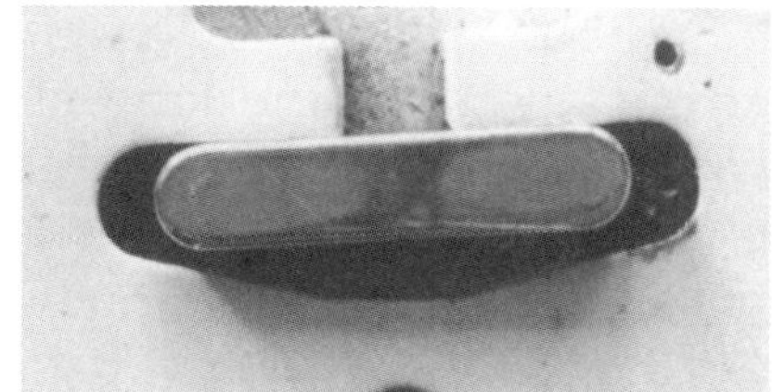

Leo Fender, used the Lap Steel as reference for sound, for the bridge position, while for the neck position he wanted a warmer, softer sound, one which jazz players would use, similar to the tone they achieved with their big archtop guitars.

The result of his research was a pickup smaller than the bridge unit, with about 8000 turns of AWG 43 magnetic wire around six cylindrical Alnico magnets, with a slightly reduced diameter compared to the ones used on the other model. These were for an average resistance of 7,8 kOhms, ranging from a minimum of 7k to a maximum of 8k. A nickel cover protected the delicate winding and cut some of the highest frequencies thus contributing to the distinctively sweet timbre of this pickup.

Probably Fender was happy with the results, because he never changed the technical specifications of this model through the years. The Telecaster neck is a pickup with a delicate balance, and the best ones have a warm but well defined timbre. Some can be too muddy sounding, but with the right unit, its warmth, coupled with the cutting power of the bridge pickup, has an impressive versatility. In the right hands it can flow through jazz, blues, country, funky and rock with ease.

The Fender Stratocaster

For the Stratocaster Leo Fender decided to design a completely new pickup, but remained faithful to the simple structure used for the Telecaster units, although experimenting for a long time with different wire gauges, number of turns and type of magnets.

The result of these experiments was a pickup, intended to be used for all three positions, with magnets a bit smaller than those of the Telecaster bridge unit and a winding range of 8000 to 8700 turns of AWG 42 Heavy Formvar magnetic wire, with a resistance of about 6 kOhms.
It had thicker insulation than the Plain Enamel used on previous models.

According to some experts, such as Seymour Duncan, Bill Lawrence and Lindy Fralin, the magnets used on the first pickups were Alnico 2 or 3 and only later Alnico 5. Cobalt, one of the components, important for military applications, and therefore occasionally less available, had its percentage in the formula changed from one batch to another, thus explaining difference in sound between different sets of pickups. The resistance actually measured on original fifties models ranges from 5, 5 kOhms to 6, 5 kOhms.

To balance the different output of the strings, Fender used magnets of different length, considering it unnecessary or too complicated to find a system for adjustable individual magnets. At first the longest magnet was under the D string, by 1956 the longest was under the G string (at the time the string set comprised a wound G), but in 1974, following the trend toward thinner gauge strings, CBS made the pickups with magnets all of the same length. Two screws permitted adjustment of all eight of the pickups in relation to the strings.

The pickups and the controls were mounted on a large, single ply pickguard, with 8 mounting screws, switching to a three-ply one in 1959 which had 11 Philips screws. Older pickguards tend to become greenish with time, but in early 1965 a different kind of plastic was used which retained the white colour better. Some Stratocasters were fitted with an anodized gold pickguard in the early fifties, while in 1962 a tortoise shell-like pickguard is used on some guitars.

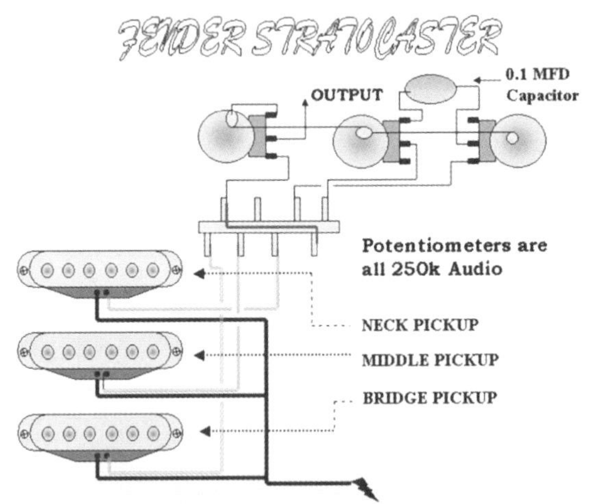

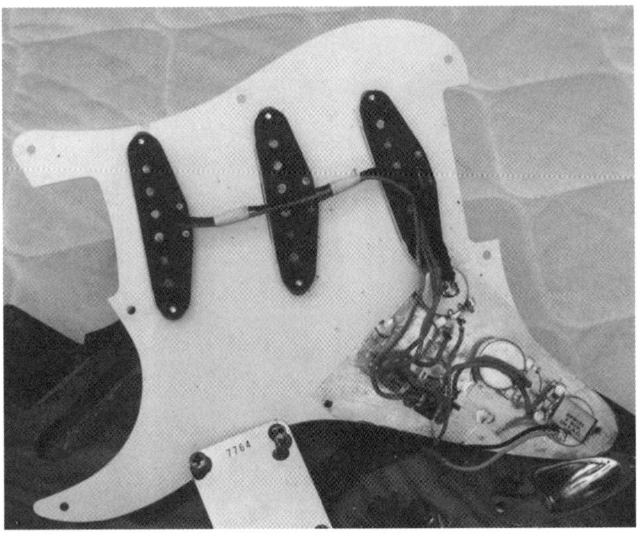
1955 Stratocaster's circuit, notice the big capacitor and the shielding limited to the control's area (Claudio Caldana).

The layout consisted of a three position switch, a master volume and tone control (with 0.1 MFD capacitor) for the neck and middle pickups. The bridge model was left without tone control for more brightness (on these models there was no base metallic plate). The potentiometers were all Audio 250k as on the Telecaster. The three position switch only allowed selection of the single pickups but their combination (when the five position switch became available Leo Fender used to say that he would not use it anyway, because he considered the sound of two units together, too "gimmicky"). As it happens, musicians, such as Buddy Guy, learned how to put the selector in a position that permitted use of the two pickups together. This made the "undesirable" sound their mark, so much so that to some it is the main reason to play a Stratocaster.

It seems that the use of three pickups was more a marketing decision than a desire for more versatility, although the Fender Company widely stressed, in their advertising, that this characteristic was another "Fender first". In reality the first guitar equipped in this way was the Gibson ES 5, and the truth is that the Stratocaster could only properly claim, to be the first "solid body" with three pickups. Another technical feature for which Fender was surely proud, was the best vibrato ever conceived for a guitar and still today an industry standard. The new pickup has a less punchy sound than the Telecaster bridge model, but has good balance in every position, with a clear, bright tone immediately identifiable with the Fender brand.

During the sixties (around 1964) a Plain Enamel AWG 42 wire substituted the Heavy Formvar used previously, and increased the tone differences between Stratocasters of different periods, which were due to the variety of wood used on the body. Ash was used up to 1956, and alder after 1957, except for blonde finished instruments and fingerboard material, which was originally one piece maple for the neck, and rosewood fingerboard after 1959. During the sixties new automatic winding machines, were available instead of hand guided ones, but in order to avoid wire breakage the tension at which the winding was done was reduced and the number of turns decreased. With the new machines the turns were also more regular.

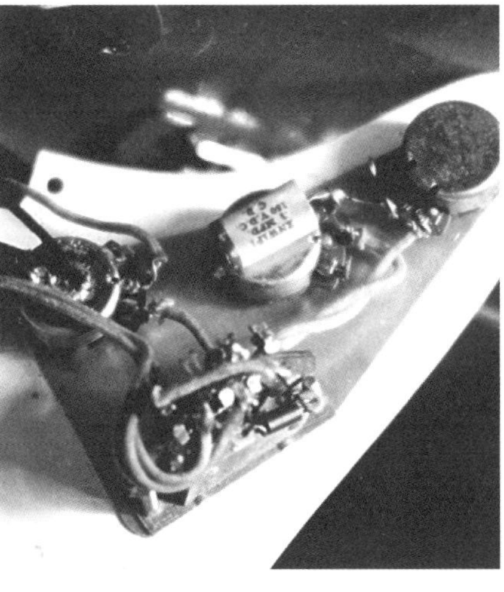

Detail of a '58 Stratocaster's circuit)Claudio Caldana).

The resistance of the pickups produced by the end of the sixties and throughout the seventies was about 5,7 kOhms. For statistic's sake, the average reading of Fender pickups was as follows: at the beginning, 6 kOhms, by the end of the fifties, 6,3 kOhms, with some exceeding 6,5 k, after 1965 about 5,7 kOhms. The base of the pickups was black vulcanized fibre up to 1965, then dark grey and clear grey in 1968. Since 1980 plastic black bobbins were used, except for the vintage reissue models.

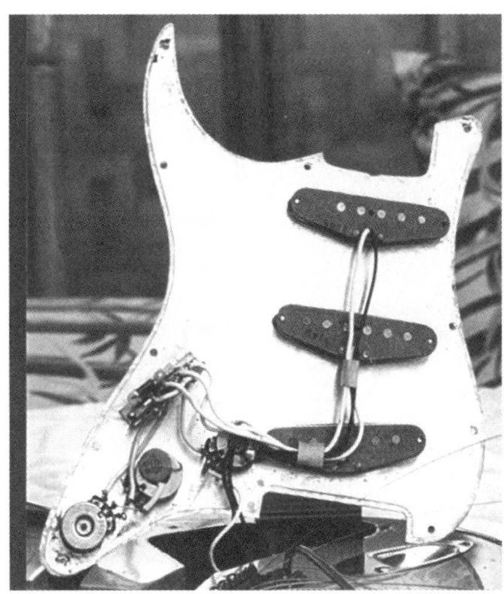

1966's Stratocaster, notice the grey base of the pickups, the shielding extended to the whole pickguard and the smaller tone control's capacitor (C. Caldana).

For shielding purposes the interior of the pickguard was partially covered with a thin triangular metallic sheet, around 1959 the whole surface was covered and in 1969 the covering was again only partial. The cables connecting the pickups to the circuit were covered in a typical waxed cloth, white for the signal, black for earth. After 1968 the cables were plastic covered.

The pickup cover was made from a hard material (ABS plastic) up until 1955, and then from more durable injection-moulded plastic, with less rounded corners, thicker sides and a less shiny look. It provided no shielding and the only purpose was to protect the delicate windings.

The tone is rooted in Leo Fender's love for country and Hawaiian music, yet, players such as Jimi Hendrix, Ritchie Blackmore and Jeff Beck proved what a powerful and expressive tool it can be for rock music. These sonic adventures Fender could never imagine, nor, we presume, even enjoy.

After the eighties Fender introduced reissues of the older models, with vulcanized fibre, Heavy Formvar wire and cloth cables, offered in different versions.
The basic version was the “Original Vintage ‘57/’62”, with specifications reproducing the average values of some units of the first years of the sixties. Then the Custom 54 arrived, a reissue of the first production units, and the Custom 69, which were copies of the sixties units. More powerful models were the Fat 50 and the Texas Special. In 1970 the value of the tone control capacitor was changed to 0.05 MFD and is still used on the American Standard model, but on the Vintage Reissues was reintroduced the original 0.1 MFD capacitor.

The Gibson P-90

Rock power! ‘63 SG TV, ’54 Les Paul Junior and ’68 Gold Top Standard with P 90s (Claudio Prosperini).

After 1941, with the availability of new smaller and more powerful Alnico magnets, Gibson worked to find a substitute for the bar pickup, a. k. a "Charlie Christian Model". The first to be introduced was a version with a metallic cover, then a longer model was made, which extended from the bass side at the end of the fingerboard to the treble side of the bridge, with four magnets under the winding and protected by a tortoise shell plastic cover.
After less than one year this model was discontinued and replaced with a smaller unit, made with two magnets and mounted slanted near the bridge for a bright tone. The war forced Gibson to suspend experiments, but in 1946 was issued a new model. Known as P 90, the new pickup had specifications similar to those of the 1941 small model, but this time with a black plastic cover. Before 1955 the cover was made in thermoformed plastic, thinner and with a more sparkling appearance than later ones, made from injection-moulded plastic.
The winding, as on the last version of the bar pickup, consisted of about 10000 turns of AWG 42 plain enamel wire, for an average resistance of 8 kOhms (actually ranging from 7,5k to 9k), with two Alnico magnets on the base.
The two magnets had the south polarity sides toward the centre, touching six screw type polepieces directing the magnetic field up to the strings, and the north polarity side facing the outer sides of the pickup.

Two lifted wings on the metallic base held the magnets firmly against the polepieces (two magnets of the same polarity drive each other back). This structure had part of the magnetic field directed toward the strings by the polepieces, plus the exterior side energy was attracted, being of opposed polarity, by the one toward the centre, thus surrounding the whole pickup. The resulting wide magnetic window is one of the reasons for the fat sound of this model.
The resonant peak, for a single coil model, is a relatively low 4800 Hz, with an inductance of 7,5 h, giving this pickup a powerful voice, with biting highs, good presence of the middle frequencies and deep low end.

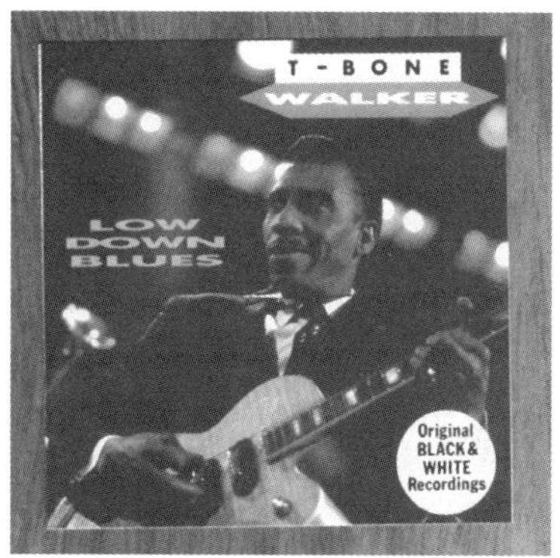

The output is strong enough to push any amplifier to a growling saturation, while on the neck position and with an appropriate tone regulation, the timbre becomes warm and soft.

Such an impressive versatility allowed the P 90 to become the favourite model for jazz, blues and rock musicians, such as T-Bone Walker, Freddy King, Chuck Berry, Scotty Moore, the first B. B. King, Hubert Sumlin, Herb Ellis, Jim Hall, Leslie West, just to name a few.

The P 90 was used on most middle and high level guitars, but for the cheaper ES 125 a simplified version was devised. In order to cut costs, six cylindrical magnets substituted for the adjustable polepieces and, of course, there were no bar magnets on the base, but the wiring was the same as on the normal model.
The sound of this version was slightly brighter and had a more pronounced attack which was due to the magnets directly under the strings (today we would say "Fender style") which gave more density to the magnetic field.

The staff leading the Gibson Company in the fifties, from left: Walter Fuller, Julius Bellson, Wilbur Marker, Ted McCarty, and John Huis (courtesy of Gibson).

During 1959, Gibson used a bar magnet directly in the winding, on the Melody Maker, which was the cheapest solid body on offer. This bar magnet was known as M56, and was slightly smaller than the bar magnets used on P 90s, (code name was M 55), although by 1960, probably to standardize production, the P 90 was also made with two M 56 on the base. Except for this substitution, the technical specifications remained unchanged at least until 1968.

During the first years of the sixties the M 55 could still be found on some P 90 or P.A.F. pickups, probably due to left over stock. In the seventies the P 90 was reissued as the Laid Back Model, with more powerful Alnico 5 magnets and a resistance of about 8,3 kOhms.

Still very popular, the P 90 is available in different versions, from the high quality reproductions made by Seymour Duncan in the Antiquity Series and Lindy Fralin, to the less expensive Duncan Vintage, Gibson P 90 "Super Vintage", Rio Grande Jazzbar and Bluesbar. P 90 style models are also offered by Harmonic Design and Jason Lollar. With similar specs, but designed to be installed in normal humbucking rings, are the Gibson P 94, the Rio Grande Bastard, both with Alnico 5 magnets, and the Duncan Phat Cat, made with Alnico 2 magnets.

The Gibson Humbucking

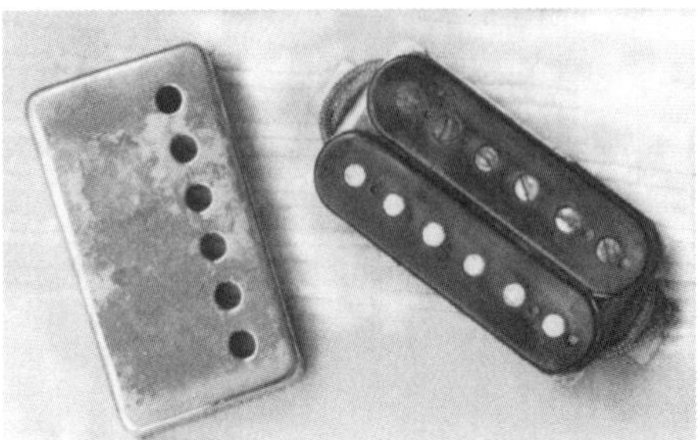

It is usually impossible to duplicate a great success, and Rickenbacker never managed to recreate the past success of the "Horseshoe".

Leo Fender also failed to produce the desired effect with models that followed the Stratocaster, the Jaguar and the Jazzmaster.

Gibson, with the popularity acquired with the bar pickup and the P 90 seemed to be in the same position.

The entry of Seth Lover in 1953 brought new energy, with the design of the Alnico Model, issued in 1954, which had small rectangular Alnico 5 magnets, each adjustable by a screw, directly in the winding, which is the same as used for the P 90. The new model had a clearer sound, more output, but did not have time to become popular because the same man who designed it soon invented a more clever concept. That same year, Lover was asked to search for a system to cut noise from the amplifiers built by Gibson. The engineer decided to use the solution devised to also make a hum-free pickup.

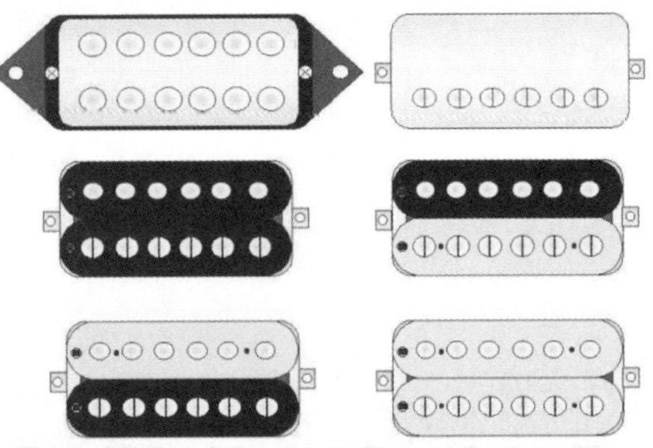

Humbucking's prototype, production model, colour of the bobbins used between '57 and '60.
Cream bobbins are introduced in '59.

The idea was to use two bobbins, connected with opposed phase and magnetic polarity, this way the two parts of the signal picked up by the polepieces would result in phase, while the hum induced by any source of interference, picked up by the coils, would be out of phase and so cancelled almost completely.
A metallic cover acting as a shield would make the pickup even quieter.

Lover made a prototype, with a M55 magnet on the base of the two bobbins and twelve polepieces directing the magnetic field toward the strings. Ted McCarty, immediately accepted the project and the only reservation concerned the non adjustable polepieces. The P 90 and the "Alnico" Model both had the possibility to adjust the output of any single string, so fixed polepieces in a new model could be seen as a regression. The solution was to put adjustable screw type polepieces through one of the bobbins. A nickel or gold plated cover gave to this model a

different look and the new mounting system, in a plastic ring, permitted adjustments for height and inclination of the unit.
Seth Lover didn't plate the prototype, imagining that a heavy plating would cut some of the highest frequencies, therefore Gibson at first tried to use gold paint, which however wasn't resistant enough.

The label applied on the bottom of the Gibson humbuckers from 1957 to 1962. (C. Prosperini)

Nickel and gold plating were more durable, although the plating had to be kept as thin as possible so as not to interfere with the magnetic field. In the second half of the sixties chrome plating proved even more resistant, and substituted the nickel plating, while on high level guitar models the more delicate gold plating was retained.

From the start the new model was called "humbucking" and Gibson applied for a patent, but it looked like a long process because other pickups using the same principle had already been proposed. The increasing competition by other manufacturers prompted Gibson to quicken the pace and in 1957 all the high level guitars were equipped with the new model, with a label attached to the base on which was written "PATENT APPLIED FOR" (some earlier units were without labels).

Gradually the humbucking pickup replaced the Alnico Model on some Lap Steels, on the L-5 CES, Super 400, ES 175, Byrdland, Les Paul Model, Les Paul Custom, ES-5 and ES 295. The lower grade models were still equipped with the P 90.

The humbucking was made using the same AWG 42 Plain Enamel wire as for the previous models, with the same number of 10000 turns, split on two bobbins, each with 5000 turns.

The system was very efficient and even with only one magnet, the output was the same as with the P 90 and sometimes even greater. Normally the pickup had south polarity on the screw side and north polarity on the fixed poles side, but on the Varitone equipped stereo guitars, such as the ES 355 DT-SV, the neck unit had north polarity on the adjustable poles, resulting, if used mono with both pickups selected, in an out of phase sound. (In stereo they are supposed to be sent to different amplifiers).

The tone had sweeter highs and more pronounced mids, compared to a P 90. As always the technical specifications were elusive, seldom reflecting the parameters, therefore although the humbucking should have a resistance of about 8 kOhms, actual measurements showed that values on original units could vary between slightly more than 7 kOhms to more than 9 kOhms. This means that "P. A. F."s, as the original humbuckers were known, could sound brighter or

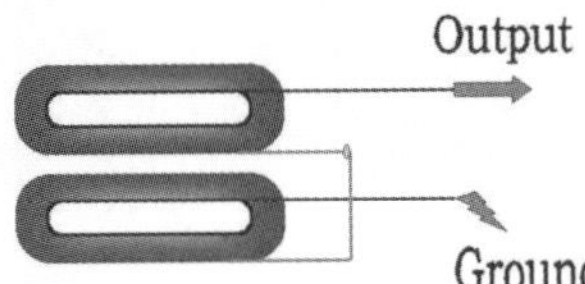

darker according to the number of actual turns, but maintained good balance between sustain, clarity and harmonic richness. All had a common characteristic which, as on Fender pickups of the same period, seemed to transcend technical discrepancies, although for most connoisseurs the best ones are those with a reading closer to 8 kOhms.

1961 Gibson ES 335 TD, Fender Deluxe Amp from the same era and a '63 Reverb unit (C. P.).

The wire was wound around two black plastic bobbins (butyrate). Both bobbins were wound in the same direction and the two windings were then connected in series with opposed electric polarity. The bobbin with adjustable screw polepieces laid on a metallic support with holes to allow the screws to pass through, while the one with non adjustable polepieces was placed on a maple insert. Under the bobbins, on the nickel-silver base plate, was the single Alnico bar magnet. A nickel silver cover protected the windings and acted as a shield. As on previous models there was no waxing, as the heat necessary for the process would have distorted the bobbins due to the kind of plastic used on them. The pickup became an industry standard.

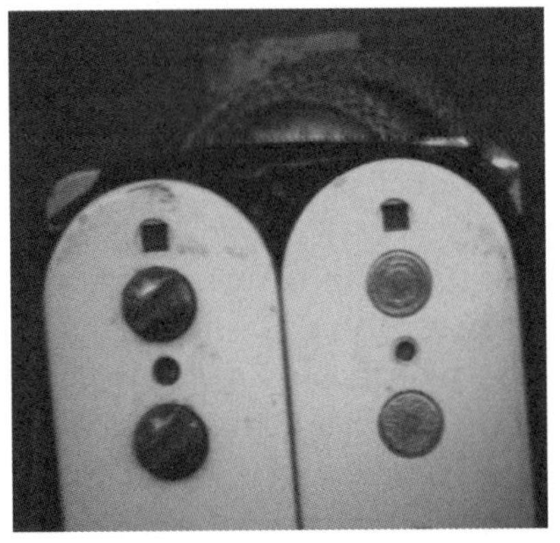

The square holes with ring on the bobbins of PAFs and early "Patent Number" pickups

In 1959 the factory from which Gibson bought the bobbins claimed a temporary lack of black pigment, so a certain number of bobbins were delivered white (actually with a light cream hue which tended to increase with time). Since the model was supposed to receive a nickel or gold plated cover, no attention was paid to the colour of the bobbins used, therefore the black bobbins already in stock and the new cream ones, got mixed on the same units. So after 1959 there are PAFs with both black bobbins, some with one black, one cream (also called "zebra"), some with both cream bobbins (nicknamed "double white" or "full cream").

In 1960 the black bobbins were again available and the white ones gradually, disappeared. The relative scarcity of double whites and zebra, compared to the most common black pickups, plus the increasing number, at the time, of units with a higher number of turns in the windings, gave these pickups a mythical status.

To find a more powerful sample from that period, or with a particularly good tone, has nothing to do with the colour of the bobbin. Myth, aesthetics and rarity increase the market value of zebra and especially full cream pickups, well above the all black units of the same period.

In 1960 the number of turns in the winding remained unchanged but the shorter M56 magnet substituted the M55, in theory causing a subtle difference in sound. In 1962 a new label, "Patent N° 2.737.842" replaced the "Patent Applied For", but for some reason Gibson decided to not use the real patent number of the humbucking pickup, but one which referred to the bridge-tailpiece designed for the 1952 Les Paul Model. Except for the label both the "Patent Applied For" and the "Patent N° 2.737.842" models from the same period are exactly the same. Another, more important change, occurred later during the sixties, when the wire delivered to Gibson was no longer plain enamel, but insulated with a polyurethane lacquer, distinguishable from the previous one for it's clear, copper colour instead of the usual reddish brown used on the "P. A. F." and early "Patent Number" pickups.

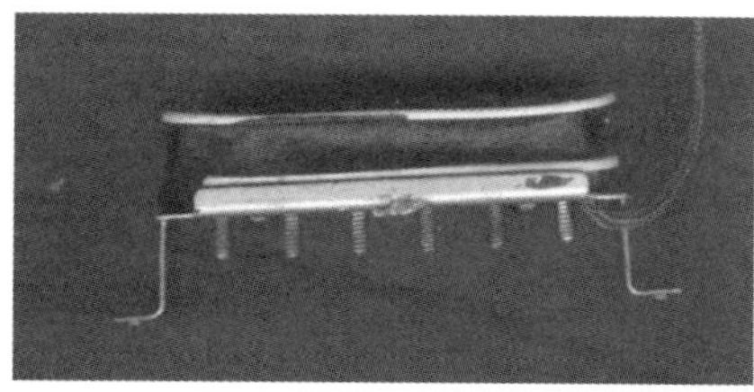

The kind of plastic used for the bobbins, on PAF pickups, was subject to distortion, over time, due to the tension of the windings.

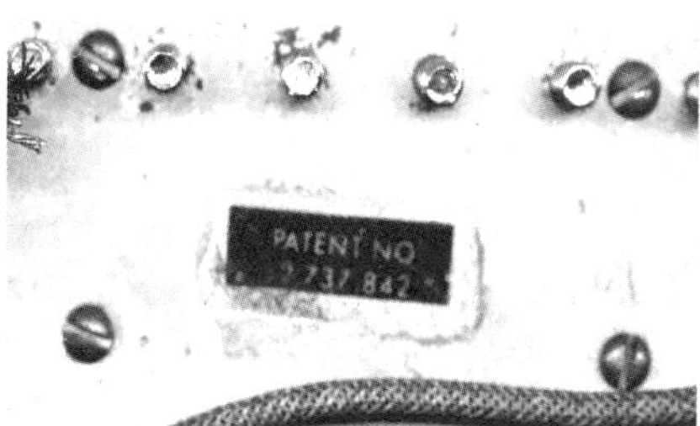

The label used on Gibson pickups after mid '62 (C. Prosperini).

The thinner insulation and the availability of newer winding machines with an automatic stop system, produced more consistent and evenly stacked turns in the bobbins, but also some timbre differences. By the end of the sixties more powerful magnets were used, probably Alnico 5 and most think that those used previously were actually Alnico 2, 3 or 4. During the seventies it seems that even the brighter Alnico 8 was used.

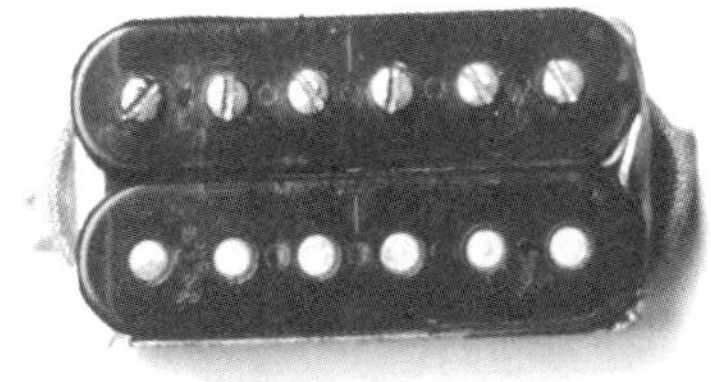

In the late sixties the bobbins lacked the square holes and a "T" mark appeared instead (C. C.).

A new variant was introduced in 1973, the "Super Humbucking", with ceramic magnets and different windings for the neck and bridge models for a broader range of sounds. Pickups from this era often have magnets of different dimensions, some similar to the old M55, others smaller like the M56. The values of the potentiometers, traditionally 500 kOhms, in 1974 was changed to 300k for the volume control, 100k for the tone control, probably to obtain a smoother sound from the new, brighter pickups.
The basic model with Alnico magnets, to distinguish it from the Super Humbucking, was now called "Original Humbucking".

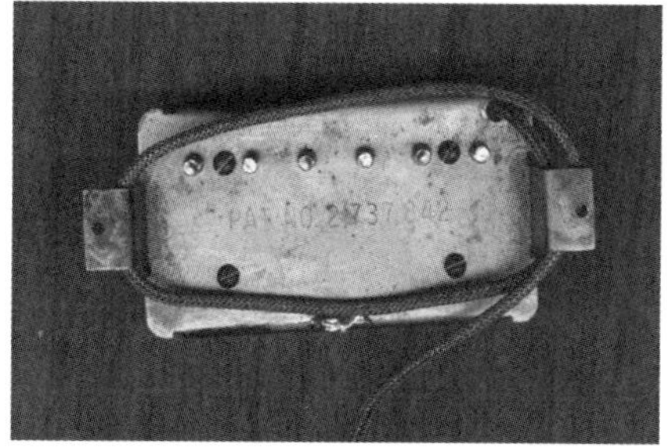

In the seventies the patent number was engraved on the pickup's bottom (C. P.).

All these variants can be recognized thanks to several small details. The "Patent Applied For" and the first "Patent Number" pickups have a small square hole surrounded by a circle at the top of the bobbins (due to inconsistencies of the stamp

Since the late seventies the pickup's base has small cuts (right), not present on previous versions (left).

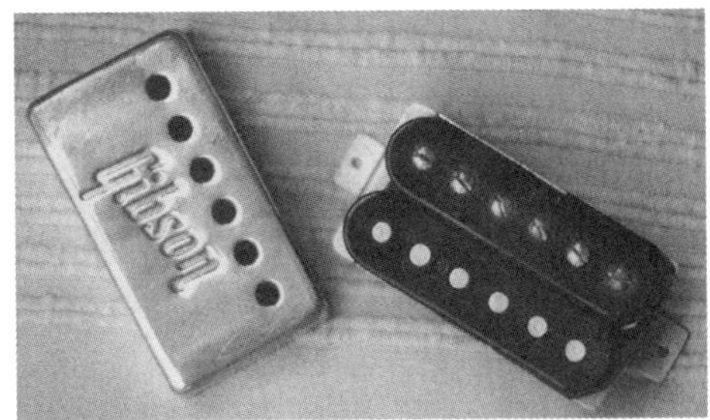

The name “Gibson”, in 1971, for less than one year, was engraved on the pickup’s cover (Claudio Caldana).

the ring is sometimes barely visible). By the end of the sixties the square hole is missing and there is a "T" mark on the bobbins. During the seventies the patent number label was no longer applied and the number was engraved on the base plate. By the end of the decade the base plate wings which received the height adjusting screws had a little cut on each side, not present on previous units. In the eighties the base plate had twelve holes, six under the adjustable poles, as usual, and six under the non adjustable polepieces.

1986 Gibson ’59 Les Paul Reissue (C. Caldana).

The metallic cover which had been nickel plated until about 1968, with a yellowish reflection, then became chrome plated, with a bluish reflection. The “Super Humbucking” looked similar to the other models, from the top, but turning it around it was possible to see that it was completely immersed in black resin.

Since 1974 the pickups had different polepiece spacing for neck and bridge models for better alignment under the strings.

In 1980 the Les Paul Heritage Standard and Heritage Elite were introduced, with pickups labelled "Pat. Appl. For". Those pickups had Alnico 2 magnets very similar to the M56, with a resistance of about 7,5 / 7,8 kOhms and a sound closer to the old ones. This was clearly an attempt to recreate the original specifications, but the overall quality and timbre were not up to the task. The use of the standard circuit of the time, with reduced potentiometer values, didn't help to recreate the sound of the old guitars.

For a short while, at the end of the eighties, some pickups were mounted on a base similar to a circuit board, which was very delicate, and made it impossible to repair the pickup if it got broken. This was not a rare circumstance for those models.

At the same time research on the characteristics of old instruments produced more accurate reissues of the original guitars while for pickups the effort was to reproduce the specifications of the “Patent Applied For”.

The result, in the early nineties, was the “57 Classic”, with Alnico 2 magnet (M55 dimensions), AWG 42 Plain Enamel wire, and, finally, a sound character similar to the unit designed by Seth Lover (it seems that the luthier Tom Holmes, maker of fine PAF copies, was consulted). On details other makers came closer to the timbre of the originals, but the “57 Classic” is without doubt the best pickup produced by Gibson since 1968.

The circuit was partially changed, with Audio 500 kOhms potentiometers for the volume controls, whereas linear 300k potentiometers were used for the tone controls. Only the Historic Collection models maintained all the original values, the capacitors were the correct 0.022 MFD value, but not the original brand, Sprague, which according to Gibson were unavailable, and only recently resumed.

Standard Gibson circuit

Super 400, L5, ES 175, Byrdland, ES 350TD, ES 335 TD, Les Paul Model, SG Standard

Potentiometers: 500 k Audio
Capacitors : 0.022 MFD

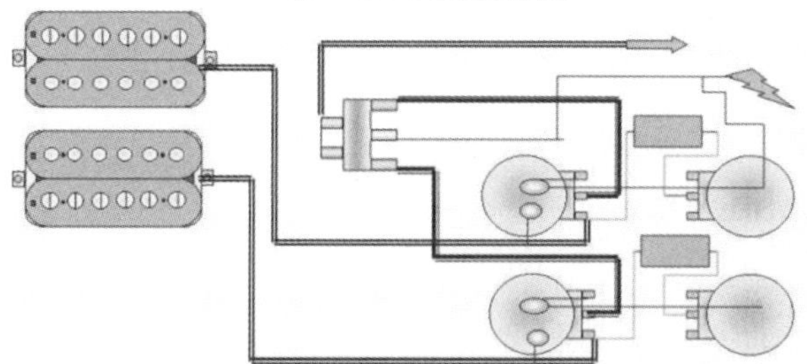

The electric layout used on two pickups guitars from Gibson since the forties and today reproduced on the models of the Historic Collection.

Like the Fender Telecaster and Stratocaster pickup models, the Gibson “Patent Applied For” has also been widely copied.

The most faithful versions are, up to now, the Duncan Antiquity and Seth Lover Model, not waxed and made using the same bobbin material as the originals. Other excellent versions are: The Lindy Fralin, Jason Lollar, Wolfetone and Tom Holmes replicas, and the less costly but good sounding Duncan Pearly Gates, the SH-1 ‘59 Model, the APH-1 Alnico II Pro and the Rio Grande Genuine Texas.

Good copies are also made by Peter Florance (Voodoo Pickups), using Alnico 3 magnets.
Gibson added a Custom Shop model, the “Burstbucker”, with Alnico 2 unpolished magnet but with slightly unbalanced bobbins and, as the original models, not waxed.
Three versions are available:
Burstbucker #1, slightly underwound for a clean sound.
Burstbucker #2, normal (with an output similar to the ’57 Classic).
Burstbucker #3, reproducing those with a few more turns in the windings for a fatter tone.

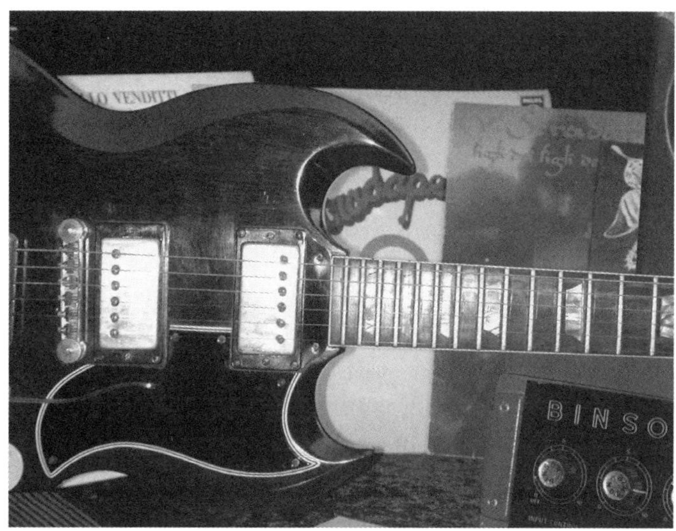

The “Patent Applied For” pickups of a ’61 SG/Les Paul Standard (Renato Bartolini).

A similar model, the Burstbucker Pro, waxed and with Alnico 5 magnets, is used as stock equipment on the Les Paul Standard since 2003.

The DiMarzio Super Distortion

In 1972 the sound pursued by most makers was still a clear and bright one. Gibson had already reintroduced the Les Paul Models, but only the Custom and the Deluxe versions, which were very different from the original series (the Standard would return in 1974) and everybody in the field seemed to ignore what was happening with rock music.

The success of bands such as Cream, Led Zeppelin, Allman Brothers Band, and Colosseum, caused guitar players to pursue a hot, fat, saturated sound. Jazz rock had the hard sound of Al DiMeola and John McLaughlin, for which the clean sounding guitars of the time seemed to be unsuitable. Larry DiMarzio had the right solution to satisfy their needs.

The Super Distortion started with a structure similar to that of the Gibson humbucking.

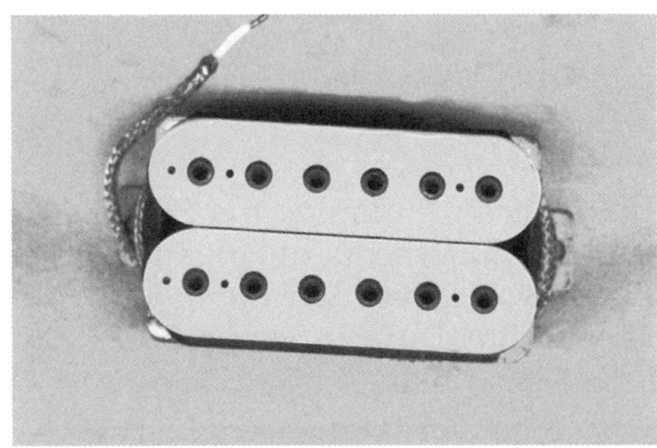

It was wound with more turns in the bobbins for a nominal D. C. resistance of 13, 68 kOhms and an inductance of 8,2 Henries, a powerful ceramic magnet substituted the Alnico one, for increased power and more sensitivity to the higher frequencies, all this resulted in a very fat, hot sound with an output level twice as loud as the Patent Applied For, aggressive mids and still enough high frequencies to avoid muddiness.

The first samples were a bit bulky, compared to normal humbuckers, and on some guitars they were fitted with difficulty, but soon the manufacturers became more organized and the pickups looked more professional. In the seventies the wings for the height adjusting screws were square, as on Gibson pickups, but were triangular on later models. The materials used were of very high quality.

The success went beyond all expectations and during the first year it seemed that every musician in New York had a DiMarzio pickup on their guitar and soon the Super Distortion was used by Al DiMeola, John McLaughlin, Paul Stanley of Kiss, John Abercrombie, Philip Catherine, Tom Scholz, Pat Thrall and other famous players. The Super Distortion became the industry standard as far as high output pickups were concerned even compared to other DiMarzio models which appeared as mere variations on a theme and it is the one used to compare new models of this kind.

The Super Distortion remained the original and although it lacks the harmonic richness of a Gibson humbucker, and has the opposite sound of the clear top end of a Gretsch Filter'Tron, it has no competitors for saturated sounds and pushes even the most refractory amplifier to the verge of distortion. The resonant peak at 6850 Hz is high enough to give a clear high end, not dissimilar to that of a PAF, even though less pronounced.

The Dual Sound version had a four conductor output cable, allowing out of phase and parallel connections and the possibility to turn off one bobbin for single coil sounds, but the main appeal remained the sustain in full power mode.

For Stratocaster players seeking more power, DiMarzio designed the SDS-1, a single coil model wound for a resistance of 8,68 kOhms, two ceramic magnets on the base of a structure similar to that of the Gibson P 90. It had Allen screws polepieces and a timbre similar to that of the Super Distortion.

Other similar models were the Super 2, a brighter version of the Super Distortion, and the TDS-1, a not very popular tapped version of the SDS-1. The Paf was inspired by the Gibson original humbucking, but the DiMarzio interpretation was brighter and louder sounding.

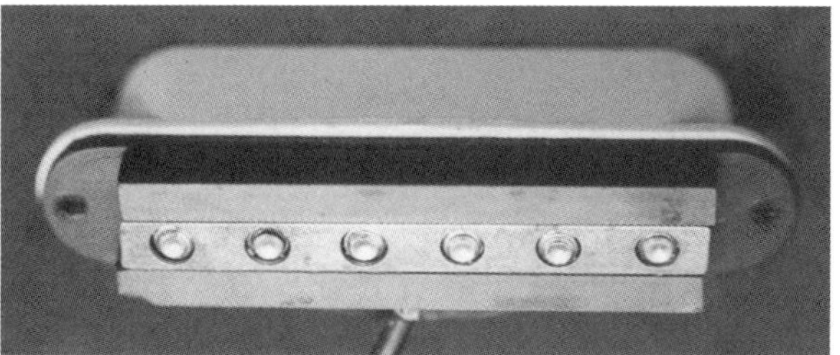

DiMarzio SDS-1 (Claudio Prosperini).

More models followed, such as the very powerful X2N, but the model on which the DiMarzio myth is based was the Super Distortion.

In 1974 Gibson changed the value of the potentiometers used on the guitars from 500k to 300k for the volume controls and 100k for the tone controls. Most musicians were unaware of this change and when they tried the Super Distortion on their instruments, the common complaint was that the sound was too dark. DiMarzio offered good quality 500k audio potentiometers with which the pickups sounded open enough, so much so, that some players used them even on the neck position.

With their strong sonic personality, the DiMarzio pickups gave good results, at least as far as loudness is concerned, even on instruments of relatively low quality. Therefore it became common practice at that time to fit a DiMarzio Paf at the neck position and a Super Distortion at the bridge to substitute the ordinary pickups fitted on Japanese guitars. However this new freedom was not limited to cheap guitars, even musicians who had a high end instrument, were no longer limited to the maker's choice of pickups. With the Super Distortion a new era started, that of the customized guitar and a new market of replacement pickups opened.

Gibson responded with the Super Humbucking fitted onto the early seventies' SG guitars, but even though they were more powerful than the standard units, the timbre was not as full, owing to the fact that the ceramic magnets were used to make their voice clearer, rather than fatter.

With the advent of high gain amplifiers, such as the Mesa Boogie, it became less important to use very loud pickups and most players were now looking for less specialized pickups, with a more traditional timbre. Seymour Duncan's J. B. Model became the choice for those desiring a classic sound with more power than traditional models.

Duncan still believed in the idea of an overwound pickup, but with an Alnico 5 magnet replacing the ceramic one for a sound closer to that of Gibson's original model, a design on which even some DiMarzio models will later be based, such as the "Paf Pro", the FRED, the Tone Zone, Norton and others.

Time would tell which models are going to become classics. Certainly the J. B. Model had its followers, if we think of the Gibson 498, the Rio Grande BBQ and several others, but for the Distortion class of pickups, the DiMarzio "Super Distortion", with its big voice, continues to maintain an undeniable place in history even after three decades.

After all even the finest handcrafted "vintage" models made today owe something to this growling humbucker for opening a new market and we believe it should sit with other innovative models such as the "Charlie Christian", the P 90, the Fender models and the Gibson "Patent Applied For".

Fat tone for the Gypsy! Al DiMeola, one of the most distinctive guitar players of the seventies, got his tone using Gibson Les Pauls outfitted with DiMarzio Super Distortion pickups. Later DiMarzio issued a set dedicated to him as one of the first "Signature" models from this brand.

PART 5 - Masters of tone

George Beauchamp

George Beauchamp (courtesy of Rickenbacker).

Born in Texas, George Beauchamp as a child studied violin, and went on to receive a solid musical education, comprised also of steel guitar lessons during the 1920's. In 1923 he played as a professional, with his brother Al and his friend Slim Hopper, as "The Boys From Dixie" band. Then he moved to Los Angeles where he made good use of his talent as a guitar player, especially Hawaiian style, also gaining a reputation as a brilliant singer, with fine sense of humour. His talent was not limited to music, as he also seemed to have a good disposition for alcohol and is remembered as being very generous with his friends.
As most guitar players of the time, George was frustrated by the difficulty to make his instrument heard in noisy places or when playing in bands with horns.

As the record players and the first amplification systems seemed to suggest, he believed that the solution would arrive with electrification. After several experiments, like putting the record player horn onto the guitar, he met John Dopyera and together they started to search for more practical solutions, though not less eccentric. In 1925 the first cone loudspeakers were introduced and to apply the same concept to a guitar, from George and John's point of view, meant being up to date with technological innovations. It seemed that Dopyera was already working on the idea, when he met Beauchamp, but the guitar player surely encouraged his research and pushed him to realize them practically, by ordering an instrument for himself.

The result was the birth, of the resophonic guitar in 1926 and then, in 1927, the founding of the National Company. The first model was the Tricone, but the range would later comprehend single cone instruments. George Beauchamp became general manager and was very active in promoting the new instrument, persuading his good friend Sol Hoopii, the most popular Hawaiian player of the time to become Godfather to the instrument.

Personality clashes and disagreements about financial problems, in 1929, pushed Beauchamp to quit the Company. Since the beginning of National, Adolph Rickenbacker, thanks to his working experience in wood and metals,

Adolph Rickenbacker, in the early seventies, with the original "Frying Pan" lap steel.
(Courtesy of Rickenbacker)

started making the metal bodies for the guitars (only about forty are presumed to be hand made by the Dopyera brothers when they started).

Rickenbacker was a friendly and kind-hearted man and got on well with the eccentric George, so when he was fired by the Dopyera brothers, it came naturally to offer him the continuation of experiments on guitar electrification. Attending evening classes on electronics, Beauchamp learned that by disturbing a magnetic field it was possible to induce current in an adjacent bobbin. his concept had already been used for generators, telephones and phonograph heads, and so he started to experiment on the subject with the help of Paul Barth. The result was a pickup made from two big magnets shaped as horseshoes, with a winding in the middle and six polepieces on top through which the guitar strings were supposed to pass.

An artisan, Harry Watson, got the job of manufacturing a neck and a guitar body from wood and the same day, using simple hand held tools from a single piece of maple, made the prototype. Because of the round shape of the body, the instrument was nicknamed "Frying Pan". Adolph Rickenbacker had the financial power, the tools and the enthusiasm to produce the new instrument and the first move was to found a company, named Ro-Pat-In Corporation, soon changed to Rickenbacker Electro.

The first lap steels were produced in 1931, under the direction of Beauchamp, and labelled Rickenbacker. The instruments produced were not made from wood, as the prototype, but from aluminium and later from Bakelite, a very hard plastic material invented in 1909. Aluminium proved to be too sensitive to changes in temperature, making it difficult to keep the instruments in tune.
Success arrived slowly, and the economic depression didn't encourage musicians to invest in unusual instruments. However orders started to arrive and the range was expanded including two electric archtops in the catalogue, plus a version of the pickup sold as a separate unit to mount on acoustic archtops.

From the start Rickenbacker built its own amplifiers and after some years Ralph Robertson was employed, who, in 1941 designed four models. One of these, the Professional, had a loudspeaker designed by James B. Lansing.

In 1940 George Beauchamp was already busy with other things that had nothing to do with music, but concerned his second big passion; fishing. Unfortunately he died of a heart attack, that same year, on the high sea.

To start it was difficult, but then George Beauchamp had reason to be proud, as, Rickenbacker instruments were used on many Hollywood movie soundtracks, they were favoured by country players as well as Hawaiian players, thanks to Sol

Hoopii. Les Paul bought a Vibrola Spanish Guitar, and Harpo Marx ordered a custom electric harp which was used in several movies. What Beauchamp failed to see was the development, only a few years later of his prediction, that all pickups designed since then, including those with active electronics, were based on the same principle as his “Horseshoe”.

Leo Fender

Leo Fender was stubborn, kind-hearted, ambitious, confident in his intuitions and, deep down possibly insecure, according to the information available. Colleagues, partners, musicians old and new all have some anecdotes to tell about this man, who was often called, probably quite rightly, “genius”. Everybody, even competitors, acknowledge his devotion to friends, his honesty and a legendary commitment to what he looked upon as a mission, rather than a job. Leo Fender was born on August 10, 1909, on a ranch near Anaheim, California. As a child he lost an eye through illness, and disliked to have photographs taken.

In the late nineties, the Fender Custom Shop built this Limited Edition copy of the prototype of electric guitar designed by Leo Fender in 1949. Notice as, with the exception of the headstock, the main elements which will define the future Broadcaster/Telecaster are already present (A. Angelucci).

When photographs were necessary he was careful to place himself in a position which made it difficult to notice his artificial eye.

When he was 13 years old Fender learned the basics about the world of radio in his uncle's shop, and soon was able to repair the radios of his schoolmates. Following his love for music, Leo even tried to learn to play the saxophone, but his difficulty with timing convinced him to give up. His interest in technology and mechanics seemed to be insatiable and soon, in 1932, he was able to build amplification systems for school parties and local bands.

In 1934, just married, he opened the Fender Radio Service, where he offered servicing for any electrical device, but also sold radios, musical instruments, amplification systems, and phonographs.

Meeting Doc Kauffman was the determining factor for Leo's interest in pickups and electric guitars. In 1944 the two men started to build lap steels and Fender designed the "Direct Strings Pickup" and the K&F amplifiers. Fender's commitment was total and the perspective of growth for the Company seemed to fuel Leo's energy even more. However Doc was unwilling to take on the increased responsibility and decided to quit. Fender bought Kauffman's share in the Company and continued alone, the two men would remain good friends for their entire life.

In 1950 Fender introduced the Esquire, destined to unsettle the market, renamed Broadcaster, then finally Telecaster (the name Esquire continued to be

1955 Stratocaster and Deluxe Amp from the same year (C. Prosperini).

used for the single pickup version), an instrument combining the characteristics of a regular guitar with some of the sonic qualities of a lap steel. The solid wood body was practical and the sound was clear and bright.

The most notable quality of Leo Fender, at the time, was his aptitude to listen to musician's comments and translate their needs into solutions applied to his instruments with extraordinary synthesis of ideas and effective simplicity. Some found the body of the Telecaster uncomfortable and Leo decided to design a new model, more versatile and comfortable to play.

The result was the Stratocaster, which was not simply a Telecaster with a more sinuously shaped body with a pickup added (an intervention carried out on some custom made instruments), but a really different model for which a special pickup was designed, similar in concept to the Telecaster units, but different in both appearance and sound.

Early sixties' Twin Amp. Leo Fender was as successful with amps and basses as he was with the guitars, bringing in any field innovations and originality of vision (C. C.).

When the increasing sales of guitars and amplifiers gave Leo more purchasing power, he started to search for better loudspeakers, becoming directly responsible for the improvements in this field achieved by Jensen and J. B. Lansing. Later it seems that Fender's confidence in his own opinions prevailed over those of collaborators and musicians.

Some of Leo's designs, imagined as progressive, were not so successful, such as the pickup for the Jazzmaster, which failed to convince jazz players to put down their chunky archtops but obtained limited success in completely different musical contexts.

New circuits were conceived for the Jaguar, the top of the line, and the Jazzmaster, much more complicated than the usual Fender's simple solutions, a trend that continued even after he left the company carrying his name. Although Leo was loosing his hearing, he was still on the lookout for brighter sounds, and founded the Music Man Company. He also designed an active circuitry to increase the highs of the already bright Sabre pickups which musicians didn't seem to appreciate.

The success of the factory was due to the basses and the amplifiers, but disagreements between the partners forced Leo to quit the company. In the eighties he then went on to found, the G & L with his old friend George Fullerton.

Fender was restless and designed more guitars and new pickups, conceived to efficiently direct the magnetic field toward the strings (Magnetic Field Design), both on single coil and humbucking models, so as to get more output and highs. On the F 200 guitar an active circuit increased the trebles even more and a passive version was also available. Without active electronics pushing their sound to the extreme, the "Magnetic Field Design" pickups, with ceramic magnets and less windings than the old Fender units, had good versatility and were appreciated for their strong attack and good sustain.

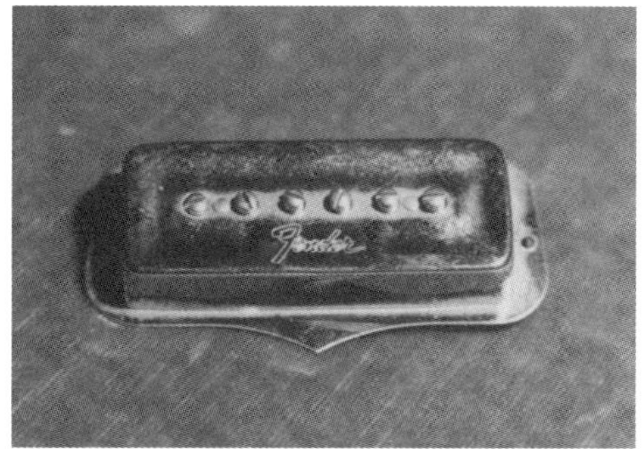

While Leo Fender, once left the Company he created, tried to solve his health problems before seeking new adventures, CBS, new owner of the brand, launched a series of hollow body electrics equipped with DeArmond pickups in the late sixties. Since then other models appeared fitted with pickups designed by Seth Lover, previously with Gibson, while more recently other units, signed by Don Lace and Seymour Duncan, were used on some guitars (C. Prosperini).

Leo Fender failed to convince most guitar players that his new models sounded better than the older ones with alnico magnets, but guitars such as the S 500, and the ASAT Classic, for a short time called Broadcaster, were fine instruments. The second one, in particular increased G & L's reputation.

The last design, in the pickup field, was the "Z" model, a humbucker with a winding for the low strings and one for the high string, similar in concept to the pickup of the Precision bass, mounted on the "Comanche" guitar. The purpose was to keep the magnetic window narrow as on single coil models but without hum.
These new designs from Leo Fender failed to convince players as he had hoped, to get rid of their old instruments or pickups, and buy the recent ones. However, many seemed to like them and respect for G & L was growing, especially due to models such as the ASAT Classic and the Legacy, even though, again, bass players appeared more open to accept innovations.

The 1959's Fender Bassman, with a Stratocaster or a Gibson les Paul, is still a reference point for tone excellence (C. Caldana).

Preference for old or new instruments aside, without any doubt Leo Fender, until his death, on March 21, 1991, continued to show an unequalled commitment, deeply involved in his untiring research for new solutions.

He continued his pursuit for excellence, and the hardest competition didn't come from other makers but from products he had designed in the past.

G & L "Magnetic Field Design" pickups

The "Z" pickups of a G & L Comanche guitar (Fabrizio Dadò).

Leo Fender, whose contribution is important for so many things, such as amplifiers, the bridge-vibrato for the Stratocaster and for developing the G & L guitars, designing excellent pickups, which were a model of simplicity of concept and efficiency, did not always understand the tastes and needs of musicians.

Even the units designed for the Jaguar and the Jazzmaster, which were shadowed by the success of the Telecaster and Stratocaster, when used excluding the complex circuits of these guitars, were fine, and proved the validity of the project.

Leo Fender, going from many unrepeatable successes to some failures due to his stubbornness, remains the indisputable king of inventiveness and produced, between 1944 and 1991, the widest range of timbres, from the "Direct Strings" pickup to the full sounding "Z" model, ever created by a single designer.

Seth Lover

Seth Lover (courtesy of Gibson)

Born in Kalamazoo, the town where the Gibson story began, on January 1, 1910, Seth Lover started studying electronics in the 1920s and was soon able to repair radio equipment. At seventeen he went into the army, lying about his real age, and later attended electronics classes which gave him the opportunity to find a job in a radio service laboratory.
In the 1930s Lover started his own repair shop.

In 1941 Walter Fuller, the inventor of the "Charlie Christian" pickup and the P 90, invited him to work for Gibson as amplifier technician. When the USA entered World War Two, Lover went back to the army and was employed in Washington as an electronics teacher. When he was finally embarked, the war was at its end.

Lover was re-employed by Gibson and designed the "Alnico" pickup, which differed from the P90 in that it had a square magnet under each string, height adjustable and directly in the winding, instead of a base loaded magnet and screw polepieces. His specialty was fighting hum, and he designed a circuit based on a photoelectric cell in order to obtain noiseless tremolo on amplifiers.

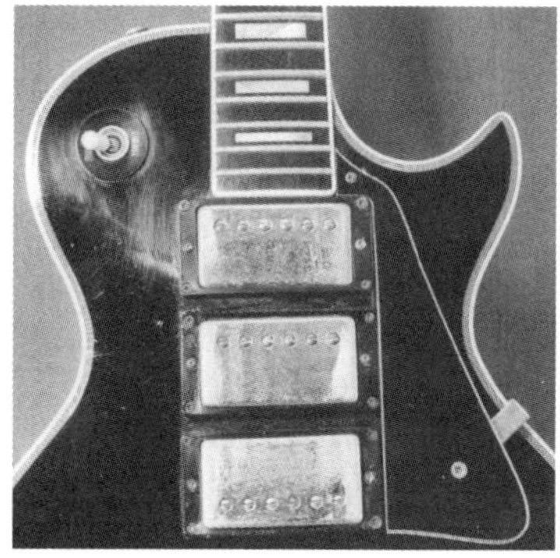

The Les Paul Custom, top of the line of the Solid Body Series, had a black finish, gold plated parts and three humbucking pickups (C. Prosperini).

Another of his jobs was to find a way to reduce amplifier hum and his solution was a choke on the mains transformer, a solution which gave him an idea for a new kind of pickup; the humbucking model. His contribution was also effective for the development of guitar models, such as the Flying V. The success of the humbucker led to another creation, a similar unit for Epiphone, which Gibson had acquired in 1957. The minihumbucking pickup was born, a smaller version of the model designed for Gibson, still with AWG 42 wire but with less windings under narrow nylon bobbins for a resistance of about 7 kOhms (a normal size humbucker had a resistance of about 8 kOhms), with the usual tolerance of +/- 20 %. Except for its dimensions the minihumbucking was structurally similar to the Gibson model, including the presence of a "Patent Applied For" label on the first specimens.

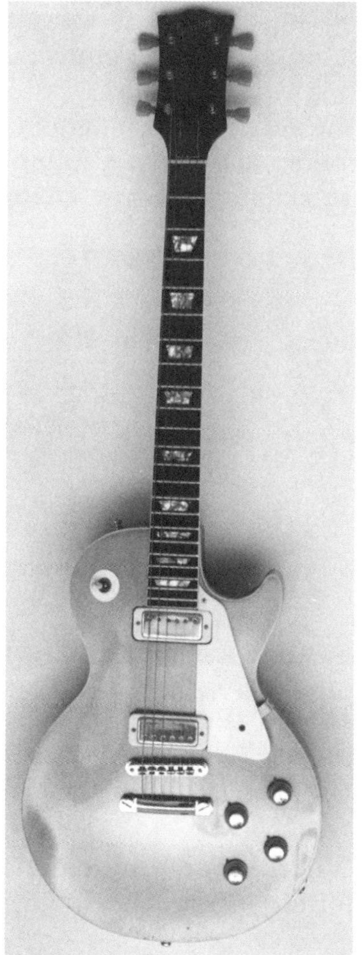

1971 Les Paul Deluxe (C. C.)

A mini-humbucker was also chosen for the Firebird series, albeit in a slightly different version than the one used for Epiphone guitars. It had the same windings, two magnets inside the bobbins, and was without adjustable polepieces. These differences gave the pickups a stronger attack, perfectly complementing the craftsmanship of the guitar, made with the neck and the middle portion of the body cut from a single table (neck-through body), a solution which favoured sustain and high frequencies and was responsible for the Firebird's characteristic sound.

A third version of the minihumbucking was standard equipment on the Johnny Smith Model guitar, which had a magnet in one of the bobbins, polepieces in the other and a thin ferrous plate on the base which transferred the magnetic field from the magnet to the polepieces. A fourth version was similar, but had three polepieces on each bobbin, on the one close to the neck for the low strings, and on the one close to the bridge for the other three.
At first this last version was supposedly intended for Epiphone, but apparently it was actually used on some Sears Silvertone and Harmony guitars.

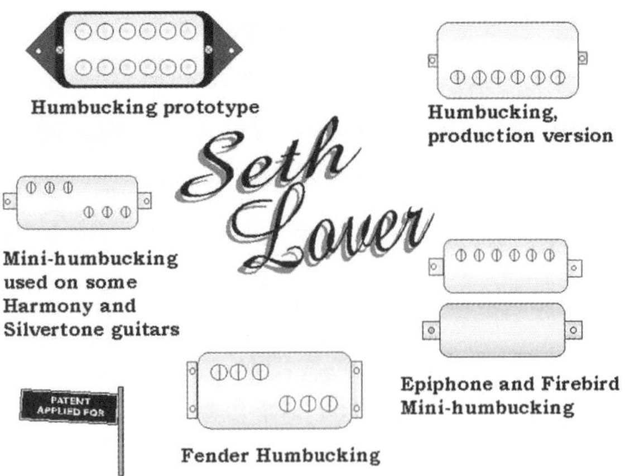

In 1967 Seth Lover resigned from Gibson after Fender had made him a much more interesting financial offer. This entailed designing, for the company now owned by CBS, a humbucking pickup with a brighter timbre than the Gibson model, which complied with the Fender tradition.

It seemed that CBS asked for a unit similar to the Gibson model, but Lover preferred to find a new solution with a more original voice.

The clear sound of the Fender humbucker was due to the use of Cunife magnets directly in the bobbins, shaped as screws for adjustability; in each bobbin three of these magnets were adjustable, and three were placed upside down to act as fixed poles. The choice of Cunife, an alloy of copper, nickel and iron, was due to it's workability and sound properties similar to those of Alnico 3. By alternating the adjustable magnets in the bobbins, it was possible for the magnetic field to follow a pattern similar to that of a Fender single coil in the lead position on a Telecaster or Stratocaster.

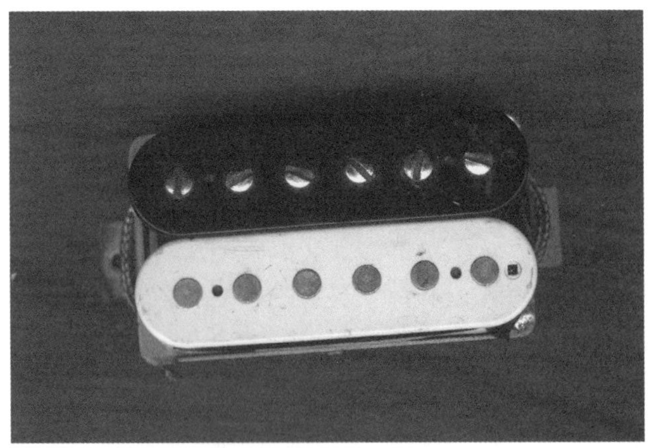

Gibson "Patent Applied For" pickup. It has the shorter M56 magnet and zebra bobbins. The Gibson humbucker was without any doubts the most successful of Seth Lover's designs.

While working for Fender, Lover designed a distortion device and other effects, but CBS didn't accept his suggestions and apart from a few prototypes and specimens given to friends, most of his ideas remained unrealized.

In 1969 the small humbucking model designed for Epiphone was used, for the first time, on a Gibson model, the Les Paul Deluxe.

In 1980 Gibson paid homage to the inventor of the humbucking pickup in advertisements for the Gold Top Reissue, which carried an imitation of his signature.

When Lover contacted Gibson to find out why they hadn't asked him personally for signature, the surprising reply was that they didn't know he was still alive!

In 1994, during the last years of his life, Seth had the pleasure to admire a model dedicated to him by his most successful disciple, Seymour Duncan, who sought his advise for the production of model SH-55 "Seth Lover", a faithful copy of the "Patent Applied For" humbucking, for which he would receive a percentage on each one sold. On January 31, 1997, after a brief illness, Seth Lover passed away.

Larry DiMarzio

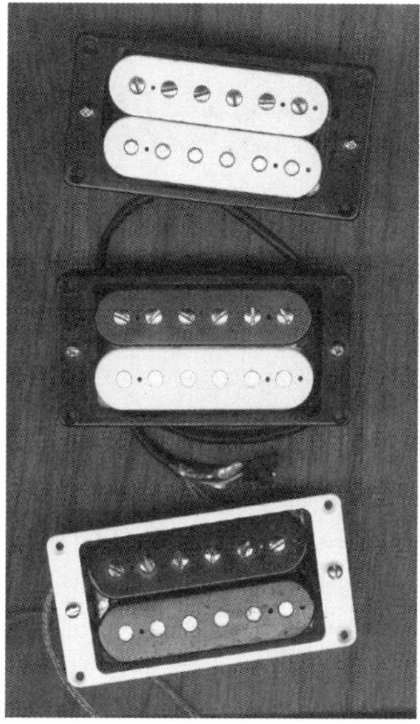

DiMarzio "PAF" pickups

Larry DiMarzio's story started, as for many pickup makers, as a musician. In his younger years he played rock 'n roll in several bands using a Kay, which he then substituted for a Gretsch Country Gentleman. He then went on to a Gibson Barney Kessel and, finally, to a Fender Stratocaster.

One day, while trying to repair one of the Stratocaster's pickups, Larry learned the basics by which they worked. Woodworking notions, acquired from his family, allowed him to earn a job in a guitar servicing shop, where he gained experience in fret substitution and other lutherie work. Confident in his knowledge of electronics, DiMarzio expounded his ideas on the subject to the shop owner, who gave him some pickups to repair.
After some difficulties and lots of notes taken on wire gauges, he perfected his winding techniques, and DiMarzio's reputation began to grow.

A meeting with Bill Lawrence, to whom he showed a Telecaster he had modified, led to a job as assistant for the famous pickup designer. This was a good opportunity for young Larry to learn many secrets about the art of pickup making.
His interest in music prevailed and DiMarzio became good friend with Gene Simmons and Paul Stanley from Kiss, and played with them on several occasions. Then he became tired of the restless life on the road and went back to pickup servicing.

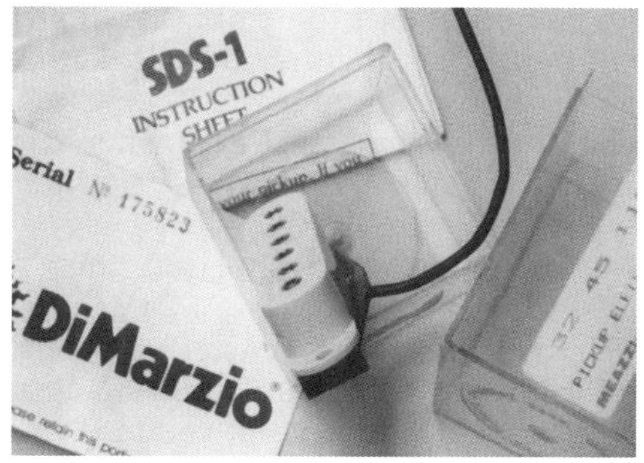

The SDS-1 (Claudio Prosperini).

In 1973 the first DiMarzio advertisement appeared in Guitar Player Magazine, showing his original model, the Super Distortion, produced since 1972. In 1975 his catalogue included the Dual Sound, the Pre-B1, the Fat Strat and the PAF. By the end of the seventies his reputation had grown outside the United States and the DiMarzio factory was now equipped with digitally controlled winding machines and produced an ever increasing number of models, including those for bass and acoustic guitar.

Several instrument makers fitted their models with DiMarzio pickups and many orders came from the Far East.

DiMarzio, was the first to conceive pickups intended to push the amplifiers into distortion, while most designers still tried to avoid it. He was the first to understand the need for high quality versions of classic designs, such as the

A guitar hand made by Stanzani & Tomassone for Claudio Prosperini with DiMarzio Fat Strat and X2N pickups (C. P.).

PAF, the first to produce a high output model for Stratocaster with a Gibson-like sound, such as the SDS-1, built with a structure similar to a P 90 but with two small and powerful ceramic magnets in place of the bigger Alnico ones used on the Gibson model.

DiMarzio was also the first to efficiently use Allen screws as polepieces, the first to offer special taper potentiometers with 500k and 1Mohm values for more brightness with hot pickups, single coil or humbucking.

Rapidly the business was extended to offer not only pickups and potentiometers, but also raw bodies and necks, all the necessary accessories and the instructions for assembling a complete instrument from the parts in the catalogues. There was also a wide choice regarding electronics and type of wood.

Models such as the Dual Sound were sold with a mini-switch and the instructions for all the wiring options available for the pickup. Good quality plastic for the bobbins, Teflon output cables and a simple but solid structure, plus attention to details, aesthetics and competitive prices, put the DiMarzio products at the top of the market. DiMarzio's success opened the door to many other makers, such as EMG, Bartolini, Duncan, but more than anything, changed the view of the guitar, or bass. It was no longer an item to be accepted simply as it had been conceived by the factory, but as an instrument on which it was possible to adapt personal preferences almost without limits. Today all major brands offer guitar models in a wide range of versions, with all possible options (just think about the embarrassing number of Stratocaster models in the Fender catalogue), therefore the market for parts, such as necks and bodies, is somewhat restricted and left to a few specialized makers. By the end of the eighties DiMarzio no longer offered bodies and necks, but included several new pickup models and today the number of models produced is impressive.

Recent DiMarzio catalogues show the "Signature" line, with special models designed for the likes of Al DiMeola, Rick Derringer, Steve Morse, Steve Vai, plus Telecaster and Stratocaster models in humbucking configuration, new "Classics" such as the FRED and the PAF Pro, to the "Virtual Vintage" for Telecaster and Stratocaster and several versions of models, humbucking or single coil, inspired by the P 90.

Although today high quality manufacture is not exclusive to DiMarzio, this brand remains a leader in an ever growing market. Most makers, these days, seem interested in creating perfect copies of famous models from the past. DiMarzio prefers to reinterpret the old recipes by adding his own flavour, for a sound that is always characterized by an edge reflecting his old love for rock and it is not surprising that most DiMarzio pickup users are, indeed, rock musicians.

Seymour Duncan

Having repaired and rewired hundreds of original vintage pickups, Seymour Duncan had gained experience, on this matter, that very few others could claim.

Seymour learned the first guitar chords from his father, while still a teenager, and two uncles stimulated his interest in music through the records of Charlie Christian, Jimmy Bryant, Speedy West, and Duane Eddy, increasing the young man's collection to nearly 2400 classic recordings. Influenced by James Burton and Albert Collins, Duncan played in his first band, the Flintstones, in 1963.

Meetings and conversations with Les Paul and Roy Buchanan stimulated his curiosity for sound and Seymour started to correspond with Fender and Gibson treasuring each answer.

In this period Duncan tried to rewind his first pickup, trying too obtain the same sound as Roy Buchanan. While playing with different bands he became friends with Elliot Randall, Jimmy Page, Robbie Robertson and Jimi Hendrix, who gave him a white Stratocaster.
In 1968 while working in television in Cincinnati he met Tut Taylor, Norman Blake, Jerry Reed, Glen Campbell and other musicians. In 1973, following Roy Buchanan's suggestion, he moved to London, where he worked as a session man and did servicing, at Fender's Soundhouse, for the Who, Supertramp, Peter Frampton, Jeff Beck and others.

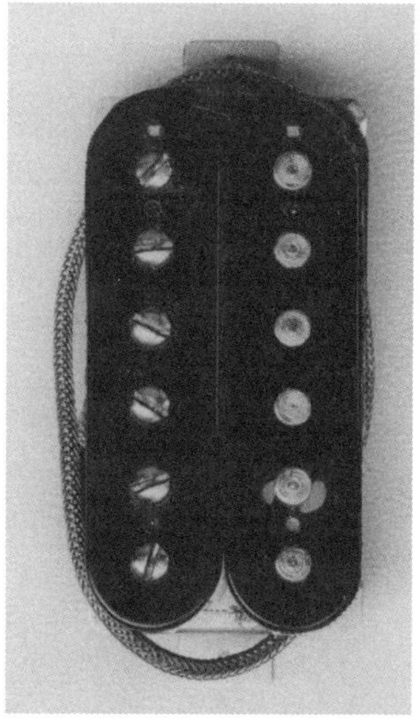

Duncan SH-PG-1 “Pearly Gates” (C. Caldana).

After a few years Seymour went back to the United States and made pickguards, knobs and guitar bridges which he sold to Mighty Mite, Schecter and Charvel. In 1976 Duncan opened his own laboratory and started making pickups, putting the ideas matured from his long conversations with Leo Fender, Bill Carson, Doc Kauffman, Seth Lover to good use, and by the end of the decade he was able to produce the best copies of "vintage" models on the market.

The most popular models were the SH-1 '59, a faithful reproduction of the old Gibson Patent Applied For, the SSL-1 and STL-1B, respectively copies of the pickups for the Stratocaster and the Broadcaster, and the J. B. Model, based on a pickup wound for Jeff Beck, on which had a medium high output level and a sound clearly inspired from the Gibson school. The J. B. became standard equipment on several guitar models made by Jackson, Hamer and others, including Fender for the "Robben Ford Signature" model.

Antiquity Humbucker set

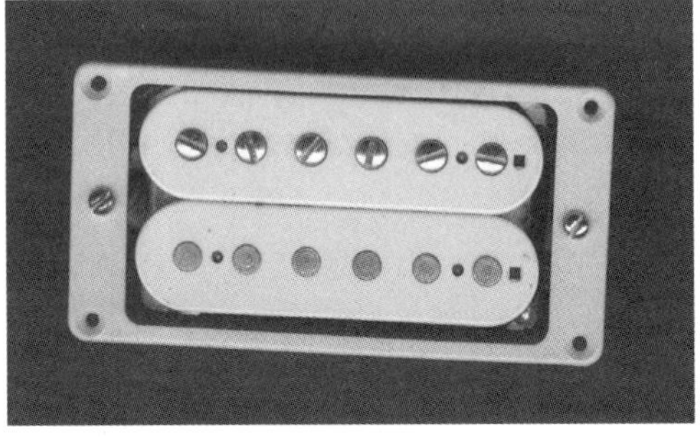

SH-55 “Seth Lover” without cover. As for the Antiquity, the bobbins are made from butyrate, the same plastic used in the ‘50s. The magnet is alnico 2 calibrated for the same magnetic field’s intensity measured on the originals.

Antiquity P 90 set

The range of models was one of the broadest on the market, with high output models and a unprecedented possibility of choice on vintage models. Duncan's curiosity failed to diminish as time went by and when he had the opportunity to examine Billy Gibbons' Les Paul, for a few days, the distinctive sound of which graced all the first records of the ZZ Top, he studied the pickups and the result was the Pearly Gates model, with an Alnico 2 magnet and a resistance of 8,5 kOhms. Billy Gibbons himself used this pickup on several guitars and Fender ordered a special version, with an Alnico 5 magnet and a resistance of 8, 65 kOhms, for the Lone Star Stratocaster.

The Trembucker models are also interesting, in that they have square polepieces, designed for guitars with vibrato (DiMarzio offered most models in "F" version, with Fender style spacing). Duncan believed that the characteristics of Alnico 2 magnets were closer to those of the fifties' pickups and introduced the Alnico Pro series, with humbucking and single coil models. These had a sweeter sound than similar models using Alnico 5.
Several other makers were now offering models with a similarly weaker magnetic field, compared to regular Alnico 5, such as Fender and Fralin. They used Alnico 3 and DiMarzio, with the "Air" series, used Alnico 5, but in a special configuration aimed at the Alnico 2 performance.

Continuing his experiments, Duncan has recently introduced, the "Nashville" series, single coils with Alnico 5 magnets for the low strings and Alnico 2 magnets for the high strings, in order to obtain a softer high end and more brilliant basses. Studying the old models, Seymour felt the necessity to acquire the technical equipment necessary to diminish the magnetic flux of the magnets to the same level as the vintage ones; this way he obtained calibrated magnets or, to use his terminology, "Duncan aged" magnets.

With these magnets plus accurately reproduced details, Duncan was able to recreate the appearance and sound of fifties and sixties pickups.

Other successful Duncan products were the pickups for bass, the Live Wire series with active electronics for bass and guitar and the very fine systems for acoustic guitar amplification.
The successful sales of these products allowed Seymour to continue his research and to find the raw materials he needed to obtain the most authentic reproductions of the old models and also to buy the complex and expensive equipment with which he could accurately control magnet specifications.

Finally in the 1990s Duncan was able to realize an old dream: to make pickups with the "appearance, the sound and smell" of the fifties' models with exceptional attention to details; the Antiquity series was born, soon followed by the Antiquity 2 series, copies of the sixties models. In 1994 Duncan paid homage to Seth Lover with the model SH-55, which was realized after consulting the old designer to whom it was dedicated. It was similar to the Antiquity but lacked the aging process and had a slightly brighter sound.

Recently Duncan makes pickups designed by the luthier Bob Benedetto and mainly aimed at jazz musicians. He continues to play the Telecaster, holds seminars, during which, with the help of portable equipment, he teaches how to analyse, date or make a pickup. Seymour Duncan, is interested in making good versions of the traditional designs, and pays attention to details which are so important for the aesthetic and sonic results, which other makers often overlook. From his Custom Shop can be obtained any model, from a "Charlie Christian" copy to an "Alnico" model, from a Filter'Tron to special design models with customized windings or magnets.
In effect his production is not limited to exact copies of old models, but his catalogues also display modern models, produced with modern techniques for the modern player, while maintaining the same quality. As the introduction of the Nashville Series proves, Duncan is not afraid to experiment new configurations bringing new life to time tested formulas.

The research carried out is impressive and ongoing, and is especially praiseworthy considering that the results are not limited to the effects on production, but shared with everybody through the pages of "Vintage Guitar Magazine", which has articles that are a mine of technical and historical information, thus spreading the knowledge of vintage pickups to a broader public.

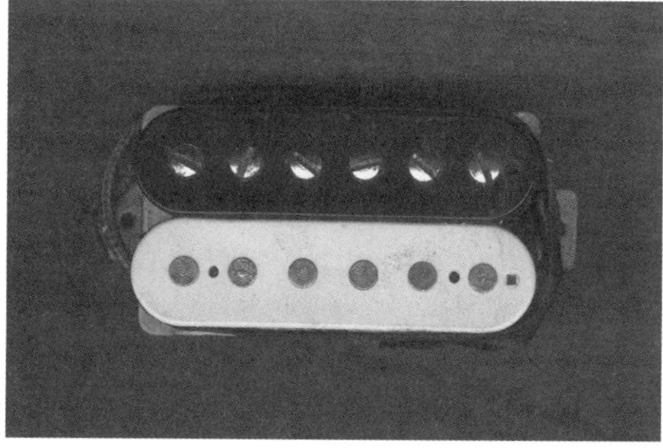

Duncan '59 Model

To have a good tone requires practice, a good instrument and, of course, good pickups. But nothing can replace culture, and listening to as many classic albums as possible is the best way to learn from the greats.
Musicians from any field, from country to jazz, from blues to rock, have documented their quest for tone on countless recordings, inspirational for their wide variety of sounds, styles, the best of them managing to balance with taste originality and tradition.
From them we can learn how tone, to be really good, has to be appropriate for the musical contest.
Some had a raw sound, some a very elegant tone, some relying on simple harmonic structures, others playing through complex chord changes. There have been players using the tone of their instrument as bare as possible, players who felt the need to process it heavily, but what's amazing is how they made it all work translating their notes in emotions, new concepts, evolving to new techniques or resuming forgotten styles, always allowing their personality to show through and so making of wire, magnets and wood, powerful tools for artistic expression.

Most of the images are credited in the related captions, all the others are by Claudio Prosperini, Claudio Caldana, Alex Angelucci and Mario Milan.
For several images in the colour section we are also very grateful to Rickenbacker Guitars, TV Jones Pickups, Lollar Guitars, Joe Barden Engineering and Lace Music Products.

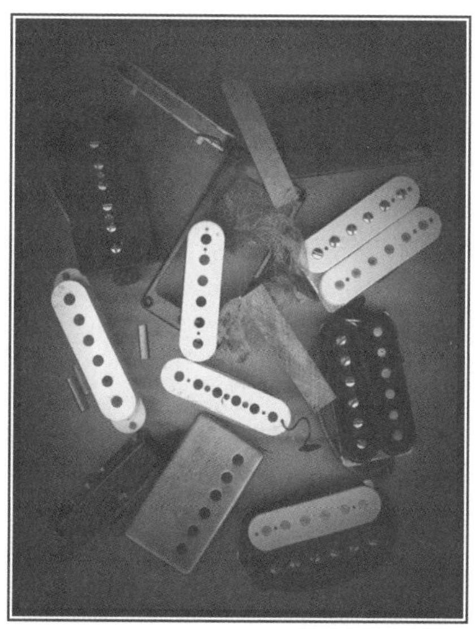

Bibliography

Magazines

Vintage Guitar (VG Inc.), Guitar Player (CMP), The Guitar Magazine (Link House Magazines Ltd).

Books

André Duchossoir: "Gibson Electrics, the classic years" (Hal Leonard), "The Fender Telecaster" (Hal Leonard) and "The Fender Stratocaster" (Hal Leonard).
Richard Smith: "Fender - The Sound Heard Around the World" (Garfish).
Donald Brosnac: "Guitar Electronics for Musicians" (Music Service Corporation).
Les Schatten: "The Book of Standard Wiring Diagrams Vol. 1 e Vol. 2" (Schatten).
Adrian Legg: "Customising Your Electric Guitar" (Kaye & Ward).
Jay Scott: "The Guitars Of The Fred Gretsch Company" (Centerstream).
Walter Carter: "Epiphone, The Complete History" (Hal Leonard).
George Gruhn e Walter Carter: "Electric Guitars and Basses, a Photographic History" (GPI - Miller Freeman Group).
Walter Carter and others: "Gibson Guitars - 100 Years of an America Icon" (GPG).
Tom Wheeler: "American Guitars" (Harper - Collins).
Richard Smith: "Rickenbacker" (Centerstream).
Hans Moust "The Guild Guitar Book" (Hal Leonard).
Yasuhiko Iwanade: "The Beauty Of The Burst" (Hal Leonard).
Paul Day: "The Ultimate Guitar Book" (Alfred A. Knopf)
Tony Bacon, Tom Wheeler, Walter Carter, André Duchossoir and others: "Classic Guitars Of The '50s" and "Classic Guitars Of The '60s" (Hal Leonard).
Jason Lollar's "Basic Pickup Winding & Complete Guide to Making Your Own Pickup Winding Machine", can be ordered from his web site www.lollarguitars.com
Giovanni Gaglio: "Il manuale di chitarra elettrica" (Alpi).
Tom and Mary Evans: "Guitars, From The Renaissance To Rock" (Oxford University Publishing).
Alan Peters, Lucinda Leech, Bill Lincoln, Jane Marshall, Aidan Walker, Bill Lincoln and Luke Hughes: "The Encyclopedia Of Wood" (Facts On File)

GUITAR INSTRUCTION & TECHNIQUE

NEW

THE GUITAR CHORD SHAPES OF CHARLIE CHRISTIAN

Book/CD Pack
by Joe Weidlich

The concepts and fingerings in this book have been developed by analyzing the licks used by Charlie Christian. Chord shapes are moveable; thus one can play the riffs in virtually any key without difficulty by simply moving the shape, and fingerings used to play them, up or down the fingerboard. The author shows how the chord shapes – F, D and A – are formed, then can easily be modified to major, minor, dominant seventh and diminished seventh chord voicings.†Analyzing licks frequently used by Charlie Christian, Joe has identified a series of what he calls tetrafragments, i.e., the core element of a lick. The identifiable "sound" of a particular lick is preserved regardless of how many notes are added on either side of it, e.g., pickup notes or tag endings.† Many examples are shown and played on the CD of how this basic concept was used by Charlie Christian to keep his solo lines moving forward. Weidlich also makes observations on the physical manner Charlie Christian used in playing jazz guitar and how that approach contributed to his smooth, mostly down stroke, pick technique.

00000388 Guitar $19.95

GUITAR CHORDS PLUS

by Ron Middlebrook

A comprehensive study of normal and extended chords, tuning, keys, transposing, capo use, and more. Includes over 500 helpful photos and diagrams, a key to guitar symbols, and a glossary of guitar terms.

00000011 .... $11.95

NEW

GUITAR TRANSCRIBING – A COMPLETE GUIDE

by Dave Celentano

Learn that solo now! Don't wait for the music to come out – use this complete guide to writing down what you hear. Includes tips, advice, examples and exercises from easy to difficult. Your ear is the top priority and you'll train it to listen more effectively to recognize intervals, chords, note values, counting rhythms and much more for an accurate transcription.

00000378 Book/CD Pack $19.95

GUITAR TUNING FOR THE COMPLETE MUSICAL IDIOT (FOR SMART PEOPLE TOO)

INCLUDES TAB

by Ron Middlebrook

A complete book on how to tune up. Contents include: Everything You Need To Know About Tuning; Intonation; Strings; 12-String Tuning; Picks; and much more.

00000002 .... $5.95

INTRODUCTION TO ROOTS GUITAR

VHS

by Doug Cox

This book/CD pack by Canada's premier guitar and Dobro® player introduces beginning to intermediate players to many of the basics of folk/roots guitar. Topics covered include: basic theory, tuning, reading tablature, right- and left-hand patterns, blues rhythms, Travis picking, frailing patterns, flatpicking, open tunings, slide and many more. CD includes 40 demonstration tracks.

00000262 Book/CD Pack $17.95
00000265 VHS Video $19.95

KILLER PENTATONICS FOR GUITAR

INCLUDES TAB

by Dave Celentano

Covers innovative and diverse ways of playing pentatonic scales in blues, rock and heavy metal. The licks and ideas in this book will give you a fresh approach to playing the pentatonic scale, hopefully inspiring you to reach for higher levels in your playing. The 37-minute companion CD features recorded examples.

00000285 Book/CD Pack $17.95

LEFT HAND GUITAR CHORD CHART

INCLUDES TAB

by Ron Middlebrook

Printed on durable card stock, this "first-of-a-kind" guitar chord chart displays all forms of major and minor chords in two forms, beginner and advanced.

00000005 .... $2.95

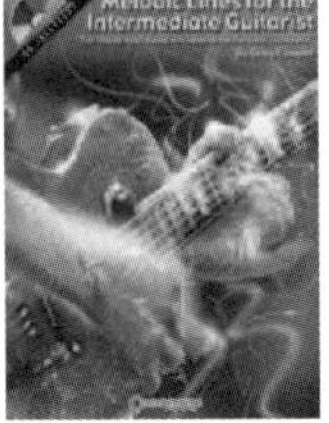

MELODIC LINES FOR THE INTERMEDIATE GUITARIST

by Greg Cooper

This book/CD pack is essential for anyone interested in expanding melodic concepts on the guitar. Author Greg Cooper covers: picking exercises; major, minor, dominant and altered lines; blues and jazz turn-arounds; and more.

00000312 Book/CD Pack $19.95

MELODY CHORDS FOR GUITAR

INCLUDES TAB

by Allan Holdsworth

Influential fusion player Allan Holdsworth provides guitarists with a simplified method of learning chords, in diagram form, for playing accompaniments and for playing popular melodies in "chord-solo" style. Covers: major, minor, altered, dominant and diminished scale notes in chord form, with lots of helpful reference tables and diagrams.

00000222 .... $19.95

MODAL JAMS AND THEORY

INCLUDES TAB

by Dave Celentano

This book shows you how to play the modes, the theory behind mode construction, how to play any mode in any key, how to play the proper mode over a given chord progression, and how to write chord progressions for each of the seven modes. The CD includes two rhythm tracks and a short solo for each mode so guitarists can practice with a "real" band.

00000163 Book/CD Pack $17.95

MONSTER SCALES AND MODES

INCLUDES TAB

by Dave Celentano

This book is a complete compilation of scales, modes, exotic scales, and theory. It covers the most common and exotic scales, theory on how they're constructed, and practical applications. No prior music theory knowledge is necessary, since every section is broken down and explained very clearly.

00000140 .... $7.95

OLD TIME COUNTRY GUITAR BACKUP BASICS

by Joseph Weidlich

This instructional book uses commercial recordings from 70 different "sides" from the 1920s and early 1930s as its basis to learn the principal guitar backup techniques commonly used in old-time country music. Topics covered include: boom-chick patterns • bass runs • uses of the pentatonic scale • rhythmic variations • minor chromatic nuances • the use of chromatic passing tones • licks based on chords or chord progressions • and more.

00000389 .... $15.95

OPEN GUITAR TUNINGS

INCLUDES TAB

by Ron Middlebrook

This booklet illustrates over 75 different tunings in easy-to-read diagrams. Includes tunings used by artists such as Chet Atkins, Michael Hedges, Jimmy Page, Joe Satriani and more for rock, blues, bluegrass, folk and country styles including open D (for slide guitar), Em, open C, modal tunings and many more.

00000130 .... $4.95

OPEN TUNINGS FOR GUITAR

by Dorian Michael

This book provides 14 folk songs in 9 tunings to help guitarists become comfortable with changing tunings. Songs are ordered so that changing from one tuning to another is logical and non-intrusive. Includes: Fisher Blues (DADGBE) • Fine Toast to Hewlett (DGDGBE) • George Barbazan (DGDGBD) • Amelia (DGDGCD) • Will the Circle Be Unbroken (DADF#AD) • more.

00000224 Book/CD Pack $19.95

ARRANGING FOR OPEN GUITAR TUNINGS

By Dorian Michael

This book/CD pack teaches intermediate-level guitarists how to choose an appropriate tuning for a song, develop an arrangement, and solve any problems that may arise while turning a melody into a guitar piece to play and enjoy.

00000313 Book/CD Pack $19.95

ROCK RHYTHM GUITAR

by Dave Celentano

This helpful book/CD pack cuts out all the confusing technical talk and just gives guitarists the essential tools to get them playing. With Celentano's tips, anyone can build a solid foundation of basic skills to play almost any rhythm guitar style. The exercises and examples are on the CD, in order of difficulty, so players can master new techniques, then move on to more challenging material.

00000274 Book/CD Pack $17.95

SCALES AND MODES IN THE BEGINNING

INCLUDES TAB

by Ron Middlebrook

The most comprehensive and complete scale book written especially for the guitar. Chapers include: Fretboard Visualization • Scale Terminology • Scales and Modes • and a Scale to Chord Guide.

00000010 .... $11.95

SLIDE GUITAR AND OPEN TUNINGS

by Doug Cox

Explores the basics of open tunings and slide guitar for the intermediate player, including licks, chords, songs and patterns. This is not just a repertoire book, but rather an approach for guitarists to jam with others, invent their own songs, and understand how to find their way around open tunings with and without a slide. The accompanying CD features 37 tracks.

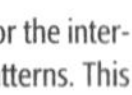

00000243 Book/CD Pack $17.95

SPEED METAL

by Dave Celentano

In an attempt to teach the aspiring rock guitarist how to pick faster and play more melodically, Dave Celentano uses heavy metal neo-classical styles from Paganini and Bach to rock in this great book/CD pack. The book is structured to take the player through the examples in order of difficulty.

00000261 Book/CD Pack $17.95

25 WAYS TO IMPROVE YOUR SOLO GUITAR PLAYING

by Jay Marks

Keep your music fresh with the great ideas in this new book! Covers: chords, dynamics, harmonics, phrasing, intros & endings and more!

00000323 Book/CD Pack $19.95

Centerstream Publishing, LLC
P.O Box 17878 - Anaheim Hills, CA 92817
P/Fax (714)-779-9390 - Email: Centerstream@aol.com
Website: www.centerstream-usa.com